# ORDINARY SITES

# ORDINARY SITES

## *Student Resistance and the 1970s Texas School Desegregation Struggle*

ARCASIA D. JAMES-GALLAWAY

THE UNIVERSITY OF NORTH CAROLINA PRESS

*Chapel Hill*

Designed by Jamison Cockerham
Set in Scala, Scala Sans
by Jamie McKee, MacKey Composition

Cover art: Woman profile © Adobe Stock / James;
chalkboard background © Adobe Stock / tonstock.



LIBRARY OF CONGRESS CATALOGING-IN-PUBLICATION DATA
Names: James-Gallaway, ArCasia author
Title: Ordinary sites : student resistance and the 1970s Texas school desegregation struggle / ArCasia D. James-Gallaway.
Description: Chapel Hill : The University of North Carolina Press, [2026] | Includes bibliographical references and index.
Identifiers: LCCN 2026017290 | ISBN 9781469697451 cloth alk. paper | ISBN 9781469697468 pbk alk. paper | ISBN 9781469695884 epub | ISBN 9781469697475 pdf
Subjects: LCSH: School integration—Texas—Waco—History—20th century | African American students—Texas—Waco—Social conditions—20th century | Public schools—Texas—Waco—History—20th century | Racism—Texas—Waco—History—20th century | BISAC: EDUCATION / History | HISTORY / United States / 20th Century
Classification: LCC LC214.23.W33 J36 2026
LC record available at https://lccn.loc.gov/2026017290

This book will be made open access within three years of publication thanks to Path to Open, a program developed in partnership between JSTOR, the American Council of Learned Societies (ACLS), the University of Michigan Press, and the University of North Carolina Press to bring about equitable access and impact for the entire scholarly community, including authors, researchers, libraries, and university presses around the world. Learn more at https://about.jstor.org/path-to-open/.

For product safety concerns under the European Union's General Product Safety Regulation (EU GPSR), please contact gpsr@mare-nostrum.co.uk or write to the University of North Carolina Press and Mare Nostrum Group B.V., Doelen 72, 4831 GR Breda, The Netherlands.

*For the Ancestors*

*For Black Waco*

*For Laura Mack, Willie "Uncle Bill" Brown,*
*and Russell Livingston*

# CONTENTS

# ACKNOWLEDGMENTS

I always tell my students that the acknowledgments section in any sole-authored monograph is where all the "juice" is, that is, where authors share intriguing details about themselves and their book composition journey. While I am not sure how "juicy" mine may come across, I have thought a lot about what mine may say about me if I were to ever be able to write them. Well, here we are.

Growing up, I didn't know anyone who wrote books—like real scholarly books. As a first-generation college student, I had few blueprints on which to base my becoming a tenure-stream faculty member. These details are an important part of this book's origin story because they pushed me to consider how so many allegedly unimportant people from allegedly unimportant places end up doing tremendous things that few, if any, people will ever pay attention to.

The peculiar thing about trying to tell a story few thought important enough to record means I had relatively little archival material to work with. This issue might vex a more conventional historian, but not me. In retrospect, I've realized that I always intended to foreground the oral histories that animate the Black struggle for educational justice, something accessible to me with this project because many Black alumni are still living. Seeing how these oral histories square with what was written about the events I cover led me to the historical files of Waco Independent School District, La Vega Independent School District, McLennan County Archives, and Baylor University's Texas Collection. I am deeply grateful for the incredible patience of the individuals working at these organizations in managing my many visits, inquiries, and requests.

Although my own K–12 student experiences, preservice teacher education, and domestic teaching venture certainly influenced how I came to raise the questions I pursue in this book, the seed of the idea that grew into this book was probably and most earnestly sown during my time teaching abroad in China (because I didn't speak Mandarin and thus read everything I could find). James D. Anderson's groundbreaking book was one of those I devoured, sparking my interest in the enduring quest for Black educational justice. Subsequently cultivated at the University of Pennsylvania, my thinking benefited from interactions with gifted scholars including Krystal Strong, John Puckett, Barbara Savage, Heather Andrea Williams, and my wider ECS cohort. My scholarly perspective was further nurtured at the University of Illinois Urbana-Champaign under the intellectual guidance of giants like James "Doc" Anderson, Ruth Nicole Brown, and Adrienne Dixson, whose steadfast mentorship complemented the insight I received from scholars like Anne Haas Dyson, William "Bill" Trent, Eboni Zamani-Gallaher, Anjalè Welton, Kathryn LaBarre, and Yoon Pak, alongside the academic mentors who have continued to pour into me along this tenure-track journey, namely Linda Perkins, Michelle Purdy, Dionne Danns, LaGarrett King, and Sonya Douglass. The community of peer scholars I found in graduate school is also unmatched, granting me fellowship, encouragement, laughs—oh, the laughs—and a space to express my academic and personal dreams. Francena, Devean, Jari, Tiffany, Isis, Verna, Ruqayyah, Melanie, Crystal, Hafeeza, Ansharaye, Teni, Gina, Chequita, Saba, Kristen, Kimberly, Autumn, Jeremy, Eliana, Brittany, and my absolute favorite, Chaddrick, are just some of the names of those who warrant my gratitude. Thank all y'all.

I am grateful for the resources afforded by fellowships from the Ford Foundation, the Baylor University Wardlaw Fund, the University of Illinois's Hardie Fund, the Texas State Historical Association, Texas A&M University's Arts and Humanities Fund, and the American Educational Researchers Association's Seed Grant from Division F, which made all the difference in ensuring I had the time and tools necessary to do my work to the best of my ability.

I was compelled to write this book because, like Toni Morrison recognized, the history my classmates and I needed as K–12 students in Waco, a history that should have been part of our prescribed curriculum, has yet to exist, until now. My charge is to attest to how history happens at home *and* in faraway, large places where "significant" people live. Endless thanks go to my family, Black Waco, and crucially, the Black Waco alumni who trusted me with their time and memories to ensure this book tells a story that documents alone could not. My mother, Adrica, deserves special thanks for babysitting her grandchild while I conducted interviews, attended class reunions, or tried to progress my writing. Similarly, her mother, my grandmother Debora, deserves special gratitude for widely publicizing my study, helping me secure so many incredible interviews, and sitting multiple times for interviews herself. I hope I've done y'all justice and given you all a history you can hold that humanizes and honors much of who you are, much of who I, a child of Black Waco, am.

Finally, the enduring love and motivation from Chaddrick, our child, and our soon-to-be newest arrival is what's gotten me here and what will continue to see me through. Working to manage all the responsibilities associated with life as a Black mother, daughter, spouse, half of a dual academic couple, sister, friend, and aunt is not for the faint of heart. Chaddrick, your faith in and unwavering support of me is an integral part of how I've gotten here, and our little one/s are, I suspect, what will help our unit keep on keepin' on, especially in times such as these.

# CHRONOLOGY

1949 Texas Legislature enacts the Gilmer–Aiken bills, which modernize education in part by raising and equalizing teacher salaries, standardizing school funding, and consolidating schools and districts

1951 After consolidating smaller Black schools, La Vega Independent School District (ISD) opens J. Newton Jenkins as the district's single Black school, which serves grades 1–8

1954 US Supreme Court rules that school segregation based on race violates the Constitution in *Brown v. Board of Education*

1955 US Supreme Court rules that school desegregation is to be implemented with all deliberate speed in *Brown II*

1956 Waco ISD votes to indefinitely postpone school desegregation, citing fear of losing funds

La Vega ISD opens G. W. Carver as an all-Black equalization school serving grades 1–12

1957 Texas Legislature issues Article 2900a, which prohibits school desegregation without a citywide referendum

The Little Rock Nine desegregate Central High School in Little Rock, Arkansas

1958 Waco ISD reallocates a formerly non-Black junior high school to Black Wacoans, and it opens as G. L. Wiley Junior High School

1962 A group of Black parents, on behalf of their children, file the first suit against Waco ISD for maintaining a segregated (i.e., dual) school system in *McGrue v. Williams*

1963 Waco ISD begins a stair-step school desegregation plan

Dripping Springs Elementary School opens in La Vega ISD as an all-Black equalization school

President John F. Kennedy is assassinated in Dallas; Vice President Lyndon B. Johnson becomes president

1964 Ruling issued from first lawsuit filed against school desegregation in Waco in *McGrue v. Williams*

US Congress passes the Civil Rights Act, which prohibits many forms of identity-based discrimination

1965 President Johnson signs the Voting Rights Act and the Elementary and Secondary Education Act

1966 Black Panther Party is founded in Oakland, California

1967 Thurgood Marshall is sworn in as the nation's first Black Supreme Court justice

1968 Waco ISD completes its stair-step desegregation plan, but fewer than thirty Black students attend historically non-Black schools in the district

US Supreme Court rules "freedom of choice" plans unconstitutional in the *Green v. County School Board of New Kent County* decision

US Congress passes the 1968 Civil Rights Act, commonly known as the Fair Housing Act

Dr. Martin Luther King Jr. is assassinated in Tennessee

1969 In a unanimous decision from the Mississippi case *Alexander v. Holmes County Board of Education*, the US Supreme Court refuses to allow school districts more time to comply with school desegregation mandates

1970 La Vega ISD closes G. W. Carver Junior and Senior High School without telling the Black community the school serves

Former G. W. Carver students stage a walkout in protest of La Vega ISD's closure of Carver

1971 Waco ISD and La Vega ISD reach a compromise to transfer 1,300 Black La Vega junior and senior high students to Waco ISD

Waco ISD transfers teachers midyear to comply with federal school desegregation mandates

Waco ISD closes A. J. Moore High School

Jefferson-Moore High School opens in Waco ISD as a nominally desegregated but majority-Black high school that ostensibly replaced A. J. Moore

Waco ISD implements busing to facilitate the transfer of 1,300 Black students from La Vega ISD

US Supreme Court rules busing a constitutionally legitimate way to facilitate school desegregation in *Swann v. Charlotte-Mecklenburg Board of Education*

1972 Waco ISD begins to see a sharp decline in student enrollment that corresponds with broader white flight trends

1973 Ruling from the 1971 *Arvizu v. Waco ISD* case requires Waco ISD to create and submit for approval a new school desegregation plan based on evidence that the school district was still operating a dual school system

Waco ISD closes G. L. Wiley Junior High but reopens it the next year

# ORDINARY SITES

INTRODUCTION

# Lessons from Black Waco

In 1971, A. J. Moore High School graduated its final class. As the only Black high school in Texas's Waco Independent School District (Waco ISD), A. J. Moore had served generations of students for nearly a century since its official inception in 1881.[1] Since the start of the 1970–71 school year, senior class officers spent countless hours imploring the white power structure to honor—at least in name—this segregated Black school's legacy in the transition to a new building. Seniors and class officers Marvin Shelton, Paula Ritcherson, and Gilbert Jackson made repeated appeals at school board meetings and in local newspapers to convince the school administrators that erasing the name A. J. Moore was tantamount to erasing Black Waco's heritage and history. Their efforts were part of a larger initiative at the behest of high school students from different Waco campuses to preserve the names of Waco's two oldest schools. Beginning in September 1970, these class officers, alongside dozens of Waco ISD alumni and current students, "band[ed] together in an effort to save Waco High School's name for the school on North Nineteenth and Moore High School's name for the Jefferson Urban Renewal school."[2] Both these new school buildings were erected as Waco ISD struggled to implement the federal school desegregation mandate originally compelled by the 1954 *Brown v. Board of Education* decision. Nearly two decades later, Waco ISD, like too many other Southern school districts, was still prolonging the elimination of a dual schooling system that treated Black and non-Black schooling as separate issues.

Representing their entire school, class officers Marvin, Paula, and Gilbert sharpened their tactics to appeal to the school board over the course of the year because they understood that this naming issue was reflective of the board's disregard for "Negro heritage in Waco," as one parent explained.[3] These Black students not only circulated petitions to document that the majority of their student body hoped to keep the school's name but also conducted original research that they presented to the board at meetings to make their case. "To prove the worth of the name 'A. J. Moore'" and "the role Professor Andrew [*sic*] James Moore played in education for blacks in Waco," these Black student leaders examined the few primary documents accessible to them to sketch a biography of Alexander James Moore, the school's founder and first principal.[4] That news reporters did not trouble themselves to identify Professor Moore accurately by name, misrecording it on multiple occasions as Andrew instead of Alexander, reflects the low regard most white Wacoans had for Black education, Black Waco, and Black children. Furthermore, at the heart of this issue was the fact that "the students of Moore High [were] wanting a place in society"; one Moore High alumna urged the school board to "encourage them [the students at Moore High] by naming the [new] school A. J. Moore," because, as she saw it, "the board never thought of the student body."[5] Moreover, proponents of this name change roused multiracial support from across the city: Alumni and "the student bodies of the three other high schools in town [Waco High School, University High School, and Richfield High School] have sent letters to the school board saying that the name should be 'A. J. Moore.'"[6] In the midst of these remarkable strides on the part of Black Waco students and their supporters, their white counterparts from historically non-Black Waco High School deployed a similar petition strategy, the results of which they presented to the board to demonstrate overwhelming support for keeping the Waco High School name as they also prepared to transition to a new school building for the 1971–72 school year.[7]

The white power structure stood unmoved by the Black students' savviness, but this obstinance could not quash the wider fight to uphold Waco's Black educational heritage. In October 1970, the board voted unanimously to accept the subcommittee's recommendation, announcing that the new school intended to replace A. J. Moore would take the name Jefferson-Moore High School while Waco ISD's other new school building would maintain the name Waco High School.[8] With this decision, the board opted to preserve the legacy of historically non-Black Waco High while effectively terminating that of Black A. J. Moore High. The October school board meeting saw the widespread support for the preservation of Moore High's name fall on deaf ears because the board, apparently in unison, "walked out on the students and wouldn't hear them"—they literally turned their backs on the Black students.[9] Such blatant disrespect of the desires of Black Waco's children was not uncommon, but this response was no less disappointing. Black Waco's frustration targeted the antiBlackness that governed the whole decision-making process. Although the Black students had gone above and beyond their white counterparts by conducting original research, attending virtually all the school board meetings, lobbying for the name change, and following nearly all the rules and regulations in place for making their case, they had little to show for their efforts. The all-white school board's presumptive concession to include "Moore" as one part of the new school's hyphenated name was marred by antiBlackness, according to longtime Waco resident Curtis Wilburn, who underscored that the name "Jefferson" paid homage to the third president of the United States, a man whom many Black Wacoans resented given his primary occupation, in their eyes, as an enslaver.[10] Combining Alexander James Moore's name with that of such a figure, many Black Wacoans felt, further sullied the legacy of Black education that A. J. Moore had come to represent in the city.

In the spirit of struggle for the sake of one's humanity, Black Waco students articulated an acute assessment of the meaning they made of their fight against a backdrop of white supremacy. Class president Marvin Shelton expressed this awareness with a question: "Why be ashamed of putting a black name on it?"[11] The shame, he perceived, was white Waco's, not theirs. Marvin knew that the legacy of Anglo schooling would live on in the name of Waco High School, as it had in prior decades when de jure segregation—segregation by law—prohibited Black students from attending it. School board president John Faulkner corroborated Marvin's critical inquiry when he admitted, immediately after the December 1970 school board vote against the name change, that "we can no longer have a Negro school."[12] Neither Marvin nor the scores of A. J. Moore stakeholders, however, would stop "show[ing] how much they care[d] for A. J. Moore High School." By the end of the school year, Marvin was able to highlight that he and his classmates, among other stakeholders, had fought for the name because a "'sense of pride hit us all at once, when we thought we were going to lose the name.' Even though the name has 'Jefferson' tacked to it, Shelton said, the students still accept it as 'Moore High.'"[13] Maybe they knew they would not win, but they fought anyway. They challenged white power anyway. This tradition, a racially realist one, has historically marked the Black freedom struggle against white domination, and Black Waco's story highlights the salient intricacies of this struggle through the quotidian aspects of Black community life.[14]

The Black-imbued salience of this particular place, one that Black Wacoans established as a home with great meaning, is undeniable. In such a place, the spatial dimension and significance of this fight transcend the simple matter of what name a community gives a school building. This exercise of Black spatial agency stood to disrupt the status quo that was rooted in antiBlackness and white supremacy. It saw Black Wacoans demand the dignity the white power structure so often denied them. It saw them refuse for history to forget them. To erase them. It saw them participate in the democratic process as the citizens they had always deserved to be should they so choose. The Black sense of place they sought to impose on Waco writ large, although ultimately unsuccessful, shook the foundations of the white racial order. And students, Black students, led the way.

*Ordinary Sites: Student Resistance and the 1970s Texas School Desegregation Struggle* offers a new story about school desegregation, one centered on ordinary Black people in an ordinary place. In part, it revises what many have come to accept as a common story about race in Southern US schools by pointing out the classed and gendered elements that shaped not simply race but Blackness. It places at the center Black Waco students of different class levels and genders to destabilize widely held assumptions about what school desegregation was and meant for Black Southern students writ large. *Ordinary Sites* accomplishes these tasks by looking at a place that is like most places across the country, one that has rarely, if ever, been considered overly large, interesting, or important. It analyzes the people of that place—its Black people—to show that their lives were complicated and significant in ways that school desegregation helps illuminate. By focusing on a seemingly unexceptional place, *Ordinary Sites* underlines commonalities across Black student experiences in formerly non-Black schools, insights relevant to a range of differently spatialized places of virtually any size. Taking seriously Black students' and communities' day-to-day struggles and identities, this local history, like Charise L. Cheney's *Blacks Against Brown*, places value in truths present in locales across the country.[15]

Using the dissolution of Black schools as a point of departure, *Ordinary Sites* grapples simultaneously with Blackness, gender, and class—observing, for instance, the ways Paula, as a Black girl, had school experiences that were distinct from those of her Black boy peers Marvin and Gilbert, as well as how their respective class positions influenced how they pursued their name change mission. More specifically, this book interrogates how gender and class status shaped Blackness in the mixed-race environments of desegregating schools. Looking from a different perspective at Paula's participation in the

Junior Future Homemakers of America club, for example, and considering what it might have meant in a predominantly white environment reveals fresh insights about this consequential chapter in US history.[16] Furthermore, the book queries how socioeconomic status functioned in mixed-race contexts for Black Waco children of different genders.

School desegregation mixed races, but how did the co-ed experience across racial lines inform Black students' everyday schooling experiences? How did class differences among Black students influence how they navigated formerly segregated non-Black schools? What did school desegregation policy reveal about Black spatial agency, the consequential ways Black peoples have conceived of and produced space despite a logic deeming them insignificant and placeless? Guided by these questions, *Ordinary Sites* reframes school desegregation as a policy shaped by Black spatial agency. I contend that Blackness, gender, and class differentiated Black students' quotidian experiences of school desegregation, a racialized site of spatial contestation. This argument is complemented by the related claim that the unique disposition of Black Waco precollegiate students represents an ontological matter of Blackness too robust for full containment or explanation by frameworks chiefly concerned with oppression or death. Afropessimism, for instance, is growing as a popular school of thought centered on Black suffering and annihilation, which certainly has an integral place in the history of African Americans but not, I argue, the only place. Destruction, deprivation, and despair on their own provide an incomplete portrayal of the fullness of Black life. Frameworks sensitive to and capable of appreciating expressions of Black life are also vital. Waco is one of many sites that scholars deem unremarkable and thus overlook; challenging this view, I mine the Black ordinary to showcase African Americans' everyday struggle against white domination in navigating a consequential policy's implementation. Although I analyze the late 1960s, the late 1970s, and the early 1980s, much of this book's focus is on the early 1970s, because that is when Waco schools ramped up their desegregation efforts—albeit not of their own volition—and Black students were involuntarily relocated to new schools in greater numbers.

## THE UNWRITTEN AS LEGITIMATE

Taking a local history approach, *Ordinary Sites* yields to, in many cases, oral testimony to illuminate new insights about Black student life in and around desegregated schools. Oral history makes it possible to uncover details about the lives of regular people, whereas official records might fail to reveal vital details about those people's daily lives, experiences, or perspectives. This point underlines why oral history is integral to everyday Black history and thus foundational to this project. Despite enduring concerns about its susceptibility to inaccuracy in comparison to textual documents, prominent oral historians, including Alessandro Portelli, have been resolute in illustrating the many ways the written record is itself frequently littered with inaccuracies.[17] Scholars who level charges of erroneousness and inauthenticity against oral history seem unbothered that ordinary people in ordinary places often escape written scrutiny and, thus, the annals of history. *Ordinary Sites* seeks to subvert these claims and position Black quotidian life, as captured orally, as interesting and worthy of historical attention.

Oral history interviews are vital to this project because the answers to the questions motivating it remain largely unrecorded elsewhere. They crucially supplement—rather than compete with—archival documents, as I principally assess the how, not the what, of memory. Placing interviews in conversation with one another as well as with historical records and historiography allows me to assess specific dates, places, events, and the significance of discrepancies where they existed. To help me paint a general picture of school desegregation in Waco, the memories of narrators—the term oral historians use for their interviewees—serve as a sort of docent for me, even as I also consult extant archival records and acknowledge that racism has a wounding effect on cities and other peopled places that colors how residents remember their past.[18]

Leveraging the ordinary site of Black memory, this book challenges typical historical methods that render oral history inferior to the written archive, exposing one of the many ways, as Saidiya Hartman has poignantly illustrated, the written archive can violently render Black life either absent or inconsequential.[19] Given how little the written record reveals about regular Black students' experiences in ordinary places, this monograph elevates oral histories to tell a more complete story of school desegregation. Hence, situating oral histories as credible sources that provide perspective often missing from other, more traditional forms of evidence—not as sources inferior to the written record—represents a necessary departure from convention that I contend is essential to narrating chapters of Black history. Rather than viewing oral history interviews and written records as being opposed to each other, this book offers a way to read these rich sources of evidence as acting in concert, yielding a more dynamic account of Black history.

The written record and oral history interviews alternate between playing a supporting role and a leading role in the book, effectively switching places in the book's second half. Chapters 1 and 2 are driven largely by written accounts, while the final three chapters of this book are rooted largely in oral history evidence. In part, this initial reliance on written documents reflects my effort to establish the context that Waco's Black students were navigating from the late 1960s through the 1970s and early 1980s. Foregrounding the traditional archive allows me to critique it and use it as a point of contrast to the oral history interviews. Inverting this approach thereafter, I rely substantially on oral history interviews in chapters 3, 4, and 5 to depict in closer detail the day-to-day experiences of Black desegregating students. Again, the memories of Black Waco students gave me access to knowledge that would have otherwise been lost to history. Thus, in the final three chapters, I engage oral history interviews as foundational to the larger narrative I am telling and draw on written sources as needed for clarification and comparison; that is, I am interested not in seeking to "verify" the memories of Black Waco's children but in exploring how they interpreted their experiences and the larger significance of their doing so in the ways they did.

## RECASTING SCHOOL DESEGREGATION

This interdisciplinary historical project recasts school desegregation from the view of Black students, thereby exposing how the dominant narrative promotes a homogeneous Black experience that obscures students' daily classed and gendered struggle against antiBlackness in ordinary places. These interventions center on identity, time period, theory, and place.

Racial analyses, top-down legal accounts, and adult perspectives overlook how Black precollegiate students viewed the way other social constructs like gender and class influenced their quotidian experiences. This assessment of peer-reviewed scholarship, which excludes memoirs written by Black students, persists in characterizing the historiography. Because segregation was a legal policy centered on Blackness, race has commanded the lion's share of scholarly attention in discussions about school desegregation. Pathbreaking studies by historians Vanessa Siddle Walker and Michael Fultz, for instance, have reformulated how scholars recognize the quality of segregated Black schools in the South and the trying conditions Black educators navigated during and in the wake of this hallmark policy.[20] As a result, giving attention to gender or class status might seem at best a peripheral endeavor and at worst a betrayal of desegregation's ultimate concern—the legal dimension vis-à-vis the long-standing "separate but equal" ruling. Only recently have scholars starting delving into explorations of gender's role in this narrative, but this literature yet lacks a comprehensive assessment of gender beyond its relevance to girls and women.[21] As pioneering political histories by Richard Kluger, Mark Tushnet, James Patterson, and J. Harvie Wilkinson III, for instance, have illustrated, many middle-class Black and other progressive communities agreed that the strategy best suited to challenge de jure segregation required revising the legal system.[22] This effort, as historians and legal scholars tell it, involved the work of many adults, mainly men, who worked primarily outside schools and had formal legal training, which has rendered students largely tangential in many school desegregation narratives. Additionally, some scholarship highlights teachers' experiences navigating newly desegregated schools and the ways in which communities contended with the fate of school desegregation.[23] The few academic accounts of Black Southern students underscore battles fought at the higher education institutions at which a small minority of Black students matriculated or in other contexts, such as elite private schools, that proved similarly inaccessible to most.[24] To gain a sense of what most Black students might have faced in ostensibly regular places, *Ordinary Sites* contributes a precollegiate student-centered analysis of the ways Blackness, gender, and class converged in Black students' everyday experiences.

The second intervention responds to how the literature has widely equated school desegregation with the 1954 *Brown v. Board* decision that only nominally outlawed racially separate schools and with the policy's immediate aftermath into the 1960s—well before many obstinate school districts implemented the mandate and transformed students' daily lives. Delays persisted even after the US Congress during the Lyndon B. Johnson administration put increased pressure on school districts to desegregate by passing the 1964 Civil Rights Act. As school desegregation scholars Gary Orfield, whose copious scholarship on this topic has painstakingly documented myriad facets of this complicated policy and its legacy, and Chungmei Lee observed, "Serious desegregation of the cities only occurred in the 1970s and was limited outside the South."[25] This historiographical concentration on the 1950s and 1960s means that most of what we understand about school desegregation excludes an assessment of the 1970s despite it being a crucial time of change for most Black students. *Ordinary Sites* demonstrates the limitations of this periodization, portraying school desegregation's prolonged implementation into the 1970s, when most Black students saw their daily school lives shift.

My third intervention recognizes that despite this policy's salience as experientially place based, many scholars have declined to interrogate that school desegregation exemplified spatial contestation as it intersected with Black students' gendered and classed experiences. Several educational studies exploring Black communities in Southern states, including those by Charles Bolton of Mississippi, Scott Baker of South Carolina, Michelle Purdy and Vincent Willis of Georgia, and Davison Douglas of North Carolina, have acknowledged, but not theoretically probed, the spatialized modes of school desegregation's implementation.[26] Historians have discussed racial conflict over space in virtually each region of the United States but stopped short of elucidating how racially marginalized stakeholders remade their new school setting in ways that refashioned the social order.[27] As noted above, historical narratives about school desegregation from a social history lens are deeply concerned with race—a focus that is merited but incomplete if in isolation. Even the many studies that have concentrated on a specific city or state to more precisely understand school desegregation dynamics have largely missed the human geography element of this policy's implementation in a way that attends to the particularities of Black spatial agency. For this reason, I provide a theoretical examination of school desegregation as an instance of racialized spatial production vis-à-vis Black agency.

Given how scholars have repeatedly studied places that dominated national headlines, the fourth intervention broadens the historiography's geographical diversity of school desegregation.[28] This emphasis has created an incomplete, skewed narrative, entailing only a few accounts from Texas's sizable Black population, none at the Texas precollegiate level, and little understanding of students' plight in seemingly insignificant cities like Waco—a place not squarely rural, urban, or suburban that for decades avoided national attention for circumventing school desegregation.[29] Furthermore, the historical narratives about school desegregation in the Lone Star State have generally followed a similar trend regarding the study of large (i.e., important) cities or those that made headlines for horrific acts of violence. In terms of people groups, Texas's extant school desegregation historiography underscores the experiences of Mexican Americans, teachers, and college students.[30] Even historians looking at more ordinary places have often taken a statewide perspective, perhaps in an attempt to compensate for what a focus on one of these state's less sizable—and thus less remarkable—cities might offer.[31] While admittedly significant, the concentration of scholarship on such locales and on such groups raises unanswered questions about what was happening in places and to Black people outside the limelight, places and people that were not necessarily extraordinary but were no less important.

There recently have been cutting-edge studies that demonstrate important progress toward addressing these gaps in scholarship. These interdisciplinary studies are enhancing how scholars conceptualize space and place in educational contexts that have historically favored "progress" and "development" narratives; they also supply methodological reconsiderations of Black oral history with respect to places widely believed to be "common" and thus uninteresting. By stressing the unique salience of local histories and investigating spatial matters as deeply racialized in and beyond the context of schooling, this work is challenging the scholarly inclination to associate virtually all Black communities with an "urban" setting while also expanding research to include Black rural communities, both historical and contemporary.[32]

Notwithstanding these advancements, scholars overall have said little about the experiences of Indigenous groups, and Texas is no exception. Any discussion of any group's racialized oppression, however, would be remiss if it did not acknowledge the Indigenous peoples whom white settlers dispossessed and attempted in most cases to eradicate. In Waco's school desegregation struggle, there are scant traces of Indigenous students in the historical record or extant oral histories. Given the focus of this project and the research questions that inspired it, the plight of Indigenous students is outside the book's scope, but more research is certainly needed to better understand how Indigenous students in Texas broadly and in Waco specifically navigated school desegregation. In particular, the Wichita people, who include the Wacos from whom the city of Waco gets its name, warrant special mention. None of the groups on whom this book focuses were the first to inhabit the Waco-area lands I discuss; thus, I refer to this Indigenous band here to counter Native erasure and historical amnesia.

Relatedly, another group that has merited notable attention is Mexican-descendant peoples.[33] Their presence and influence in Texas are evident across many of the state's cities. As was the case in Waco and several other Texas cities, however, ethnic Mexicans were viewed and treated as though they possessed whiteness, which afforded them access to schools that by law excluded Black students. Although they were not Anglo, they were in the law's eyes white and, therefore, like their Asian counterparts, able to attend segregated non-Black schools in Waco. Their history, then, stands apart from that of Black Waco's children, who were unable to access schools reserved for non-Black students.[34] As a result, the story this book tells is centered on the unique experiences of Black Waco students in part because their circumstances were so disparate from those of other racial groups.

Black students' entanglement with school desegregation has continued to be a focus of both racial and, more recently, place-based analyses. Legal scholars have long interrogated school desegregation in its relationship to racial equality and its special significance to Black educational stakeholders. Originally, legal scholars used the critical legal studies framework to make these and related critiques but quickly found it inadequate. The group of legal scholars perhaps most critical of the ways that *Brown v. Board of Education*—both the 1954 decision and the 1955 follow-up decision known as *Brown II*—proved unable to remedy racial inequality in education have come to be known by many as critical race theorists. Not long after the civil rights movement, they started grappling with the *Brown* decision's legacy and its shortcomings for Black communities in particular, which had implications for most students racialized as non-Anglo. Founding critical race theorist Derrick Bell went so far as to reject the stated rationale of the decision, asserting with his "interest-convergence thesis" that the United States supported the desegregation of schools mainly because it stood to gain more than it was forfeiting in doing so; specifically, he argued that the Cold War context during which much of this legal fight unfolded forced the nation's hand, in that it had to desegregate schools given how its poor treatment of African Americans rendered it hypocritical on the global stage in its fight against communism. Desegregating schools, from that vantage point, seemed like low-hanging fruit. Having himself provided ample legal support for the desegregation of schools in the South throughout the 1960s, Bell questioned this legal strategy's efficacy relative to the interests of the Black families with whom he had worked. He came to recognize how legal victories failed to ensure the higher-quality education Black stakeholders were actually seeking.[35] This struggle for school desegregation brought into sharp relief the pitfalls of the larger civil rights strategy.

These critical school desegregation insights were foundational to what has since crystallized into critical race theory, an attempt to explain why racism persisted after the monumental gains of the civil rights movement. In this book, I engage critical race theory to interrogate the function of race, specifically Blackness, in the school desegregation implementation process. A central proposition of this theory is that racism is an endemic, normal feature of the United States that is evident across its institutions, structures, and systems, especially the education system.[36] It emphasizes the structural rather than the interpersonal manifestations of racial injustice and is deeply concerned with power's role in maintaining oppression. Additionally, critical race theory focuses on the perspectives of those experiencing racial injustice, elevating their insights to illuminate the ramifications of racial oppression, with an eye toward redress. Some critical race theorists also identify with racial realism: They accept the inevitability of antiBlack racial oppression but choose to fight it anyhow; they measure their humanity by the strength of their will to assert themselves in the struggle against white domination despite the outcome.[37] Rejecting ahistoricism, critical race theory reflects a deep consciousness of historical context and embraces narrative as a compelling form of examination.[38] In this same vein, many critical race theorists have authored counterstories as a way to undermine the authority frequently given to dominant narratives that uphold the status quo of racial inequity.[39] This theory also criticizes the ways ownership rights and property interests have historically intersected with and refashioned racial categorization practices to sustain white superiority, Black inferiority, and racial capitalism.[40]

As much as school desegregation was a legal issue, it was also a spatial matter. This aspect of school desegregation discourse has been less appreciated, however. The emerging body of work on Black geographies furnishes a way to analyze the special role of Black geographic subjects in the implementation of this policy. Black geographies grow out of the discipline of human geography and critical geographies of race. Principally, this perspective opposes conventional geographic beliefs that position Black peoples as perpetually placeless or displaced by dramatizing the ways they have persistently acted consequentially on the places they create and inhabit.[41] While this lens is cognizant of the role of antiBlack oppression in shaping the lives of Black peoples, it is not wholly consumed by or interested in Black suffering. Acting in many ways as a counter to Afropessimistic views that position violence, oppression, and death as comprising nearly all, if not most, of Black life, Black geographies underscore how Black life is as equally deserving of analysis as Black death.[42] More precisely, I view Black geographies, given their insistence on Black aliveness and livingness, as a rebuttal to central propositions of Afropessimism concerned acutely with Black mortality. In this study, Black geographies facilitate a meaningful spatial analysis of school desegregation in Waco from the vantage point of the city's Black students. The analysis clarifies the importance of examining not only ordinary places like Waco in which Black people have lived and do live but also the seemingly mundane ways Black students asserted themselves in new, largely hostile schools. Highlighting both the physical and nonphysical places Black students have occupied, the field of Black geographies is a generative perspective for detecting the nuances of Black life as a spatial endeavor.

As products of Black Waco, Black students operated from a Black sense of place, which geographer Katherine McKittrick describes as "a set of changing and differential perspectives that are illustrative of, and therefore remark upon, legacies of normalized racial violence that calcify, but do not guarantee, the denigration of black geographies and their inhabitants."[43] This recognition of the normality of racism, antiBlack racism in particular, demonstrates Black geographies' alignment with critical race theory, both of which converge to highlight antiBlack racism's influence on Black Waco students' school lives. Additionally, a Black sense of place involves "the process of materially and imaginatively situating historical and contemporary struggles against practices of domination and the difficult entanglements of racial encounter."[44] Few places better illuminate these racial encounters than newly desegregated schools. Black Waco students knew their lives would be forever changed in leaving—forcibly—their segregated Black schools for formerly non-Black ones. They predicted there would be turbulence. They also accepted that their doing so would constitute a spatial enterprise that would likely demand resistance, a key feature of both critical race theory and Black geographies. These spatialized assertions of Blackness represent Black spatial agency. Acting on their autonomy, then, was less about its effectiveness and more about what such an act symbolized—that they were fully human and deserved to be treated as such.

Consistent with critical race theory and Black geographies is the notion of antiBlackness, which is fundamental to the experiences of Black Waco students. I use the terms "antiBlack" or "antiBlackness" to refer to antiBlack racism that constitutes "structural or institutional acts and supporting ideologies that oppress, subjugate, or subordinate Black peoples."[45] The goal of antiBlackness is predicated on the subjugation of Black peoples; it goes hand in hand with white supremacy, which seeks to bolster the status quo of white power and domination. While the objective of antiBlackness is specific in its targeting of Black people, white supremacy's aim is to embolden white dominance, which can employ antiBlack tactics but may not do so exclusively. Moreover, racism, more generally, is not necessarily specific to Black peoples but can, and often does, implicate them. Stated differently, antiBlackness is specific to Black people in that its goal is typically Black subordination but not always for the sake of white supremacy, which can be served through both antiBlack and more general racist means. Although the relationship between racism and antiBlackness is slippery, antiBlackness is a distinct brand of racism that requires Black peoples to be the target of racial malice. This special contempt for Blackness and Black peoples marks it because, as some argue, it is the fulcrum of white supremacy, making it possible for this and for other non-Black-specific manifestations of racism to flourish.[46]

Although Blackness was certainly at the center of Black Waco students' experiences in these schools, race was not the sole defining feature. Gender and socioeconomic status, which I use interchangeably with class status and references to income level, also overlapped with Blackness to shape the students' day-to-day lives in significant ways. Growing out of the Black feminist tradition, both critical race theory and Black geographies emphasize the contextual temporality of oppression and the ways groups experience simultaneously different forms of oppression. Both are sensitive to the ways the consideration of gender complicates racial analyses and, further, how class interests tend to reflect the hold capitalism has historically had on society. Gender as an analytic category is well established in scholarship, and it considers how social issues differentiate themselves along gendered lines that reflect the misdistribution of resources and power. Although at times across the book I engage sex-based language (e.g., *female, male*), my doing so serves to stress commonalities across those labeled as such a sex despite their gender identity. In a similar fashion, class as an analytic category raises questions regarding financial capital to ascertain how it affects the level of resources and power that different groups can access. These lenses enable the careful assessment of the ways multiple forms of privilege and oppression operate simultaneously. In lieu of an intersectional framework that is more beholden to evaluations of oppression exclusively, these views enable a more dynamic assessment of Black Waco students' complicated lives, which included features of advantage and disadvantage, experienced concurrently.[47]

Importantly, these perspectives converge to reveal that antiBlack racism was—and in many ways remains—ubiquitous regardless of which geographic region of the country one might find oneself in. Despite the myth of Southern exceptionalism, the popular view that the South is the only place where racism has historically festered, the notion of the "good, liberal North" is a farce.[48] "Northern states," historian James D. Anderson points out, "designed complex institutional arrangements to sustain day-to-day segregation and racial inequality."[49] Boston in the 1970s, for instance, presents a telling example of Northern obstinance to desegregation, specifically to busing. Shortchanging Black children's access to a well-resourced education, anti-Black violence animated white resistance against the implementation of this policy in a fashion some historians argue rivaled what occurred below the Mason-Dixon Line.[50] My focus on the South here aims not to argue for its especially pernicious nature but to demonstrate nuances related to the gendered and classed idiosyncrasies of antiBlack racism in the process of reconfiguring schools. *Ordinary Sites* represents what I hope to be the first of many studies to recast this and other familiar historical chapters in a new light, one that carefully considers the normalization of antiBlackness as it interacted with other forms of oppression and privilege in any number or variety of sites in and outside schools.

The terms "desegregation" and "integration" signify different parts of a process related to mixing peoples whom society has assigned to different racial categories. For the purposes of this book, "desegregation" refers to the sanctioned process of interrupting the ongoing practice of racial segregation or racial separation. In contrast, "integration" refers to an outcome of desegregation. It is much more difficult to achieve than desegregation, because it requires the thorough mixing of racial groups in meaningful ways across different levels of an organization or society. In the case of schools, for instance, one might use the term "integration" as an apt label if or when the number of faculty, staff, administrators, and students have a racial composition reflecting that of the wider school district, city, or county and have a similar distribution within each academic course level and across extracurricular activities. Because few if any schools actually achieved integration—certainly not Waco schools—I usually employ the term "desegregation" to indicate this distinction.

Given the history of non-Anglo students who were able to attend segregated white schools in Waco, I employ the terms "Black schools" and "non-Black schools" throughout this book. In large part, I was inspired to make this decision by NAACP attorney Thurgood Marshall, who would go on to become the nation's first Black Supreme Court justice, and Howard University professor Charles Thompson, both of whom articulated this observation upon their visits to the University of Texas in the 1940s. They witnessed how every racial group except "Negroes" could be found on the campus.[51] This departure from convention, which has typically seen scholars refer to racially separate schools during school segregation as either white or Black, aims to deploy more precise language to describe the racial context that shaped which schools Black Waco's children could and could not attend. It also challenges arguments about the irrelevance or restrictive nature of the Black/white racial binary in discussions about racism's multifaceted nature. As Nobel laureate Toni Morrison contended, Blackness, even when it goes unnamed, has always been implicated in any discussion about race in the United States because the construction of other groups as racialized in their own right rests on a spectrum between whiteness, the epitome of the society's racial order, and Blackness, which Derrick Bell described as the very nadir of this order.[52]

In each chapter, after initially introducing Black "students," a term I use interchangeably with "alumni," by their first and last names, I thereafter refer to them by their first names. The absence of a racial descriptor for an individual or group, especially in reference to students or alumni, presumes their Blackness. If ambiguity threatens which students with the same first name I am referring to, I address them by their first name and last initial (e.g., Connie S. and Connie O.). I chose to use this first name convention as a way to remind readers, and myself, that these students, even as high schoolers, were children, who were navigating an incredibly complex web of racialized violence, further complicated by sexism and classism. Their youth marked their journey through Waco's desegregated schools. Thus, refraining from the urge to call them by their last name or place a courtesy title prefix (e.g., Ms.) before either of their names is an invitation to remember that this is a story about children. I employ this practice while wrestling with the legacy of disrespect that largely defined how white society engaged with Black people with regard to their names; that is, I recognize that Black adults were historically stripped of the respect paid to other groups, particularly Anglos, when being addressed. This practice aimed to dehumanize and demean Black people. In an effort to counteract the social impulse to disrespect Black adults and elders, *Ordinary Sites* underscores that these individuals were once children, and using their first names invokes their youth. This expanded conceptualization of children—in which high-school-aged youth are children—has been infrequently applied to Black peoples, and some historians argue that childhood, as a social construction, was rarely if ever extended to enslaved children.[53] Thus, my emphasis on their youth serves to counter the plethora of impulses that routinely "adultify" Black children with little regard for their life experiences, numerical age, psychological development, or emotional maturity.

In a similar vein, I refer to the Black girls in this narrative by their surname at birth, not the surname they used during our interview. This name is the one they carried when they started school and the name most of them still used when they graduated. In the few cases of students who got married during high school, I make note of that within the text and discuss it as relevant. It was largely under original, or in some cases unmarried, surnames that their school desegregation experiences transpired, so it is fitting for these names to be used in a historical account of their time as students.

I also capitalize certain terms throughout the book, as I have done in this introduction, including "Black/ness," "antiBlack," "East Waco," "people of Color," and "Southern" or the "South," to stress the authority I assign these qualities and entities. In contrast, I decapitalize, or lowercase, other terms, including "white" and "west Waco," to revoke some of the authority writers often lend to such qualities and entities associated with wealth or whiteness. My choice to do so is political. I accentuate certain groups and places in an effort to render them autonomous and distinct—to acknowledge them as integral to this story in a way that traditional capitalization practices may otherwise understate. Additionally, I view Blackness as always worthy of special recognition and respect via capitalization any time the term or its derivatives are used, including in reference to ideas about antiBlackness. To signal the seamless and familiar manner in which so much of society regarded Blackness as something warranting extreme opposition and condemnation, I forgo hyphenation (as in "antiBlack") to underscore how natural this ideology was and arguably still is for many—how the prefix and the word were more often than not fused together in the psyches of many of the non-Black individuals with whom Waco's Black children interacted.

Finally, although I use the terms "Black," "Black American," and "African American" largely interchangeably, the following distinction clarifies how these differ from one another and applies to my usage in this book: The descriptor "Black" is used to refer to racial identity, whereas the descriptor "African American" signifies the specific ethnicity of a people who are Black, namely those with ancestors enslaved in the land now known to many as the United States and whose lineages prove difficult to trace back to a specific sub-Saharan African country. I use "Black American" synonymously with "African American" as a way to acknowledge this group's native-born status and their inability to lay claim to any other specific place or nation-state. As a note, all alumni who contributed to this study identify as Black, Black American, and African American, meaning no one was able to lay claim to a specific non-US country and had descended from persons enslaved in the United States.

## WHAT'S TO COME

My concentration on place—that is, the spaces to which humans assign meaning—compels me to characterize Waco widely, and Black Waco specifically, from the perspectives of the Black community under study. This focus indicates the community history *Ordinary Sites* offers, much like that furnished in historian David Cecelski's riveting account of a Black North Carolina community's resistance to school desegregation in *Along Freedom Road.*[54] This depiction constitutes much of the focus of chapter 1. Accordingly, Waco and Black Waco represent central characters in this historical narrative, and tracing the education of Black Waco's children requires analysis of not only Waco ISD but La Vega Independent School District (La Vega ISD) as well. La Vega ISD was and remains a relatively small school district adjoining the city of Waco that for decades educated many of the city's Black children. Located primarily in the city of Bellmead, La Vega ISD was unique in that its boundaries expanded beyond the city limits of Bellmead and into East Waco, one of the few places in Waco that Black Wacoans could live. Thus, a story about Black education in Waco would be incomplete without La Vega ISD's story, which, as I show, converged with that of Black Waco ISD students to comprise a history of Black Waco education.

Setting the stage for this narrative, chapter 1 analyzes twentieth-century Black Waco as a rich assortment of spaces that holistically nurtured its Black children in a distinctly Southern context that defied categorizations of Texas as Western or Southwestern. This chapter argues that despite the long-standing antiBlack racism that prefigured the antiBlack implementation of school desegregation in Waco, Black Wacoans established a Black sense of place that challenged conventional pairings of Blackness with dispossession and whiteness with freedom. Although I characterize Black-segregated Waco as a vibrant, thriving community amid systemic racial subjugation, I take care to not romanticize de jure segregation. I begin by contextualizing the racial landscape of Waco as it influenced the two school districts and cities under scrutiny, Waco ISD in Waco and La Vega ISD in (mostly) Bellmead. Emphasizing the historical import of the 1916 lynching of Jesse Washington in Waco, this chapter connects the enduring significance of such antiBlack violence as it overlapped with gender and class to shape Black students' expectations for how they would engage with white Wacoans in the school desegregation process. Analyzing residential, population, income, and occupation data, I provide a spatial analysis of Black Waco linked to school desegregation across Texas to contextualize La Vega ISD's implementation of it and the legacy of its Black schools.

Against this racialized, spatialized backdrop, *Ordinary Sites* pivots to how the two school districts under scrutiny went about desegregating. In chapter 2, I examine the La Vega school board's duplicitous decision to shut down the district's only Black high school—without warning—revealing how white supremacy and antiBlack structural racism rendered immaterial the African Americans' sense of spatial belonging. I underscore the humiliating way most residents found out about this closure and how adjoining Waco ISD and La Vega ISD colluded to abruptly close their Black schools and subsequently arranged an inter-district transfer of Black students. This handover included La Vega compensating Waco ISD for accepting new students, that is, for the "burden" of assuming additional Black bodies; Black students, nonetheless, resisted in gendered and class-centric ways. This chapter's central assertion is that school districts negligently used Black schools and children as pawns, but Black students staked their new territory by publicly protesting their mistreatment, bucking gender conventions and class mores. Before exploring these topics, it begins with a focus on the 1970 walkout that Black students led within the first weeks of the 1970–71 school year at La Vega High School to protest the undignified way La Vega ISD had closed its Black high school. Although official activism was certainly important, especially during this era, Black Waco students' resistance was largely informal and unorganized, making me careful to frame these Black students not as activists but as everyday resisters. Additionally, none of this study's alumni identified as activists, so for me to place that label on them would betray their capacity for self-definition. Nonetheless, three distinct yet compatible versions of the walkout's origin, which subvert mainstream narratives about the absence of Black agency, illuminate the ways that Blackness, gender, and leadership capacity colored each account. Next, I illustrate the harrowing school year that followed and the social class tensions, both intra- and interracial, that animated it. Ultimately, I demonstrate how white segregationists worked tirelessly to sustain white domination and Black subjugation and how Black students enacted spatial agency by repurposing formerly non-Black schools as places where they could reclaim their dignity.

In contrast to *Ordinary Sites*' first two chapters, its final three provide a closer, more microlevel look at Black Waco students' day-to-day lives. These chapters offer a reading of school desegregation widely absent from more conventional primary sources. Throughout the book, I strive for a balance in the subjects of my analysis, between the oppression Black students faced and their resistance to it. Chapters 1 and 3 furnish an account of the subjugation that Black students had to contend with, while chapters 4 and 5 stress their multifaceted, heterogeneous resistance strategies; chapter 2 supplies a combination of the two.

Shifting focus from overt acts of structural antiBlackness and Black student resistance to the conditions Black students encountered in desegregating Waco schools, chapter 3 explores the pervasiveness of centuries-old tropes that structured Black children's treatment in school. This chapter posits that white school stakeholders applied what I refer to as the Mammy, Problem, Mascot, and Black Buck stereotypes on Black children in desegregated schools—distortions that revealed more about those imposing them on Black students than about Black students themselves. These controlling images exposed the depravity inherent in white supremacy and what it meant for Black personhood to be undermined, sometimes through paternalistic praise, with nonchalant regularity. I highlight that despite Black students having every right to claim victim status, many refused to do so, turning instead to craft analyses of whiteness and racial power based on their experiential knowledge, their agency, and their capacity to critically read their new social world. Texturing the mosaic of Black thought and action in desegregated Waco schools, other Black students, as I demonstrate, embraced the application of these slanted conceptualizations. I portray how the time and place—the when and where—of Blackness, alongside its gendered and classed dimensions, gave new meaning to common stereotypes that shaped Black students' experiences as a result of school desegregation. Bringing Black students face-to-face with racism and heightening their vulnerability, school desegregation created an opportunity for gendered and classed Blackness to take on new meaning in a new educational setting.

From these accounts of mistreatment, I transition to the various ways Black girls negotiated these fraught conceptualizations in their new milieu. Chapter 4 highlights the marked determination of Black Waco girls in newly desegregated schools, particularly as cheerleaders, homecoming queens and queen nominees, pregnant students, and young mothers. Asserting that Black girls were visionaries who expanded white people's notions of femininity and capability, chapter 4 demonstrates how Black girls achieved their goals through tenacity and audacity by believing they could hold titles ostensibly reserved for their white (girl) counterparts. Their visionary acumen redefined and expanded traditional, hegemonic notions of femininity and capability, making their new schools, the South, and the nation more inclusive and representative of their dynamic experiences. Framing them as shapeshifters, this chapter follows a group of Black girls who occupied different ends of the class status spectrum, from their elementary school days through high school, to understand the attributes they shared, how they viewed themselves and their circumstances, and what their bodies symbolized. In analyzing the stigmatization of the Black female body, discourses around sexual activity, the importance of the Black racial collective, and what it meant to make history, I subsequently demonstrate that Black girls with seemingly incompatible experiences had far more in common than one might expect. This exploration of femininity and morality, notions that were deeply classed, illustrates how Black girls used school desegregation as a stage on which they expressed themselves as whole, sufficient, and unique on their own terms.

Turning to Black Waco students as a whole, chapter 5 continues the theme of self-determination, providing an account of how Black students evoked and developed care practices in their new racially mixed schools. This chapter underscores how school desegregation diminished the holistic care that had defined the ethos of segregated Black schools and how Black Waco students re-created key elements of this care by renegotiating how and where they practiced, sought, and mirrored care in their new schools. First, I show how some Black Waco students transferred from majority-white desegregated schools to a high school that was technically desegregated but (still) majority Black. Second, I demonstrate how Black Waco students mirrored the extent to which they felt cared for by their school, adjusting the level of their school engagement to be either highly involved, disassociated, or somewhere in between. Third, I show how Black Waco students, to re-create key elements of the communal education that school desegregation took from them, deliberately changed the way they cared for one another. That is, many started to view the salience of their race and how, in this new racial context, that trumped any class divisions among them. I illustrate how unifying across different class statuses served as a safeguard against racial violence and repelled breakdowns in racial unity that could be exploited. Although their class differences were rather slight in comparison to those between them and white students, African American pupils grew increasingly aware of what their socioeconomic level meant in these new schools.

Stepping back to bring together *Ordinary Sites*' key elements, the conclusion summarizes the book's key ideas, linking them to current issues such as resegregation trends, Black students' sense of belonging in predominantly white institutions, policies penalizing Black hair, and discipline disparities across race and gender. I highlight how this book expands knowledge about African American education history in Texas, pushes readers to consider race as well as other categories of social difference, and raises the larger question of school desegregation's success. In particular, I explore school desegregation's capacity to meet its stated aims, suggesting ultimately that considerations of power—on the school board, in administration, on the legal bench—were largely missing from the wider concern with Black student well-being. We are still learning what these vestiges of quotidian antiBlackness and Black students' unwillingness to be defined by such sentiment have meant for ordinary Black life across space, race, gender, and class.

Now, let's get to it.

# 1

# Spatializing Black Waco and School Desegregation

*The school board took advantage of the black community. Some of the black schools were just as well equipped and some of the white children should have been displaced like the black children were. We shouldn't have had to bear all the burden.*

BETSY FANCHER, *VOICES FROM THE SOUTH*, 1970

On learning that she would be attending formerly non-Black Waco High School, Debora Wilkerson considered what everyday encounters with white students would mean for her schooling experiences. She brought with her to school her family's placed-based memories of white racial terror—horrific in their routine nature and the unexceptional nature of their perpetrators. These memories animated how Debora thought about her hometown and made her cautious about engaging with her white counterparts. Home, as she had known it, would suddenly be redefined. These ordinary practices of brutality weighed on the psyche of many Black residents. Historians have illustrated how Black girls like Debora sought to balance such trepidation with courage.[1] Thus, desegregation was not simply about a change in the student body or the location of one's school; rather, for Debora, it was about a disruption to her sense of safety that respatialized a place she had long called home: Waco. For her, "some of that fear [was still present during school desegregation] because many of our parents or our grandparents had lived during the time of the lynching. Some others had lived during the time of the tornado, where it talks about [how] the tornado traveled—the tornado that tore Waco apart—traveled the same path that they used to drag this young man's [dead] body."[2]

Jesse Washington was that young man.[3] Scholar-activist W. E. B. Du Bois dubbed this barbarous spectacle "the Waco Horror" and dedicated an entire supplement of *The Crisis*, the NAACP's periodical, to it.[4] White locals lynched Jesse, a Black seventeen-year-old, on May 15, 1916, after a sham investigation and hasty trial in which an all-Anglo jury found him guilty of raping and killing a white woman, Lucy Fryer, for whom he worked. Having allegedly violated Fryer's white womanhood, Jesse was tortured and mutilated for hours. Before roasting his corpse and claiming pieces as souvenirs, a raucous crowd of white men, women, and children numbering in the thousands cut off Jesse's fingers, ears, toes, and penis while they doused him in oil to set him ablaze. In the post-Reconstruction era, as historians have shown, lynching transformed from a primarily punitive activity into a cultural practice of leisure predicated on spectacle, torture, and sadism.[5] Hours later, these white locals brandished Jesse's charred remains by dragging them through the downtown area, along the same path that in 1953, thirty-seven years later, a tornado would take and raze downtown Waco, as Debora recounted. Some Black Wacoans believe that the catastrophic tornado, which caused at least $57 million in mostly white property damage, 114 casualties, and nearly 300 injuries, represented the Black community's retribution for Jesse's senseless murder.[6] Standing out as one of the few historic events for which Waco is known, the spectacle of Jesse's 1916 lynching was tragically typical.[7]

The connection between Jesse's lynching and schooling in Waco is, in part, spatial. "Students from nearby Waco High School," according to historian James SoRelle, some of whom were the same age as Jesse, "rushed to the scene during their lunch hour [to] witness this exhibition of horror," his lynching.[8] Unlike Jesse, these children were white, as Jim Crow prohibited Black children from attending Waco High en masse until the 1970s. Besides *The Crisis*'s feature, one of the only written reflections by a Black local resident about Jesse's barbaric extralegal murder was published in Paul Quinn College's newspaper, the *Paul Quinn Weekly*. Located in East Waco for most of its life, Paul Quinn College was established in 1872 as Texas's first historically Black college. The article's author, A. T. Smith, stressed Jesse's innocence and accused the white woman's husband of her murder. This accusation found Smith serving a one-year sentence of hard labor in a convict labor gang for criminal libel.[9] Such atrocities rarely escaped the purview of students—Black or white. And Debora's comments underline the crucial importance of oral history in Black communities that were unable to wield the written word in their defense. Her reflections also highlight how Black communities often embed critical notions of space in the oral histories they pass down. Their doing so makes it nearly impossible to separate the where from the what. This act of survival, and perhaps even resistance, reflects not only the value of oral history but also the deeply intertwined nature of space and race—more precisely, of space and Blackness.

The racialized intersections of memory, space, and place coalesce to form this chapter's argument: African Americans in the small, Southern, presumably unimportant city of Waco established a Black sense of place that challenged conventional pairings of Blackness with dispossession and whiteness with freedom. While Black segregated life often saw underinvestment and suffering, Black Waco's myriad cultural assets reveal what the community lost in school desegregation and what some Black students fought to keep.[10] These efforts exemplify how life—aliveness—rather than death, framed much of their existence.[11] Furnishing an account of Waco's racial history as it manifested in the city's development, planning, economics, Black education, and early considerations of school desegregation, this chapter contextualizes the backdrop against which more full-scale school desegregation took place in the 1970s. Tragically, both Waco's and Bellmead's long-standing antiBlack racism prefigured school desegregation's antiBlack implementation. These factors converged to peculiarly spatialize Waco such that the implementation of school desegregation transpired as a contested site on which educational stakeholders asserted spatial claims. Encompassing both singular and representative characteristics of other schooling sites, these circumstances fostered the blend of Blackness, gender, and class I argue mediated Black students' experiences therein.

Black students' feelings about school desegregation were predicated on looming anxieties resulting from centuries of racialized violence in Waco. Although white Wacoans slaughtered Jesse several decades before Black students desegregated non-Black Waco schools, Debora's remarks illuminate how the shared memory of his fatal brutalization shaped their anxiety about school desegregation in Waco—anxiety that was acutely gendered and classed. Analyses of Southern school desegregation have underscored the well-warranted apprehension with which Black students entered newly desegregated schools.[12] Adding to this anxiety, gendered antiBlack stereotypes—such as the myth of the Black Brute with an unbridled appetite for white women—played a central role both in Jesse's lynching and throughout Black students' school desegregation experiences.[13] Jesse and his brother William were hired hands on the Fryers' farm; these positions reflected their low socioeconomic status and reliance on a white family for their livelihood.[14] In this instance, being a poor (and illiterate) Black boy made Jesse extremely susceptible to the lynching that white Waco meted out on him. The place-based significance of his execution reflects what Black geographies scholar Katherine McKittrick argues is "the interconnectedness of race, place, and violence," which, in the school desegregation of Waco, also came into play in Black students' courage to confront the dangers associated with close contact with white people.[15] White segregationists fretfully decried the peril that Black students represented, particularly Black boys, in sharing intimate schooling space with their white peers, especially white girls; however, those most vulnerable, I posit, were Black students, whose lack of sociopolitical power gave them little to no defense against the antiBlack violence many met in their new schools.[16]

Situating Waco as firmly Southern represents one of *Ordinary Sites'* critical departures from scholarship arguing that Texas as a whole is part of the West or the Southwest. Midcentury media and prevalent lore are largely responsible for shaping the popular notions of Texas as part of the "wild Wild West" with "cowboy and Indian" propaganda, mythology patterned after places in the western and southwestern regions of the state where African Americans were scant—places unlike Waco.[17] These imagined places hosted Anglo cowboys, "Indian savages," and Mexicans, all folded into a "vaquero" cultural landscape in endless, unrelenting desert marked by tumbleweeds and expansive stretches of cattle ranches. Although Texas's size and proximity to Mexico make it difficult to neatly situate within conventional conceptions of the South, an individual community like Waco can fit that label—because Waco is the South. Unlike other parts of the land now known as the United States, the South has historically been marked by de jure segregation policies (e.g., Jim Crow), sociopolitical restrictions that both constrained Black life and provided opportunities for it to thrive both in and beyond education. These mechanisms of segregation influenced how antiBlack racism was enmeshed throughout the area's political, social, cultural, and economic fabric and remains so today. Black alumni echoed this nuanced characterization of Waco as being Southern but not of the Deep South. Moreover, central Texas's political economy, especially its fundamental dependence on enslaved labor and, later, the significance of sharecropping, showcases Waco's Southern character.[18] Central and eastern portions of the state—where enslavement thrived and African Americans were concentrated—operated like other former Confederate states. Texas, however, distinguished itself because it is the only one of those states seated on the US-Mexico border. After white settlers worked to disappear the Lone Star State's Indigenous groups—the original stewards of Texas sky, land, and water, who included, among others, the Karankawa, Wichita, Tawakoni, and Tonkawa—Texas's peoples evolved into a robust tripartite population of African Americans, ethnic Mexicans, and Anglos. Texas historian Walter Buenger's analysis of antiBlack violence in the Lone Star State is worth quoting at length:

> No western state had almost 400 lynchings of blacks by whites between the 1800s and the 1930s, as Texas did. Racial violence of the most horrific scale should remind us that Texas was not a movie scene. It was not an imagined world. It was a place that trailed only Georgia and Mississippi in the number of recorded lynchings, as in those states, participants in those events numbered in the hundreds and occasionally in the thousands. The torture inflicted on Jesse Washington by the huge white mob at Waco in 1916 matched the brutality and sadism of anything that happened anywhere in the South. Segregation continued long after lynching stopped, and in 1969 the University of Texas [at Austin] was the last all-white football team to win a national championship.[19]

This violence, however, was ordinary in many ways; it reflected the reach of unrelenting white domination that marks the US racial project. These systemic acts of brutality were a response to the pronounced presence and perceived threat of Blackness, which ironically has a diminutive presence in the written history of Waco and the county to which it belongs, McLennan.[20] In Waco, however, Black students viewed the personal meaning of desegregation and what it implied about their safety—that the implementation of this policy would diminish it—through a spatial prism that made it difficult to separate the land from what happened on it.

The small, urbanized area of Waco is representative of communities across the United States with protracted legacies of systemic violence against African Americans for alleged sexual crimes. McLennan County, where Waco was and remains the county seat and most populous city, had the second most lynchings of all Texas counties from 1877 to 1950.[21] Jesse's brutal lynching occurred one year after the release of D. W. Griffith's iconic film, *The Birth of a Nation*, in 1915 and coincided with the rise of the Ku Klux Klan in central Texas—efforts intended to annihilate the so-called Black Brute.[22] Waco's long history of acute racial violence contextualizes how gender and class mixing across racial lines unprecedentedly challenged Southern mores, especially during the fraught period of school desegregation. These occasions of violence, however, were unsuccessful at fully circumscribing Black life in Waco.

Black (segregated) Waco, which extended east into the adjoining town of Bellmead, was shaped by the political landscape of both cities, a dynamic that influenced the community's educational experiences. White power holders weaponized educational policy to disregard the deep significance that Black Wacoans assigned to Bellmead's Black schools, which were part of La Vega ISD. Despite conjectures that it would enhance life for Black Wacoans, desegregation disrupted or shuttered many of the Waco area's signature cultural and educational spaces. In 1968, the relationship between Waco and Bellmead displayed what a federal representative from the Office for Civil Rights called "a rather unusual situation, wherein part of [Bellmead's La Vega] school district lies in another city."[23] Living in two antiBlack, white supremacist school districts, African Americans persisted despite living in, as recorded in 1962, the largest school district in a Texas city without a school desegregation plan, which took more than a decade to fully implement.[24] Waco ISD served a student population that was more than four times that of La Vega ISD, whose Black students made up nearly half of its student body.

## RACIAL DEMOGRAPHY, SPATIAL DEMOGRAPHY

Segregation afforded Black people a measure of spatial autonomy that desegregation threatened and largely upended. By assigning meaning to and producing racialized space, Black Waco and scores of other segregated Black communities across the country routinely defied conventional geographic beliefs and disproved the notion that African Americans are constantly displaced interlopers. The class-level distinctions between Black Wacoans felt materially significant to some, but they did little to shield any African Americans from the ravages of white supremacy.[25]

Residential segregation and school segregation are tightly connected, working together in many cases to propel a form of antiBlack structural violence perhaps more stealthy but no less detrimental than a lynching. Because a large portion of public school funding comes from property taxes, educational inequities reflect the funding structures that have historically advantaged schools in more affluent, whiter areas.[26] Throughout Texas, residential segregation was not exclusive to large, urban metropolitan areas, historically separating Anglos, African Americans, and Mexican Americans. In Waco, this separation appeared most acutely in Black and Anglo separation, closely linking residential segregation to patterns of school segregation. The residential patterns of African Americans in and around Waco reflect the history of both Waco ISD and La Vega ISD vis-à-vis Black students, the composition of Black communities, and what these factors meant for Black schools once both school districts eventually desegregated.

Population, income data, and spatial analyses portray the centrality of structural racism that shaped group experiences and Waco neighborhoods. Rather than train tracks dividing the city by race, in Waco a river performed this task. Following the legal prohibition of enslavement, a mix of antiBlack housing covenants and de facto practices forced many Black Wacoans to settle on the east side of the city's main river, "as the Brazos River divided the city in half" and served as a boundary line between Black Wacoans and white residents, who came to be concentrated farther west and north.[27] Referred to by many as East Waco, this area sits where the city limits of Waco end to the east and those of Bellmead begin. This eastern portion of the city was more rural in nature compared with Waco proper.[28]

Like elsewhere, antiBlack racial logics drove Waco's residential organization and directly implicated education.[29] In the early 1930s, the Federal Housing Administration, in collusion with other federal entities, started practicing redlining, an "assessment of urban neighborhoods . . . [that] was racially and ethnically discriminatory . . . [and] used the power of the federal government to formalize patterns of segregation and discrimination."[30] A 1934 redlined map of Waco shows the area east of the Brazos River bordering Bellmead almost completely red, meaning it was deemed by banks to be too risky in terms of mortgage lending or insuring, as were the pockets of south and north Waco where African Americans were more likely to lease but widely restricted from purchasing; their mere residence in these parts of the city rendered certain neighborhoods too Black and thus too risky for banks to support.[31]

Black geographic praxis, "the everyday habits, spatial lives and geographical claims" whereby "residents claim and reclaim Black geographic space in a city that strove to actively deny the promise of freedom through property and spatial regulations and violence," complements conventional spatial analyses centered on the revocation machinations of a meaningful Black emplaced existence.[32] Enriching important yet traditional views that often stress the residential covenants, codes, and redlining policies, laws, and city ordinances African Americans confronted are the intangible ways Black Wacoans cultivated spaces and places of living despite these barriers. By establishing lives of meaning "beyond the scope, gaze and mark of white oppression," Black Wacoans engaged an "everyday Black geography" consumed largely with deliberate Black emplacement, or where Black people find themselves and create place.[33] This practice "is grounded in lived experience" and predicated on Black place-making.[34] Any brief exemplifications, therefore, of the widespread, structural impediments Black Waco met in striving to create lives of meaning serve as reference points for Black Wacoans' will to live despite systemic subjugation. Determined to create homes and places of pride and importance in the face of these obstacles, Black Wacoans "create[d] sites of endurance, belonging, and resistance" that allowed them to "privilege the creative, celebratory, playful, pleasurable, and poetic experiences of being black and being around other black people in the city."[35] Although scholars have deployed this Black place-making framework to theorize Black urban communities, less squarely urban areas including Waco also engaged in such Black geographic praxis. Desegregation, however, compromised these practices of personhood.

Students' memories complement US census data indicating that the area demarcated as Bellmead featured white, agriculturally oriented residents of a lower socioeconomic status as compared with those in west Waco, who were of a more urban and affluent ilk; nevertheless, Blackness overlapped with class to make Black Waco residents more susceptible to subjugation. According to the US Census, in 1970 the median income in Bellmead was approximately $7,400 per household annually, nearly half that of white households in west Waco.[36] For context, the national median family income at this time was $10,236 for white families and $6,279 for African Americans, so Bellmead's white families had significantly less than the national average, and their incomes sharply contrasted with those of white Wacoans living in the western part of the city.[37] Black families nationally and in Waco—East Waco, specifically—had incomes below those of the low-income white residents populating Bellmead.

From the late 1940s into the mid-1960s, the city of Waco established a group of East Waco neighborhoods that concretized socioeconomic differences among Wacoans, and the legacy of the funding that facilitated these changes is complicated. Carver Park, Gholson Heights, Sharondale, the additions to Hollywood Park, and the Estella Maxey Place subsidized housing project

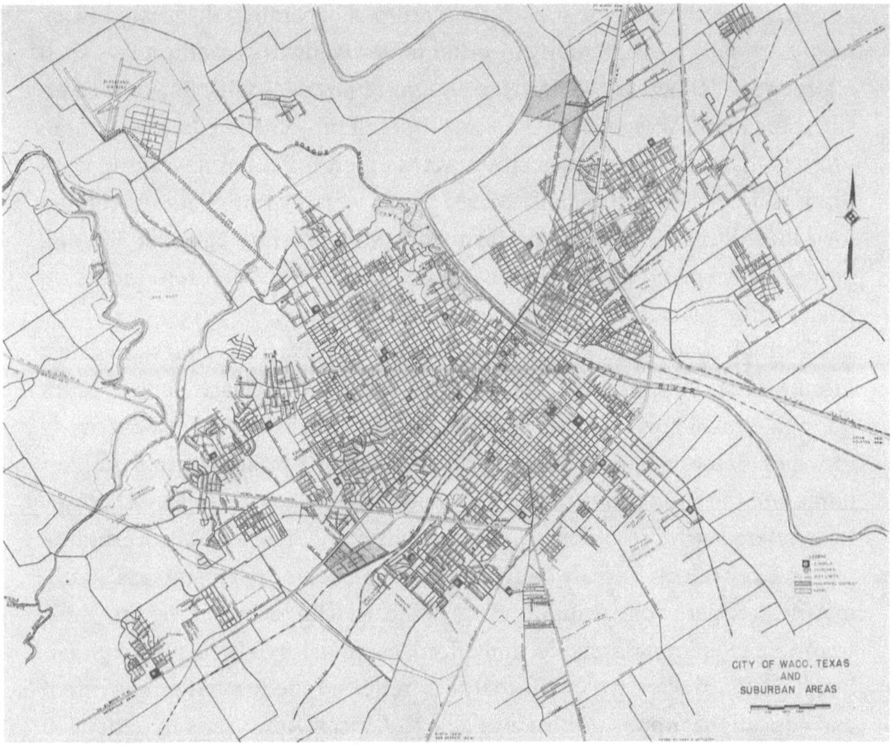


This 1974 map of the city of Waco, Texas, and suburban areas shows that the area historically known as East Waco is situated in the northern portion of the city, east of the Brazos River. Farther east sits the city of Bellmead. The area considered west Waco sits in the southern part of the city, and the area considered by locals to be north Waco is technically located in the western part of the city. Last, the area referred to by locals as south Waco sits in the eastern portion of the city. *Courtesy of the Texas Collection, Baylor University, Waco, Texas.*

were places Black Wacoans called home.[38] Before the 1970s, when Waco's population was 95,326 and Bellmead's was 7,698, these East Waco neighborhoods were upward of 90 percent Black.[39] To fund Estella Maxey Place and surrounding neighborhood construction, Waco used a multimillion-dollar grant under the program for so-called urban renewal to "clear slums" and neighborhood "blight." This program was made possible by the Housing Act of 1949 and the Housing Act of 1954, and it facilitated the relocation of underserved Black residents to income-based housing projects like Parkside and Estella Maxey Place, which opened in 1959 and was expanded in 1965.[40] The largest across the state, Waco's "urban renewal" operation decimated Black neighborhoods, giving validity to writer James Baldwin's assertion that such efforts were deliberate programs of "Negro removal."[41] With Baylor University at the helm, Waco finished Texas's first full project and completed more projects than any other Texas city, upward of ten.[42] Poor and working-class Black residents lived in Estella Maxey Place, which white Wacoans named for a local Black singer who performed mostly for white patrons. She did, however, give piano lessons to local Black middle-class children, including Baylor's first Black professor, Vivienne Malone-Mayes.[43]

The high concentration of African Americans in Waco's largest segregated, income-based, subsidized housing project, Estella Maxey Place, demonstrates the high rates of poverty in the city's African American community, but overly focusing on the socioeconomic aspect overlooks the pride they took in their home and the strong community they built therein. For some, Estella Maxey Place offered better resources, like indoor plumbing. The federal government played a key role in initially denying and later extending housing assistance to African Americans, including Black Wacoans who, many for the first time, were able to enjoy safe, stable, and affordable housing. The Black neighborhoods of Waco were typical in that they reflected the limited employment and educational opportunities available to African Americans in general at the time.[44] These oppressive conditions, however, did not fully define Black Waco. Students reminisced about the close connections they had with their neighbors in these life-giving spaces, where they reared families, celebrated birthdays and anniversaries, cooked their favorite meals, and cared for one another.

With support from the federal government, and aided by a pronounced rise in Waco's population, Black East Waco neighborhoods began to be codified in the late 1940s as part of the nation's postwar building frenzy.[45] To facilitate the effective sequester of Black Wacoans to this area, especially those who aspired to homeownership, city planners and developers advertised the Carver Park neighborhood, for example, as a Black-only neighborhood within La Vega ISD. Local newspapers throughout the 1950s shamelessly publicized the Carver Park addition and other East Waco neighborhoods as places featuring "colored properties" and "GI Homes for Colored Only."[46] Officially known as the Servicemen's Readjustment Act, the GI Bill of Rights was passed by Congress in 1944, and its housing provision promised veterans low interest rates for home loans at affordable prices with low to no-cost down payments—benefits that few Black veterans received. Waco was seemingly unique in granting these entitlements to Black veterans—provided that they were willing to settle in wholly segregated Black neighborhoods.[47] It was expected that veterans would look to settle in Waco after one of the world's largest military training bases, Fort Hood, sitting roughly sixty miles southwest of Waco, was established in 1942.[48] The de facto system of segregation could not be detected in local housing notices and documentation, as the deeds for East Waco properties in the River Oaks and Carver Park additions, for instance, excluded mention of race.[49] Instead, it was residential covenants that included language stipulating that only white persons could purchase land or homes.[50] Stated differently, the allocation of certain neighborhoods for Black Wacoans was unnecessary because they were effectively barred from purchasing land or homes elsewhere in the city, forcing them to settle in virtually the only place they could: East Waco.

In these spaces, Black families made and lived lives full of meaning and purpose; homeownership was only available to a select few, and among that small group, economic precarity was common. Connie Sadler, Willie Williams Jr., and Richard Jenkins were young children when their families moved into these neighborhoods. Willie remembered his family being the fourth to settle in Sharondale when they moved into their home, one his parents still own as of this writing. Constructed in 1966 just as Stokely Carmichael was taking over the Student Nonviolent Coordinating Committee, Sharondale celebrated Black entertainers by naming streets after them, such as (Nat) King Cole Drive, Mahalia (Jackson) Drive, and (Louis) Armstrong Drive.[51] Connie recollected that when her father, a veteran, purchased their Carver Park neighborhood home, the streets were not yet paved, and the accumulation of dust inside the house necessitated the installation of carpet. In attaining the homeownership status that the white power structure had denied many Black veterans, the Sadlers found an on-ramp to the middle class that capitalized on Jim Crow segregation by incentivizing the maintenance of segregated, and thus less valuable, housing.[52]

Although many African Americans lived in East Waco, a few settled in north Waco as well. Neighborhoods in this area contained a roughly 40 percent Black population.[53] Those living in north Waco, like Connie Oliver and Anslum Hudlin, were more likely to live in mixed-race neighborhoods, where their families had to lease rather than own their homes.[54] Connie O. recalled many of his white neighbors terrorizing him and his Black peers as children in the 1960s when they played outside. The only African Americans he remembers living in his vicinity at that time were on his block, which was surrounded by white neighbors. By the mid-1970s, other African Americans living in north Waco tended to be concentrated in two newly constructed, subsidized housing projects, the Villages and Parkside, located on the cusp of north and East Waco. Little racial mixing, as recalled by students, occurred once these housing projects opened and residents moved in.

Although only a few Waco neighborhoods included racial restrictions—all of which were in wealthy, white west Waco—these covenants informed practices that ordered the city's racial geography. As noted, by and large, Black Wacoans were precluded from purchasing homes in neighborhoods outside East Waco, restrictions that allowed them to lease—but not buy—particularly in north Waco. The few documented restrictions, however, paint a clear picture of these racial dynamics. From the 1940s onward, wealthier Waco neighborhood additions—primarily in west Waco, including Hirsch Heights, Ridgewood, Belmont Gardens, Hillcrest, Terrace Heights, Castle Crest, Ryals, Sycamore, and Tanglewood—were established with deeds, complete in many cases with plats; these documents featured language similar to that in the plat generated in 1947 for Hirsch Heights: "Lots are . . . for white persons exclusively, except schools and churches which offer facilities for white persons."[55] Similarly, the 1950 deed for the west Waco Sycamore addition read, "All lots in such addition aforesaid shall be used for residential purposes only, and by persons of the white or caucasian [*sic*] race only."[56] Such restrictions were vivid in the minds of low-wealth Black Waco students like Anslum, who recalled that the individuals who owned the north Waco home that he and his grandmother leased, as well as those around him, "were all white people, who [had] probably lived there for years, and when [Black Wacoans] started coming that way, they kept them houses and they rented them out."[57] Positioning their families to continue bringing in passive income that allowed them to build generational wealth, white Wacoans over time left the city center for its edges and soon-to-be suburbs.[58]

For their safety, Black Waco's children had to pay close attention to the racial rigidity of their landscape. This focus forced them to develop sophisticated geographic knowledge that reflected the spatial production of race, especially in areas like north Waco, where white Wacoans routinely viewed Black bodies of any age as displaced threats.[59] As Anslum, Connie O., and some of the other Black boys in their school traversed north Waco in the 1960s—around the time that the Supreme Court's first Black justice, Thurgood Marshall, was confirmed—to get to their newly desegregated school, they faced increased vulnerability to racial attacks, something Waco ISD either failed to consider or dismissed altogether. Anslum's upbringing in Waco gave him intricate racialized spatial knowledge. It taught him, for instance, that "Sixth Street [was] the main street for us as Blacks, that we could travel there freely, up until Colcord. From downtown to Colcord was like a color boundary." This "way of life" for Black Wacoans, something "you just know," as Anslum described, dictated,

> that you just don't go past Ninth Street unless you stay on Colcord. Don't venture off into Tenth Street and Eleventh Street because . . . that's where white people lived. That's their part of that area. And when we were told to go to [our new school] West Junior, my grandmother told me—and the group of young men, their parents also had told them—"Y'all stay together when y'all meet at Ninth Street, and you go straight up there to Fifteenth Street. Don't venture off; go straight to school." One block off of Colcord is West Junior, on Fifteenth Street.

This keen insight represented a racialized knowledge about Waco's built environment that compelled Black children not only to map avenues for their safety but also to read race into the landscape in a way most white children did not.

Given these exclusions and threats to safety, Black Wacoans were less likely to call south and west Waco home. The households of south Waco, which had two housing projects, South Terrace and Kate Ross, were somewhat racially mixed. Many African American residents, like Darrick Bledsoe, called these places home. This area also featured a significant Mexican-origin population that distinguished it from other Waco neighborhoods.[60] Carol Haliburton and Calvin Jones are two other students who grew up in south Waco. West Waco housed virtually no African Americans. Census records show that the median income in 1970 in this area was around $14,000 annually per household, which was over one third more than the national median white household income at the time, and that African American residents made up only 0.3 percent of the population.[61] Students accurately remembered this area, including its schools, as ultra-white and affluent. Despite school desegregation, efforts to maintain this status persisted well into the 1970s.

Regardless of which part of Waco African Americans lived in, many attended churches with roots in East Waco dating back to the nineteenth century. As scholars writing about African Americans in the twentieth century have shown, these churches, many founded shortly after enslavement, were an essential feature of Black life, giving residents spiritual guidance, community, and respite from the antiBlackness that marked the broader city.[62] Some of those to which students' families belonged included New Hope Baptist Church, Carver Park Baptist Church, Antioch Baptist Church, Second

Missionary Baptist Church, Greater Ebenezer Baptist Church, Toliver Chapel Missionary Baptist Church, St. Luke African Methodist Episcopal Church, St. James United Methodist Church, and Pleasant Olive Missionary Baptist Church. Across the Southern Freedom Movement, leaders and members of these religious institutions played integral roles in school desegregation, serving in entities like the local branches of the NAACP, Waco's Black Federation, and local school boards.[63] Their efforts were reflective of wider trends in twentieth-century African American history.[64]

Additionally, Black Waco held education in high regard, intentionally naming its segregated schools and streets in veneration of Black male leaders of local and national prominence. This practice served to remind Black Waco's boys in particular of the legacy on which they could build. Such naming practices were an important demonstration of Black spatial agency and self-determination, which held special meaning to Black people whose lives were deeply constrained by the quotidian indignities of Jim Crow. R. L. Smith Elementary School was named for Robert Lloyd Smith, a middle-class educator, politician, and entrepreneur who worked closely with Booker T. Washington and founded the Farmers' Home Improvement Society, an organization that promoted African Americans' economic independence and whose signature feature was its Waco-based bank. During the final decade of the nineteenth century, the South Carolina–born Smith was elected to the Texas Legislature.[65] G. L. Wiley Junior High School was renamed in 1958 in honor of Mississippi-born Gen. Lawrence Wiley, whose tenure as a mathematics teacher began in 1910 under Principal Alexander James Moore; Wiley would go on to serve as an assistant principal at A. J. Moore High School, where he worked for a total of thirty-five years.[66] In 1952, the Black community changed the name of East Waco Elementary School to J. H. Hines Elementary School. The school's namesake was the Texas-born James H. Hines Jr., who had served as the elementary school's principal from 1898 to 1928.[67] Kirk-Wilson Elementary School, which opened in 1952, was named for three of the four principals to serve A. J. Moore: J. A. Kirk, principal in the years 1905–25; B. T. Wilson, 1925–34; and J. J. Wilson, 1935–71, at which point Waco ISD closed A. J. Moore High. Thus, all of A. J. Moore's principals (including its founder and first principal, Alexander James Moore) had Waco ISD schools named for them.[68] Jesse J. Flewellen was the principal of La Vega ISD's segregated Black school, G. W. Carver, named for the eminent Black scientist and professor George W. Carver; Flewellen was the school's only principal for the span of its life from 1956 to 1970. Dripping Springs Road, the street on which the Carver school was located, was renamed J. J. Flewellen Road in his honor.

La Vega ISD's elementary school, J. Newton Jenkins, was named in honor of Rev. Dr. Joseph Newton Jenkins, who pastored New Hope Baptist Church from 1907 until his death in 1950; a Black middle-class leader and former educator, he, like many of his contemporaries, figured integrally into many notable religious and racial organizations across the city, such as the Baptist Ministers Union and the Texas Commission on Interracial Co-operation.[69] Nearly all these men had Black wives who taught in schools alongside them during their tenure as educators. What is striking, however, is that no schools were named for Waco's Black women leaders.

Bold naming practices, nonetheless, were unable to stem the tide of racism and employment discrimination, which persisted during this era. Waco's occupational data, which is generally on par with that of other African American communities, also sheds light on the city's social and cultural life in the 1970s.[70] Nearly 27 percent of African Americans living in East Waco worked in the service industry, including private household labor such as that performed by domestic workers. In comparison, less than 7 percent of white Wacoans living in west Waco were employed in the service industry. Similarly, women's employment rates reveal that one-quarter of all employed Black East Waco women worked in private households, whereas only 3 percent of the white employed women living in west Waco held that type of job. When looking at the highest and most lucrative tier of occupations (i.e., professional, technical, and kindred workers, managers, and administrators, excluding those on farms), racial disparities emerge once again. While 40 percent of the white people living in west Waco occupied these positions, only 17 percent of the African Americans in East Waco occupied them. Differences in second- and third-tier occupations further clarify that Black Waco citizens' access to quality educational opportunities and high-paying, nondiscriminatory employment paled in comparison to that of their white counterparts.[71]

Students' remarks corroborate these data. Willie Brown, Connie Sadler, Katherine Sanford, Anslum Hudlin, Pamela James, and Debora Wilkerson shared recollections about women in their families working as domestics in white people's homes during their childhood, adolescence, and young adulthood. The dramatic overrepresentation of Black women in private household positions and the contrasting dearth of white women in those positions bolsters the validity of these memories.[72] It also raises questions about the expectations some white students, parents, teachers, and administrators might have had for African Americans given that whites' only interactions with them might have been in such contexts. Minnie Washington, the first Black teacher at Viking Hills Elementary School, which opened in 1968 in west Waco just months before President Richard Nixon would take office, recalled a rather colorful exchange between her and the white father of one of her white students. The student's father resisted believing she was indeed his son's teacher, telling her he anticipated that anyone who looked like her—a Black woman—would occupy a janitorial role.[73] Likewise, these work-related interactions were some of the students' only substantive interactions with white people before schools desegregated. Racism and white supremacy, however, advantaged white actors and disadvantaged Black ones, so while the novelty of such interactions may have been equal across the color line, its consequences were not. Although members of a few Black families, like those of Russell Livingston and Willie W., attained higher education and secured professions as educators, they represented a minority. The small Black middle class included diverse African Americans that resided across different East Waco neighborhoods, what working-class and impoverished Wacoans called "old-money Blacks."

## THE STRUGGLE FOR AND SIGNIFICANCE OF BLACK EDUCATION IN WACO-AREA SCHOOLS

As Reconstruction waned in Waco, "education for Blacks began in 1875, four years after the state organized a public school system, with the establishment of Howard Institute by a group of Northern missionaries."[74] This chronology with respect to Black education is similar to that of many Southern communities, where the Christian missionary presence was common after the Civil War.[75] By the 1880s, when "Colored" students constituted over 40 percent of the district's enrollment, at least three schools were operating in Waco to educate Black children, the Howard Institute, East Waco (Colored) School, and First Street (Colored) School. Alongside his wife Mary E. Moore, professor Alexander James Moore worked as principal of both First District (Colored) School and Second District (Colored) School. The Moores served as educators in Waco from the 1880s into the twentieth century.[76] It was in such communities that Black schools, especially Black high schools, were erected, as more rural areas with more sparse Black populations rarely had schooling options for African Americans.[77] As historian James D. Anderson has shown, Black high schools were slow to arrive to many Southern communities, an insight that explains why this school served such a broad array of students and grade levels across McLennan County.[78] This "Colored High School" included grades 1 to 12 until 1952, when Kirk-Wilson Elementary

School absorbed grades 1 to 6, making A. J. Moore a junior and senior high school until 1971, when Waco ISD closed it.[79]

Although on the whole more rural than Waco ISD schools, La Vega schools were in essence similar. For Black Americans, Black education was a cherished tradition they invested heavily in through a variety of financial and nonfinancial resources; but for white power holders and the systems they created, it was a tool for maintaining separate and unequal schooling. La Vega ISD was established in 1927 through the merger of three separate districts: Pecan Grove, Oak Grove, and West Brook.[80] According to records from 1940, Black students in La Vega ISD at that time attended at least two different schools up to ninth grade, Old Zion School and Olive Heights School.[81] In 1951, La Vega ISD built a new "Colored" elementary school, which combined Old Zion and Olive Heights to serve as the only school for Black children in the district until 1956; this move was triggered by the 1949 Gilmer–Aikin bills passed by the 51st Texas Legislature.[82] Consolidating these schools in the postwar era reflected both statewide and national trends that saw the acceleration of such modernization efforts.

The Black communities situated outside Waco ISD's boundaries were invested in activities typical of many Black rural, agricultural residents with pronounced commitment to religion and education in segregated societies. Before J. Newton Jenkins Elementary School became La Vega ISD's only school for Black children in 1951, Old Zion and Olive Heights, the rural Black communities served by this school, had been dedicated to food cultivation and preservation—something on which the school capitalized with its canning kitchen, which had been recently constructed in 1946.[83] Its rural nature also meant that student attendance ebbed and flowed with the demands of cotton planting season.[84] On August 26, 1951, just before the school opened, the La Vega ISD board of trustees "approved the change of the [Olive Heights School's] name . . . to honor the late Dr. J. Newton Jenkins," who had died on December 17, 1950; his passing happened to coincide with the erection of a new building.[85] The principal of Olive Heights, J. W. Yancy II, remained in his leadership post following the death of this beloved community leader.[86] Opening its doors to students on Monday, September 10, 1951, this Black elementary school amounted to $141,241 in construction costs for the district, much lower than the $526,036 the district spent at virtually the same time to build a new white elementary school, La Vega Elementary School, which opened in 1953. Both schools, however, served a comparable number of students.[87] Thrilled about the new school, Waco's Black community celebrated its opening the entire first year, hosting a cornerstone ceremony, an opening rites ceremony, and a dedication ceremony.[88]

Throughout the mid-1950s, La Vega ISD school board members frequently discussed ways to manage the enduring "negro [*sic*] high school student problem," as construction of new Black neighborhoods increased the Black student population. La Vega ISD's growing Black student population followed statewide trends that saw Texas's population increase by over 50 percent from 1940 to 1950.[89] In 1954, La Vega Superintendent P. W. Shelton spoke with Waco ISD Superintendent Eric N. Dennard about continuing to pay for transfers to A. J. Moore High, which would cost approximately $100 per pupil.[90] Annexation was also a possibility, given that, as Superintendent Shelton admitted in 1955, "most [i.e., 92 percent] of the La Vega Negro scholastic population lives in Waco or on its fringes."[91] Seeking resources for "approximately 150 high school students," the board considered asking "Waco School District [to] annex . . . part of the negro [*sic*] section of the La Vega Independent School District in order to relieve this problem" and eliminate a significant number of its Black students.[92] Because education for Black La Vega ISD students stopped (as of 1955) at ninth grade, the district "transfer[red] the rest [167 high schoolers in 1955] to Moore High School in Waco. The La Vega school board knows the arrangement can't last and it will have to build a new school . . . because La Vega's white high school could not house the Negro pupils if segregation is abolished in the district."[93] The 1954 *Brown v. Board* decision nevertheless failed to move these Texas school administrators, as with too many of their contemporaries, to make the necessary provisions to desegregate their schools.

At the time that the US Supreme Court decided the *Brown* cases of 1954 and 1955, Waco ISD was operating two separate school systems, one for Black students and one for non-Black students, in keeping with the structure of most Southern school districts.[94] Black students could attend only four of the district's twenty elementary schools—Oakwood, Kirk-Wilson, J. H. Hines, and R. L. Smith—and one of the six junior high schools, G. L. Wiley. School board minutes suggest the board did not discuss desegregation until over a year later in August 1956, and after contemplating acceptable desegregation policies, it decided to postpone implementation indefinitely because the Texas Legislature had passed Article 2900a, which required a citywide referendum to overturn segregation.[95]

Advocating strategically and persistently for their children's education, the small, tight-knit community of Black East Wacoans positioned certain individuals to play an integral role on its behalf in La Vega ISD. Black Southern communities, especially middle-class ones, regularly relied on school leaders to perform such tasks. It is likely that much of this effort occurred behind the scenes through unofficial, oral agreements, as it would in the next decade with the desegregation of Waco's public facilities.[96] Although not necessarily the norm, other cities, such as Louisville, Kentucky, employed similar, more quiet tactics in the desegregation of public facilities.[97] According to the scant documentation available regarding Black education in Waco, it appears that some of the most engaged individuals were school leaders such as J. W. Yancy II and neighborhood groups. In addition to leading Black La Vega schools for decades, serving as Paul Quinn College's president in the 1940s, and being highly involved in Black Waco civic organizations, Yancy worked to leverage the J. Newton Jenkins school building as a community resource. Although both Yancy and homeowners were invested school district stakeholders by virtue of the taxes they paid to fund La Vega schools, school board records suggest they were not permitted to physically attend school board meetings, as the meetings' minutes contain multiple written requests to the all-white board that were read aloud and replied to after meetings. Yancy regularly submitted requests to use the school building for a variety of community initiatives, including free adult education classes, banquets, and college scholarship fundraisers.[98] The use of spaces like school buildings and churches in such innovative ways represented not only a strategic repurposing of space but also a response to the degradations of Jim Crow that prohibited African Americans from taking up and using space in sites more commonly known as public venues.[99]

Deference to the white power structure appeared to be part of a calculated way to secure crucial educational and community resources. In a 1955 letter Yancy wrote to the all-white La Vega school board, he stated, "We are asking you please to let us use the Cafetorium." Yancy ends the letter by assuring Superintendent P. W. Shelton that he will "always [be] present" at the event and will "see that the Cafetorium things that are used will be cared for."[100] It is likely that Yancy assumed a submissive tenor in securing approval as part of a strategy to further the social and professional activities that Waco's Black middle class deemed vital to the city's advancement of racial equity. In a 1954 written request to the board from the McLennan County Colored Teachers' Association to hold its monthly meetings at the J. Newton Jenkins building, the members expressed "their appreciation for the past favors rendered through the use of this building."[101] The following school year, the Carver Park [neighborhood] Committee sent a letter "requesting a date set for them to meet with the Board of Trustees for the purpose of discussing school needs."[102] Roughly two weeks later, this group gave to the board a petition it read aloud that expressed urgency for "build[ing] adequate school facilities for all pupils living within the La Vega Independent School District."[103] The previously scheduled $600,000 bond referendum passed nine days later, providing the funding for the new Black high school Black Wacoans were cautiously demanding.

While Black La Vega ISD stakeholders were scraping for resources, some Texas school districts, often those with relatively small Black populations, were going against the grain by taking early, though generally unsuccessful, initiative to desegregate. Following the desegregation of San Antonio schools, the 1955 case of *McKinney v. Blankenship* out of Big Spring, Texas, resulted in a Texas Supreme Court decision permitting school desegregation.[104] However, the Texas Citizens' Council, which formed in November 1955 in the wake of this ruling, requested an injunction to withhold state funds from Big Spring School District for trying to desegregate. Historians have described the local citizens' council as a "protective society" of militant white segregationists committed to prohibiting Black sociopolitical advancement across the South.[105] Although the citizens' council ultimately failed to halt school desegregation, Governor Allan Shivers and Attorney General John Ben Shepperd stated that "no school district should feel compelled to take hasty or unnecessary action" in the way of racial mixing.[106] These political figures would continue to thwart Black progress in the years to come.

Progress in building La Vega's new high school was swift, and its erection reflects its complicated legacy. At a December 20, 1955, school board meeting, trustees passed a motion for the district to purchase fourteen acres of land.[107] In March of the following year, Jesse J. Flewellen, then J. Newton Jenkins Elementary School's assistant principal, was selected as the new high school's leader, a decision the board made without his attendance at the meeting, given the strongly antiBlack politics of the era that mandated spatial segregation.[108] By April, the school began being informally referred to as Carver—with no explanation as to why.[109] Given the long-standing, pointed admiration Black communities had for George W. Carver, a pioneering Black scientist and college professor with a degree from the institution that would become Iowa State University, it is no stretch to presume they had a hand in venerating him by naming the school in his honor. Decades later, a local news story would highlight that two graduates of the school went on "to achieve great things because they pulled inspiration from [his] name."[110]

In the weeks before the 1956–57 school year began, the board held its August meeting at the newly constructed G. W. Carver High School to inspect the new school plant. Still, the admission policies of both school districts reflected their commitment to upholding a dual education system for Black and white students. As the only Black high school in La Vega ISD, Carver represented an "equalization school." Historians analyzing Southern school desegregation describe such schools as part of a scheme that in the postwar era saw all Southern states "beg[i]n or enhance . . . programs to improve black education."[111] Seeking to pacify Black residents who simply wanted, in this case, a high school education, this circumvention tactic drew out the implementation of school desegregation after the 1954 *Brown* verdict.[112] By building an equalization school after the 1954 *Brown* verdict stuck down *Plessy v. Ferguson*'s "separate but equal" requirement, La Vega ISD finally actualized the latter, having ignored it for decades like Mississippi and other Southern states had done.

G. W. Carver High School was a hallmark of Waco's Black community that provided a multipurpose space for community building. After finally convincing the district to build a Black high school, local community members used the physical building, erected in 1956, as much more than a school, as they had J. Newton Jenkins. In part, they were obligated to do so because Jim Crow laws barred them from renting or using spaces nominally deemed "public" but designated for whites. In this new Black school, they held various community meetings, fundraisers, and performances for fellowship and to center and celebrate Black life.[113] For instance, in 1957 G. W. Carver's parent-teacher association presented an "Evening of Music" for the whole Black community of Waco that featured musical groups from Black schools and churches across the city.[114] Additionally, the East Waco Neighborhood Association met there regularly throughout the 1950s and 1960s to discuss avenues for community enhancement.[115] Other East Waco stakeholders sought to tap into the spatial affordances G. W. Carver offered. In 1963, Mr. Van Pell Evans, who was instrumental to providing African Americans in Waco more and higher-quality housing options in the 1950s and 1960s, attempted to use the school to host a fundraiser for this neighborhood organization.[116] At the helm of establishing the Sharondale and Gholson Heights neighborhoods, Mr. Evans worked with L&M Corporation to expand housing options for Black Wacoans who had the resources for homeownership, an effort that incited the rise in La Vega's Black student population.[117] As housing expanded in the 1950s, with public and private investment spurring the construction of more than three hundred homes, residents from the Carver Park addition of East Waco formed a neighborhood association that advocated for the education of Black Waco's children. Having a dedicated space in G. W. Carver symbolized expanded educational opportunity and a familiar meeting place where African American life could flourish outside the white gaze.

As G. W. Carver opened, other Texas high schools trying to desegregate transformed into scenes of antiBlack bedlam. What became known as the 1956 Mansfield crisis preceded, and likely inspired, the Texas Legislature's creation of an article that systemically circumvented school desegregation mandates under federal law and another so-called crisis.[118] Located eighty miles north of Waco and just outside Fort Worth, Mansfield School District was placed under a federal court order in 1956 to desegregate, becoming the first Texas district obligated to do so.[119] With the help of the NAACP, Black students had successfully sued the district for the right to enroll. A raucous crowd of over three hundred white protesters physically blocked Black students from entering Mansfield High School. The protesters enjoyed the local police chief's and mayor's support, which was reinforced by Governor Shivers, who called in the Texas Rangers, a white supremacist state law enforcement agency that would later aid La Vega ISD in managing its "troublesome" Black students.[120] A resolution subsequently sent Mansfield's Black students to school in Fort Worth, while the district evaded its court order to desegregate for nearly a decade. The following year, in 1957, the 55th Texas Legislature passed Article 2900a.[121] As the state legislature well knew, most cities in Texas lacked sufficient votes to desegregate schools, given that many of them had white voting majorities who benefited from superiorly resourced schools.[122] Inspired by Virginia's 1956 campaign of massive resistance initiated by Senator Henry Byrd, this article employed a comparable antidesegregation strategy.[123] The effort in Texas sought to avoid desegregation by purportedly letting the majority of an electorate decide the issue.

Like other Southern school districts, Waco ISD used various tactics to avoid thorough desegregation, feigning compliance to maintain funding via token desegregation—that is, sprinkling a few Black students in formerly non-Black schools. Initial efforts in Waco to desegregate began in the 1960s with complicated transfer policies intended to dissuade legitimate desegregation, as well as freedom-of-choice plans that encouraged de facto segregation practices. These policies and plans were popular mechanisms that resulted in a smattering of Black students in previously non-Black schools but rarely the inverse of that trend. As was the case in the school system in Charlotte, North Carolina, elaborate transfer policies made it difficult for Black students to successfully move from Black to non-Black schools, as most applications that were submitted—even when completed correctly—were denied.[124] In a similar vein, freedom-of-choice plans purported to allow families to choose which school their children attended, but this policy widely maintained the status quo of separate schooling systems for Black and non-Black students.

As the only two Black high schools in the area, G. W. Carver and A. J. Moore maintained a crosstown rivalry that animated Black community relations in Waco. Both schools competed in the Prairie View Interscholastic League (PVIL), and from 1956 to 1970 they battled in athletic and academic competitions.[125] PVIL was the segregated Black counterpart to the better-resourced University Interscholastic League, which until 1967 excluded African Americans. PVIL oversaw athletic, typing, declamation, music, and extemporaneous speaking competitions among more than five hundred Black Texas high schools, serving as an outlet for students at segregated Black schools to interact and partake in standard school experiences.[126]

Students looked on G. W. Carver High School with the utmost respect and admiration. One graduate described it as "a family school."[127] Having attended G. W. Carver from grades 1 through 10, Willie Brown grew a deep fondness for the school, expecting to complete all his education there. He lauded the closeness of the entire East Waco community. "I remember it being like family, and we [Willie and his nuclear family] actually stayed right across the street from the school. I only had to walk across the street to get to class. . . . From first grade up into the tenth grade, all of us lived in the neighborhood."[128] The fortification and assurance Black students garnered from G. W. Carver stretched beyond the rigid parameters Black Waco students would soon encounter in desegregated schools.

Nearly a decade after the Supreme Court banned racially segregated schooling, "on 7 September 1962, seventeen Negro students staged the first attempt in Waco ISD to enter white segregated schools."[129] Their endeavor occurred together with that of another school desegregation pioneer, James Meredith, who registered that year at the University of Mississippi, and sparked significant racial turmoil in Oxford, Mississippi. Predictably, school officials denied the Waco students entry to University Junior High School, University High School, South Waco Elementary School, Waco High School, and West Junior High School. From Texas to Mississippi and beyond, little desegregation occurred in the decade after the *Brown* ruling. Two months later, Robert L. Penrice, attorney for the plaintiffs, filed suit with the US District Court to end segregation in Waco ISD, which resulted in the case *McGrue v. Williams*. Two years later in 1964 and resulting from this case, a court order initiated the desegregation process in Waco ISD.[130]

This order set out to gradually desegregate all twelve grades by the 1968–69 school year, but it ultimately failed.[131] Waco ISD Superintendent Avery

Downing shared his enthusiasm for the school district's so-called integration plan, noting that US Office of Education officials would support it if the plan proved to "mix the races."[132] By the point in 1964 that first and second grade were supposed to be integrated, only thirty-three Black students were attending four historically non-Black elementary schools in the district.[133] This slow pace goaded US District Judge Homer Thornberry to instruct Waco ISD to accelerate its "stair-step" pace, a common strategy that school districts used to desegregate gradually.[134] Typically, it involved desegregating a single grade each year—as if progressing up a set of stairs.

Lagging behind many Southern school districts nearly a decade after the federal prohibition of school segregation, La Vega ISD expanded its segregation practices while beginning to recognize its imminent inability to continue doing so. By the summer of 1963, the same year civil rights activist Medgar Evers was assassinated, La Vega ISD was still segregating Black and non-Black students; at this point, school district administrators acknowledged that if they were to continue resisting desegregation, they would likely lose federal funding. Meanwhile, they were planning to open yet another segregated Black school to relieve overcrowding. Waco ISD's superintendent lamented that the housing construction boom was decreasing Waco ISD's enrollment by pushing "Negro families to find new homes in the La Vega school district."[135] In need of a new elementary school as a result of this population increase, the Black community made its case for one, and La Vega ISD opened Dripping Springs Elementary School in 1963, the same year Rev. Dr. Martin Luther King Jr. delivered his "I Have a Dream" speech at the March on Washington for Jobs and Freedom. Opening the final year the district practiced segregation, Dripping Springs, which could have been considered at least initially another equalization school, took G. W. Carver's first through sixth graders, thereby making G. W. Carver a junior and senior high school.

Waco ISD employed comparable circumvention tactics, like most Southern school districts did, to avoid meaningfully mixing Black and white students. After asking the "Negro principals" present at a school board meeting what they knew concerning desegregation, and then engaging in further discussion among themselves, board members unanimously voted to have their attorney, Sam Lanham, "assist in drawing up a plan for consideration relative to integration."[136] Lanham's role was to present a plan that encouraged the community to commit to desegregation on a voluntary basis, as district leadership presumed it would save taxpayers money and quell the threat of conflict. Administrators reasoned that freedom-of-choice plans would give white parents less cause for retribution against a unitary school system.[137]

Contrasting with a dual school system, as the contemporary nomenclature described, a unitary school system supplied a single, supposedly integrated school system for all students. The popular freedom-of-choice strategy, however, allowed Southern school districts to nominally practice school desegregation by allowing students and their families to choose which schools they would attend; however, it maintained the status quo of separate schooling systems (i.e., unequal Black schools and overresourced non-Black schools) and was struck down by the ruling in the 1968 *Green v. County School Board of New Kent County* case in Virginia.[138] In Texas, this policy operated under the pretense of voluntary desegregation and (false) choice. Implementing policies such as these required the revocation of the Texas Legislature's Article 2900a, which prohibited desegregation without a referendum.[139]

Seeking to preserve spaces dedicated to whiteness, white La Vega ISD administrators concocted a nominal plan to desegregate the district's schools. This symbolic endeavor left intact treasured Black schools, which inadvertently became a cause for celebration for Black communities. In 1964, the same year that President Lyndon Johnson's Great Society program was announced, La Vega ISD launched this voluntary desegregation effort.[140] By the 1964–65 school year, Black students officially constituted 44 percent of the student population in La Vega ISD.[141] The board failed to explicate, however, particular strategies or draw maps to clarify neighborhood zones intended to facilitate the assignment of all students living in a specific area to a certain school. This deliberate omission suggests that the La Vega ISD board never intended to thoroughly desegregate its schools and explains why at the start of the 1964–65 school year, only forty-one Black students were attending "formerly all white schools."[142] Furthermore, owing to residential segregation and the concentration of Black residents in East Waco, the neighborhood zones were already being used to sort students into racially identifiable schools. Therefore, little change happened after the district passed its resolution to desegregate.

La Vega ISD's desegregation plan reflected that it was likely compelled by national legislation. The 1964 Civil Rights Act and the 1965 Elementary and Secondary Education Act marked a turning point, as both pieces of legislation "allowed the federal government to withhold federal funding from those school systems that discriminated based on the categories of race, religion, or national origin."[143] The Civil Rights Act and the Elementary and Secondary Education Act sought to destabilize racially separate educational systems by tying federal funding to the elimination of de jure segregation, thereby forcing the hand of uncooperative school districts.[144] The effects of prolonged legal struggles to equalize public schooling varied across the South, intensifying in some ways after 1968 in places like Mississippi, where white parents and politicians demanded federal funding while refusing to follow the law.[145] Amid this avid white resistance, school desegregation, as historian Charles Bolton explains, "occurred largely on white people's terms, typically with a diminution of black control over education, a loss of black institutions nurtured during years of enforced racial segregation, and a thinning of the ranks of black teachers and administrators."[146]

Despite the additional costs incurred, the district remained committed to its antiBlack evasion tactics, which were widespread and soon evident to federal officials. In 1965, La Vega ISD Superintendent Henry Cranfill wrote J. W. Edgar, commissioner for the Texas Education Agency, to inform him that the US Department of Health, Education, and Welfare considered the district's voluntary desegregation plan unsatisfactory and that it had yet to fully desegregate.[147] The guidelines that the US Department of Health, Education, and Welfare released in 1965 and 1966 started the process of delineating precise measures of school desegregation, which would be further solidified later in the 1968 *Green* ruling.[148] In response, the superintendent provided maps and zoning details, which were missing from the initial resolution, of the district's full-scale plan. The way that the segregated communities and school sites overlapped—with G. W. Carver High School within the city of Waco's boundaries and La Vega High School squarely in Bellmead—complicated the school desegregation process.[149] A "Description of La Vega Independent School District" document noted that La Vega ISD had forty-four Black students in formerly non-Black schools—three more than the previous year—but no white students in Black schools.[150] It also admitted to operating a dual transportation system alongside a dual schooling system but vowed to bring both to a halt by the 1965–66 school year. Ceasing faculty segregation and limiting zone transfers was also to help propel desegregation in the district.

Weighing their options for circumventing desegregation mandates, the La Vega school board considered "forming a separate school district for the East Waco area" after US Department of Health, Education, and Welfare attorneys lambasted the district for its continuous delay.[151] Doing so would have eliminated nearly all of the district's Black students, most of whom lived, in the board's words, in "the Federal Housing Projects," which the board asserted "added to the problem of making the G. W. Carver-Dripping Springs Campuses more congested with all negro [*sic*] residents."[152] Negative terms like "problem," "congested," and "projects" conveyed conventional anti-Black beliefs many white Bellmead residents held about African Americans.

Removing Black students, who in 1965 made up 48 percent of La Vega ISD's student population, from the equation altogether would have enabled white La Vega ISD to maintain its whiteness.[153] White stakeholders in La Vega ISD needed the numbers and funding that Black students afforded but shirked the responsibility of respecting them or dealing with them justly.

Amid these tensions, Blackness was flourishing in the portion of East Waco that bordered Bellmead. By virtually all accounts, G. W. Carver represented the very best of Black Waco and East Waco, faring well in numerous athletic and academic competitions in which students garnered state, national, and international recognition. The G. W. Carver school band featured talented musicians and a drill team led by Mr. Robert E. Lee Jr., who was known in the community as "the best band director around."[154] In the spring of the 1966–67 school year, the G. W. Carver band qualified for a regional competition that it won by a landslide in Enid, Oklahoma. The Thirty-Fifth Tri-State Music Festival saw the band earn four first-division ratings and recognition as "the best looking band in the contest."[155] Raising $3,000 to make the interstate trip, G. W. Carver "was the only Negro band in the state this year [1967] to win double sweepstakes" against "more than 12,000 high school bandsmen, drill team members, choral groups, and other music organizations [who] participated in the contest."[156] No stranger to success, "the Lee-directed band ha[d] won regional sweepstakes for the past five years in the PVIL competitions and state sweepstakes for four of the past five years."[157] Following G. W. Carver High's transition from PVIL to the University Interscholastic League, newspaper reporters expressed surprise that the school's band fared as well as it did, presumably doubting its ability to compete with better-resourced, all-white bands. Accomplished and thriving, the G. W. Carver band helped galvanize the community around its accolades and received well-deserved veneration from local and distant fans.[158]

A high point for many Black Wacoans was the G. W. Carver band's trip to Canada, which destabilized provincial assumptions about the talent and capability of Waco's Black children. Inundated with an impressive stream of invitations after winning in Enid, Director Lee accepted an offer to compete at Expo 67 at the world's fair in Montreal in July, a year after the Black Panther Party was established. "The band [was] the only Texas school band—and the only Negro band—so honored" with a solicitation to compete. With just over a month to raise $10,500 to cover expenses for the international trip, the band rallied community support around its cause to secure the necessary funding.[159] Upon arriving in Canada, yet again the G. W. Carver band blew away spectators and its competition, winning the first-place prize of $1,000.

Thousands of Canadians were mesmerized by the band's performances, requesting encores and interviews with students.[160] Financial support for the G. W. Carver band came from the broader, white Waco community as well. In a demonstration of the significance of these trips and the G. W. Carver band's success, a local newspaper sent one of its reporters, Roger Cantrell, to "accompany the band on its 12-day trip to Canada."[161] This attention and international acclaim cast Waco in a positive light, but it required Black students to be exceptional to receive the meaningful support they had always deserved.

The space Blackness occupied spanned different mediums and culminated in an exhibition of the special energy Black girls brought to bear. The G. W. Carver band's drill team, a key part of the band, had to be just as dynamic and skilled as the musicians. Reflecting on her time as a G. W. Carver drill team member, Wanda James said that she had aspired from an early age to become a member of this group. She recalled, "Carver was so popular, and the drill team . . . it was just fascinating to me to see [an] all-Black drill team. Everybody was just [moving] together, and it was hard to get on [i.e., become a member]. You had to go to the practices; you had to make sure you got the routine down."[162] The drill team captivated young Black girls like Wanda, and these assiduous Black girl dancers commanded the field and performed precisely choreographed routines. The prospect of participating and succeeding, of spending one's high school years under the "Thursday Night Lights," compelled many Black Waco students to work hard toward that goal.[163]

The sacrifices Black Wacoans made to maintain initiatives like the school band and drill team were tremendous. As a historically oppressed community with relatively few financial resources, Black Waco rallied around this school and its causes, seeing them through to their desired goals. Wanda recollected how fundraising enabled her to participate as a drill team member because her family's meager means alone would not have allowed her to do so. The band's welcome-home celebration from Canada was made possible by the community's time and support, which manifested in "piles of bacon" and a red carpet at the school, where parents had been waiting for hours in eager anticipation.[164] Community efforts to support the band also included purchasing concert tickets and barbecue dinners from band members.[165] This excitement trickled down to younger students, too, who watched their older peers ascend to great heights and yearned for comparable experiences of their own once they reached high school. Many of these young people, unfortunately, would never get the chance to have a G. W. Carver High School experience.

# 2

# Nobody Asked Us

## SCHOOL CLOSURES AND STUDENT PROTEST AS SETTINGS OF STRUGGLE

*What seems most evident from all their comments is that black youth in the South will no longer play a passive role in decisions affecting their lives and futures.*

BETSY FANCHER, *VOICES FROM THE SOUTH*, 1970

On Monday, September 14, 1970, 130 Black students marched out of La Vega High School, traveling toward East Waco. They were headed to their former segregated school, G. W. Carver High School. According to reports, this walkout's central aim was to contest La Vega ISD's abrupt and underhanded closing of G. W. Carver, the only school many Black students from this community had ever attended. This closing left an indelible mark on La Vega ISD, which would soon discard most of its Black students to Waco ISD. The walkout and the events that catalyzed it are part of a larger narrative of institutional, antiBlack, classist racism. Ultimately, this chapter contends that Black schools and children served as the school districts' pawns, but Black students staked their new territory by publicly protesting their mistreatment in expressly gendered ways. Their perspectives of the 1970–71 school year at

La Vega High speak to the chaos and racial animus that engulfed them, and the subsequent turmoil in Waco ISD that displaced Black students proved to be a continuation of the same.

This school closure opposed the plans of La Vega ISD administrators, discussed at school board meetings in the late 1960s, to keep the school open. Black students slated to attend G. W. Carver in the 1970–71 school year hence found themselves with little warning at previously non-Black La Vega High School, where they were met with great hostility. The suddenness of this closure indeed propelled their protest against it, and in the school years that immediately followed, Black Waco students would encounter—and resist—some of the harshest antiBlack racism many had ever witnessed, much less experienced. These encounters unfolded amid the revision of boundaries and the shuffling around of Black bodies to facilitate a school desegregation process between two school districts that showed little interest in maintaining Black dignity, which its Black students had come to see as integral to their education.

## DEPRIVATION AND INDIGNITY: ELIMINATING BLACK LA VEGA SCHOOLS

After going without a high school for decades, African Americans finally saw G. W. Carver open in 1956, a joyous occasion that was, however, short-lived. A court order from the federal government forced La Vega ISD to fully desegregate by the end of the 1960s. This process, however, would be hard to carry out in a district that maintained a dual schooling system with three of its seven schools virtually all Black.

Court battles were integral to the wider struggle for more than just schooling. In October 1969, the US Supreme Court heard the *Alexander v. Holmes County Board of Education* case out of Mississippi, which in a unanimous decision overturned the lower court's ruling to provide more time for schools to desegregate. The Supreme Court ruled that the "all deliberate speed" directive from the 1955 *Brown II* decision was no longer permissible and that districts were to desegregate all schools immediately.[1] The court, then, required reorganization by a firm deadline of February 1, 1970.[2] Additionally, the 1969 Alabama case of *United States v. Montgomery County Board of Education* addressed faculty assignments, which represented a significant matter for Black educators, given that too many found themselves unemployed or demoted as a result of school desegregation.[3] The Supreme Court ruled that the racial ratios of schools' faculty members had to be consistent with those across the entire district.[4] Unable to postpone faculty desegregation any longer, the

Montgomery County school district was forced to implement a plan at the beginning of the spring semester of the 1970–71 school year.

Placing increased pressure on Waco-area school districts and the many others across the country that refused to desegregate, the 1968 *Green v. County School Board of New Kent County* case in Virginia confronted a popular strategy that only nominally committed to school desegregation by preserving dual systems—one for non-Black students and one for African Americans.[5] In 1965, New Kent County implemented a freedom-of-choice plan that maintained the status quo of racially separate schooling common across many Southern school districts.[6] The Supreme Court ruled the freedom-of-choice plan unconstitutional and asserted that desegregation needed to happen in a timely fashion; in fact, Justice William J. Brennan wrote that the phrasing of the mandate in the 1955 *Brown II* ruling that segregation happen with "all deliberate speed" actually served to postpone the creation of substantively integrated schools.[7] Deciding that there should be no such thing as a "white school" or a "Black school" and instead often using the phrase "racially identifiable schools," the court called for full desegregation and an end to the deliberately sluggish pace of school integration plans.[8] Justice Brennan established six specific categories for school districts to achieve "unitary status," that is, for them to be considered fully desegregated: (1) student assignment, (2) faculty, (3) staff, (4) transportation, (5) extracurricular activities, and (6) physical facilities.[9] This ruling saw the NAACP rush forward in filing motions to enforce desegregation across the South.[10] Against this backdrop, Waco schools scrambled to reconcile their commitment to antiBlackness with legal mandates that prohibited demographic expression of their contempt for Blackness.

In the 1968–69 school year, La Vega ISD made public its plans to close J. Newton Jenkins Elementary School but to keep open G. W. Carver High School, demonstrating slightly less than full disdain for Black spatial matters in education. In a letter to Dr. Lloyd Henderson, the education branch chief of the Office for Civil Rights, the La Vega ISD superintendent addressed the district's noncompliance with federal desegregation orders and spelled out how La Vega ISD planned to fulfill its court order to desegregate at the end of the 1968–69 school year, the same year Shirley Chisholm (D-NY) became the first Black woman elected to the US Congress. The school board, the superintendent explained, proposed to keep G. W. Carver open after renaming it and implied that it would close Jenkins. He also detailed how all La Vega ISD students would be reassigned to specific schools across the district based on their school grade.[11]

As discussed in chapter 1, five years before G. W. Carver was erected, J. Newton Jenkins Elementary opened for La Vega ISD's Black primary-school-age students, and its all-Black status positioned it for closure once federal school desegregation mandates intensified; thus, like G. W. Carver and too many segregated Black schools, it also had a short life.[12] Immediately before shutting down G. W. Carver, the La Vega ISD board, which included at this point one Black man named Rev. LaDell Thomas and no women, unanimously passed Superintendent Henry Cranfill's motion for "the complete abandonment of J. N. Jenkins Elementary School."[13] The motion was passed on May 28, 1970, a few weeks after members of the Ohio National Guard fatally shot or wounded several Kent State University students protesting the Vietnam War. It also was passed presumably just as high school yearbooks in the district were made available, and a message inside the La Vega High School yearbook forecast a new, spacious, desegregated high school: "The Board and Mr. Cranfill were making plans for a new central high school to serve the entire district. Promises were announced that the new building would be a reality within three years."[14] There would be, however, no such building. Instead, the board decided to close J. Newton Jenkins at the end of the 1969–70 school year, giving school board members all summer to inform affected families that students would attend a different school the following year. As La Vega ISD's first new school constructed for Black students, built in 1951, Jenkins was significant to Black Wacoans, who had used the school as a community hub along with G. W. Carver. Little social unrest followed this decision, however, in part because the school board announced its intentions to shut it down. This news was unfortunate, but at least the board was transparent and gave the community due notice about the closure.

La Vega ISD had assumed that the Black students in the district, along with their education, were collateral, discardable tools for achieving desegregation. Although J. Newton Jenkins was newer than one of the other non-Black elementary schools and the same age as the other non-Black elementary school, it was on the chopping block. According to Superintendent Cranfill, closing a school built in 1951 and not even twenty years old "would save the district much money in needed repairs at that campus . . . [and it] was further recommended that said campus be sold, and the proceeds therefrom spent in repairing and renovating the other schools of the district."[15] Based on the typical flow of funds, however, Black students were unlikely to see any direct or immediate benefit from the sale of Jenkins. If Cranfill's comments reflect any truth, it was that in building Jenkins, the board had constructed a substandard building not intended to last, signaling that Black students were not worth quality school facilities. Such a move may have also conveyed that African Americans, as aspatial and placeless people, had no claims to specific spaces. What Cranfill's observations did not explicitly convey, but can still be easily surmised, is that the board likely agreed that Black people contaminated the spaces they used. So rather than close the district's oldest elementary school—which served a largely non-Black student body—the board decided to eliminate Jenkins.

Business continued as usual for La Vega ISD that summer, giving G. W. Carver stakeholders little reason to fear or anticipate the school's eradication or that such a move would be accompanied by negligence and callousness. In 1970, the board met twice in late July to discuss integration but omitted the details of their discussions in the official records.[16] Meeting a few weeks later on August 13, it shared an outline of another desegregation plan; if the plan was approved at this meeting, the board planned to present it for review ahead of the official start of the school year to Judge Jack Roberts, who served on the US District Court for the Western District of Texas.[17] Thus, a meeting had been scheduled with Judge Roberts to discuss desegregation plans for the 1970–71 school year a mere ten days before the first day of school on September 3. Additionally, less than two weeks before the first day of school, teachers were still being assigned to teach at a school the board was days away from closing forever. The board had approved Theresa Ann Williams as a teacher at G. W. Carver on August 18. As a late hire, Ms. Williams was set to join the forty-some teachers who had been similarly slated before or on April 21.[18]

Revealing these plans at a meeting on August 25, the board couched its announcements within a subtle set of others that only intimated G. W. Carver's coming demise. It was a convenient venue for the board members in that there were few Black community members in attendance to whom they had to answer. Principal assignments for the next school year were noted, but there was no explicit mention of who would lead G. W. Carver. There was no need, however, to discuss who would be G. W. Carver's principal because Jesse J. Flewellen had served in this role since 1956 when the school opened, and records reflect no demands that he be replaced. Flewellen, who attended the meeting, was appointed to a new position as assistant superintendent for curriculum and program development, but there was no record of discussion about his successor as principal.

Flewellen's promotion is notable vis-à-vis the scores of Black educators who faced termination with school desegregation.[19] A caveat to this pattern, as one historian studying Mississippi school desegregation noted, is that "school districts generally demoted or reassigned black principals rather than fire them, many . . . given impressive-sounding though essentially meaningless titles, such as director of buildings and grounds."[20] It is unclear how much power Flewellen wielded in his new role, but white supremacist education administrators sought, as one Mississippi superintendent pointedly stated in 1964, "to work through the negro principals and teachers to try to help us keep our schools segregated." "This kind of attitude, common in some districts well into the late 1960s," according to historian Charles Bolton, "continued to chill civil rights activism among black educators."[21] Such context suggests white district leadership may have notified Flewellen before the closure and effectively baited him with a promotion to dissuade him from inciting broad Black protest against sunsetting G. W. Carver. If so, Flewellen's decision reflected his interest in maintaining employment and continuing to address his financial responsibilities, an option infrequently offered to many Black educators, alongside his will to seemingly betray the Black community of which he was a part.

Additionally, on August 25, which was the day after the board's meeting with Judge Roberts, Superintendent Cranfill asked that the district's two high school band directors collaborate by working as a teaching team, with one, Harry P. Miles from La Vega High, focusing on ensemble activities and the other, Robert E. Lee Jr. from G. W. Carver, attending to the marching band. Such delegation of tasks between Miles and Lee, who served different high schools, indicates a measure of school reorganization. Cranfill also requested funding to staff overnight guards at G. W. Carver, suggesting that the board failed to rule out the potential for G. W. Carver stakeholders to act on any aggrievement they felt for the unjust termination of their school.

La Vega ISD's closure of G. W. Carver violated the spatial significance that the vestiges of Jim Crow manifested, important spaces created by Black communities in the Waco area in the face of white supremacist terrorism. Black G. W. Carver stakeholders of all stripes and proximities to the school board were strategically misled about the school's dissolution. These brazen acts of disregard showcase the board's willingness to preserve whiteness and neglect Black spatial agency.

Soon enough, the board realized that Black G. W. Carver stakeholders were unwilling to quietly accept the school's closure or the spatial indignity it demanded of Black Wacoans. Refusing to openly admit having done so, the La Vega ISD board shut down G. W. Carver and forced its Black students into La Vega Junior and Senior High school. The board's first official meeting of the 1970–71 school year, an unplanned one, occurred on September 15, nearly two weeks after the first day of school. This special meeting took place the day after a walkout of 130 Black students from La Vega High School.[22] At this moment, messages of Black Power, which encouraged dissent on racialized grounds, were motivating Black Waco's students to believe that they, too, were as capable as anyone anywhere to openly denounce their subjugation. Situating themselves squarely within—rather than on the periphery of—the Black freedom struggle, Black Waco students responded to G. W. Carver's closing with a walkout, claiming their spatial consequentiality. The board addressed the walkout during this special meeting without naming it while exhibiting its flawed perception of the issues that provoked it. Board members noted, for instance, a discrepancy with football coaches, which was a tangential issue but not central. After the closure, administrators ousted G. W. Carver coach Clarence Chase in favor of less qualified white coaches.[23] The board, however, refuted this issue's legitimacy. Despite Black community members' objections, officials failed to acknowledge or show concern about how abruptly and underhandedly the board carried out the closure decision or its implications for the spatial autonomy of Black Waco.[24]

Less than two weeks before the 1970–71 school year began, neither Waco's Black community nor all members of the La Vega ISD school board were aware of G. W. Carver's end. In a deceitful maneuver, the majority of the La Vega ISD board marginalized and isolated its only Black member, leaving him unaware of the closure plan. Mere days into the school year and just after the walkout, LaDell Thomas revealed that "he did not know the school board was going to present a plan to the court."[25] Thomas reported having driven to Austin on Monday, August 24, only to later "discover [that same day] that a plan calling for the closing of G. W. Carver was endorsed by the 19th District Court"; according to an ad hoc committee of Black Waco stakeholders, the grassroots Better Schools Committee, "the desegregation plan adopted by the court was drawn up without the knowledge of all members of the school board, in particular Rev. La Dell Thomas."[26] The presiding Judge Jack Roberts's office was in Austin, and it seems Thomas drove there on August 24 for a meeting with him and their legal counsel about next steps in La Vega ISD's desegregation plan. Following this meeting, newspaper reporters described the creation of this plan as an "endorsement" by Judge Roberts, a "decision [that] Judge (Jack) Roberts has approved," and a "plan [that] was accepted by the court [that] was hurriedly put together," all language indicating that the La Vega ISD board—without their sole Black member's knowledge—proposed an arrangement that called for the elimination of G. W. Carver.[27] Thomas's token place on the board, like those of Black trustees on other school boards during this time, helped nullify his power to meaningfully protest. His history of advocating for Black students, for instance, in the days following the walkout saw him demand that Black walkout participants receive amnesty.[28] Keeping Thomas in the dark about their plans to close G. W. Carver enabled white board members to move forward with their duplicitous scheme. Despite leaders in the Black community, such as Robert King and Robert E. Smith of the local NAACP, demanding answers and major revisions to the desegregation plan, La Vega ISD did and said little. Accounts noting that white members of the La Vega ISD board ostracized Thomas to concoct a desegregation plan that closed G. W. Carver contrast with others that blame the federal government for "impos[ing]" such a plan on the district.[29] It is clear, nevertheless, that at neither the local nor federal level did La Vega ISD consult the African American community in the decision-making process to eliminate the district's Black high school.

Although recollections vary regarding how students learned the news, not one alum in this study recalled receiving word from La Vega ISD about G. W. Carver's closure before the 1970–71 school year began. In July 1970, Marshall Baldwin, a rising G. W. Carver senior, was excited about his final year of high school. A few weeks into preseason football practice, however, a coach rendered shocking and upsetting news: "After practicing [for] a couple of weeks," Marshall recounted, "all of a sudden the coach came and talked to [the team]. He said, 'Well boys . . . they're shutting the school down.'"[30] The coach then directed the team to La Vega High a few miles down the road. Betty Stewart recalled the "crushing" feeling she and her classmates contended with when they found out, because, as she explained, "we had been together eleven years. For the transition that we had to go through, some just quit and got their GED later."[31]

Because G. W. Carver's school plant was notably newer than La Vega High School, it proved even more challenging for G. W. Carver stakeholders to understand the rationale supporting the district's decision, which exposed its disregard for Black space and Black children. Marshall was especially upset given the respective ages of the two schools. He asked, "Why would you shut down a school that was less than twenty-something years old and send us out to a school that's sixty-something years old? Building falling down in some place[s] and all of that, but they did."[32] Marshall and his teammates were rightfully angry. They had just been discussing the football schedule and proposing new tactics they could use to defeat teams they were to face in the upcoming season. Feeling disposable, they were left to try to make sense of what felt like robbery—of their school and all they had hoped their senior year would be.

In some cases, Black caretakers had to underline the disastrous implications of G. W. Carver's decimation to their children, a painstaking effort that laid bare the lengths La Vega ISD was willing to go to in order to undermine Black spatial agency. Like so many others, Carver alumna Beverly Rickford and her family viewed the school as a meaningful community institution that had cared for her since her schooling began. Beverly's abrupt displacement from G. W. Carver to La Vega happened as she approached junior high. She remembered attending a community meeting with her mother and brother where community leaders announced La Vega ISD was closing G. W. Carver—a notice that came from them and not directly from the board. As Beverly recalled, "I remember the walk back [from the community meeting] they probably held at Carver. The walk back home was very somber, and me and my brother were kind of . . . goofing around playing and whatever. And I remember [my mother] saying there's nothing funny about this; it's going to happen whether we like it or not."[33] In the coming years, she would learn how negatively consequential the school's closure was, but at the time of her family's discovery, she was a carefree child enjoying what felt like a normal summer walk.

The indirect, haphazard way in which the Black community received notice about G. W. Carver's end spurred rightful indignation. Many linked the board's negligence directly to the ensuing protest, identifying it as the central issue motivating the walkout. Willie Brown's mother found out G. W. Carver was closing while watching the news on television late that summer. When she told Willie, a rising junior who had spent his entire academic career at G. W. Carver, the news crushed his spirit and expectations for his junior year while planting in him a yearning for answers—or at least accountability. Similarly, Wanda James said that her family was informed at the "last minute. . . . I cannot even remember the notices being given except 'Hey, you can go there.' It was like the next day, [then] bam! you were gone." She added, "We [the Black community] were not told; everybody was very angry and mad because they were not . . . told or informed about it. And as a result, there was a riot."

La Vega ISD made so few strides to respect G. W. Carver stakeholders that some students did not find out about G. W. Carver's dissolution until the year began. Some teachers were stationed at G. W. Carver on the first day of school to redirect students to La Vega High. One of these bearers of bad news, Michael Bass's former homeroom teacher, informed him of the closure on the first school day. Disappointed that La Vega ISD did not "wait one more year" to disband the only school he had ever attended, Michael, like most other Black students, braced himself for the treacherous year ahead in a previously non-Black school.[34] In Waco as in many other places, race and class converged to produce residential segregation, further oppressing an already vulnerable community. Contained to East Waco, many Black Wacoans engaged Black geographic praxis, doing their best to make theirs a cherished community by investing in local improvement projects, including Black La Vega ISD schools. "Separate" was never equal, but Black communities worked to secure the resources necessary to reduce the disparity between Black and non-Black schools. Unfortunately, these efforts mattered little to La Vega ISD officials, who swiftly and clandestinely shut down a prized community institution and rid themselves of most of their Black students just one year after desegregating. Because the Black Waco community viewed segregated Black schools as valuable community institutions, Black students perceived the school closure and desegregation process as a spiteful incursion that warranted protest. Their perception shaped how Black students navigated school desegregation across Waco. Viewing Waco as a Black space showcases it as one in which emplaced African Americans worked to create and live meaningful lives while battling antiBlackness and white supremacy, a struggle made public in the 1970 walkout from La Vega High School.

## WALKING OUT

Black student resistance played an important role in the Southern Freedom Movement. Communities in the North and the South saw increasing instances of young African Americans broadcasting their dismay about the inadequacies of traditional education systems that failed to serve them.[35] In line with this resistance, Black Waco students asserted spatial agency through protest by calling out the indignity they faced in La Vega ISD's school desegregation process. Black geographic praxis recognizes how La Vega ISD schools functioned as contested sites of un/belonging and mis/representation for Black students; in ways conventional spatial analyses may overlook, this lens attends to the intangible, spatialized meaning-making practices that animated Black student resistance.[36] Black Waco was no stranger to organizing against racial discrimination. One notable, successful example occurred in the early 1960s, when the McLennan County NAACP and the NAACP Youth Council organized a boycott of a 7-Eleven convenience store in East Waco, near the Paul Quinn College campus. This type of protest fell directly into the purview of NAACP Youth Councils in particular, which, as historian Thomas Bynum's work shows, have roots reaching back to the 1930s, long before the timeline traditionally associated with the civil rights movement and more well-known groups like the Student Nonviolent Coordinating Committee. NAACP Youth Councils were composed of activists who advanced a tradition of grassroots youth mobilization in the North and South and used nonviolent direct-action tactics that often put them at odds with the broader NAACP.[37] Despite these tensions, in Waco the youth council and the local NAACP chapter joined forces to challenge 7-Eleven's refusal to hire Black employees despite welcoming Black patronage.[38] This boycott was well within memory for many Black Waco students, and they drew on this legacy in their own appeals for redress.

In large part, Black Waco students were openly rejecting the antiBlack notions of space the white power structure imposed on them. In ordering this reallocation of space—dispossessing Black La Vega students of their school home—white power holders strove to render them educationally displaced. Contesting this sense of unbelonging, Black La Vega students joined a loud chorus of Black students across the nation unwilling to be doormats for white supremacy. Historians have examined how during this era Black high schoolers in Cleveland and Boston, for instance, engaged in protests to reclaim educational spaces by forcing school administrators to contend with their needs.[39] Black high schoolers in Virginia, as Alexander Hyers illustrates, foregrounded the importance of and agitated for the inclusion of Black studies coursework that reflected their history and experiences in a newly desegregated context.[40] On college campuses as well, Black students boldly opposed their marginalization and subordination.[41] Black Waco students uniquely illuminate how Black students who did not identify as activists, like many of their contemporaries documented in scholarship, nonetheless drew on civil disobedience tactics to advance similar goals. In large part, they were challenging dominant ideas about their ability to belong to a school that they had historically been prohibited from attending. Black Waco students were set on making their new school respond meaningfully to their needs, to their personhood, and such a reply brazenly negated long-standing ideas about their supposed displacement in previously non-Black places. Such courage stood to destabilize white supremacy's power to control Black destiny.

At least three distinct stories explain the origin of the September 1970 walkout. Although the accounts of the walkout's genesis differ and may seem contradictory, they are compatible and help demonstrate the tense and racist environment into which Black students were thrown at the start of the 1970 school year. This racial hostility was consistent with Bellmead's reputation. Marshall Baldwin recounted that at this point in "the history of Central Texas . . . Bellmead was Ku Klux Klan headquarters."[42] Desegregating Black students routinely faced such vitriol in the North as well. As historian Dara

Walker demonstrates, in Detroit in the late 1960s, "white students and local residents met Black students with bottles, cans, bats, and chains," and a local white nationalist hate group consistently threatened Black students' physical safety.[43] Central Texas's reputation, coupled with the lower socioeconomic status of Bellmead's white residents, exacerbated an already chaotic environment.[44] Critical race theorists writing about school desegregation described this racialized class dynamic as one in which "poorer whites committed themselves . . . to keeping blacks down even at the sacrifice of their chance to rise," primarily because "many working-class and poor whites had acquired an investment in white racial privilege" that was predicated on antiBlack, often violent, subordination.[45]

Written documents about school desegregation in Waco depict a majoritarian, or dominant, narrative about the long struggle for human rights that largely discounts Black students' perspectives—alongside the Black community's writ large. This chapter's counterstories of Black Waco students, then, subvert the racial power dynamic underpinning those stock stories that leave unquestioned white supremacy and antiBlackness. One critical race theorist describes majoritarian stories as a "description of events as told by members of dominant/majority groups, accompanied by the values and beliefs that justify the actions taken by dominants to ensure their dominant position."[46] Groups who hold significant political, economic, and social power in a society employ these stock stories to "naturaliz[e] . . . their superior position," "present a picture of the world that best fits and supports their positions of relative power," and "avoid any blame or responsibility for society inequality."[47] A majoritarian perspective holds that Black La Vega students protested without just provocation. With regularity, Black students across the country faced such accusations of frivolous protests. The early 1960s, for example, witnessed Black Georgia students employ direct action to demand equal resources for their drastically underfunded schools, grievances white stakeholders disparaged.[48] It is telling that La Vega ISD's school board minutes made no overt mention of the student-led walkout but were intent on labeling Black students "problems" that needed to be handled and that the few extant accounts came from news reporters with no known relationship to the school district or the Black Waco community. These points make elevating the counterstories of Black La Vega ISD students essential to a more comprehensive narrative about the district's history vis-à-vis Black education.

Although the walkout centered on the closing of G. W. Carver, other indignities likely influenced the decision to stage it. Black students were dismayed about what they felt was the undue termination of Black faculty;

shorter and inadequate lunch facilities and times; and La Vega High's dress code policies, which they felt disproportionately targeted them.[49] Northern desegregation struggles related to staffing propelled similar direct action by Black students. In Chicago in 1967, a Black social studies teacher and Afro-American History Club adviser, Owen Lawson, faced removal from his position for "emphasiz[ing] in his classes African people's contributions to US and world history," making his instruction appear, according to parents, "too militant" with too many "Black power overtones." His dismissal inspired a Black student–led walkout.[50] Additionally, dress code issues exemplified cultural oppression, as "black students claimed the school's rules on clothing and appearance [were] mainly for white students and that black [students were] neither allowed to wear clothes in which they fe[lt] comfortable or wear Afro haircuts."[51] Outlawing such essential aspects of Black students' physical aesthetic threatened African American ontology, or what it meant to be identifiably Black. Through this policy, La Vega ISD was attacking a fundamental component of the Black aesthetic by prohibiting a natural hairstyle that had both cultural and temporal (i.e., the 1970s) significance.[52] These issues trailed the pronounced assault that was the school closure and further motivated Black students in their effort to reclaim some of their dignity and pride. Because newspaper accounts highlighted these other, more minor issues while failing to mention G. W. Carver's closing, any narrative about school desegregation in Waco would be remiss to exclude the firsthand testimony of Black students, especially given that no students recalled any of these less pressing matters as the main impetus for the walkout.[53]

### *Organized Refusal: We "Decided That We Were Going to Boycott"*

Though some stability did come within the first few weeks of the school year, La Vega ISD had already wronged Black students; the damage was done. Marshall Baldwin explained the social turbulence that became a staple at La Vega High in 1970; he, like several other students, insisted the walkout was preplanned, not spontaneous:

> After two or three weeks of just chaos, we finally got some semblance of normalcy in that school, because at the end of the second week of school, we had decided—several of us . . . in fact, a lot of us had decided—that we were going to boycott because we didn't like the way things were at that school. . . . We were going to walk out of the school because we didn't like things, the way things were happening

> in the school. . . . I can't even remember what day of the week it was. . . . We did it one morning at ten o'clock. . . . At ten o'clock, the bell rang, and we looked at each other and said, "Well, are we going to do it?" . . . And we decided, yeah, we're going to do it. So we got up, walked out of class. By this time, we had spread the word to all the other kids. . . . And we were outside the school, you know, boycotting. And we refused to go back to class, because we didn't like the way things were being done. We didn't like the way we were being treated.[54]

Deciding to walk out beforehand and following through inspired little tumult inside the school, according to this account. The uneventful yet significant nature of this version contrasts with newspaper reports in which Superintendent Cranfill decried the Black students' demands as "fantastic," suggesting they were making too much of G. W. Carver's illicit closing and their treatment at La Vega High.[55] However, the ardent sense of protest is evident in Marshall's retelling, which suggests Black high school students in Waco were absorbing the messages about civil disobedience circulating at the time, which helped them believe they could openly challenge their mistreatment.[56]

Superintendent Cranfill's issue with Black students repurposing school spaces for protest exemplifies his sense that they should not have used their new school as a site to express ownership and demand accountability. Apparently, Cranfill thought very little of the Black students and their community. His character was further exposed in his remarks to newspaper reporters, to whom he stated, "I wish I had 100 National Guardsmen, but they say you can't have them unless local protection breaks down. . . . I guess someone will have to get killed first."[57] Wishing for death as a pretext for quashing legitimate student dissent, Cranfill showed himself to be incapable of managing the blowback from helping to underhandedly close G. W. Carver and reroute Black students from G. W. Carver to La Vega High. Seeking the same support Arkansas Governor Orval Faubus received to manage violent segregationists in 1957, what history now knows as the Little Rock Nine debacle, Cranfill assumed this walkout warranted the same. He added, "I don't think the situation can get much worse without bloodshed." While this remark could be interpreted as hyperbole, Cranfill's deeds otherwise suggest he was speaking literally.[58]

Once the walkout ensued and students left the school building, they stood outside on the school's front lawn. Doing so upset school administrators and teachers, who tried to get the students to go back inside. However, returning to class was not what any of the 130 participating students had in mind. As Marshall noted, "We finally decide[d] to leave the school grounds. As we stepped across the street onto the grounds of the school district building . . . we had a lot of whites in pickups and different things with shotguns. And I would say that the only thing separating us was the area from that wall to that wall [here he points]. They had guns. We didn't. We were just angry kids. And we weren't running; we weren't afraid."[59]

AntiBlack violence by white locals was an enduring feature of Waco's racial climate. They openly brandished guns, stoking fear in Black students. According to Marshall, these individuals expected Black students to cower and defy their own moral imperative to demonstrate how mistreated they felt. In kind, wanting to participate in the walkout but scared to leave his car unattended at La Vega High, Willie Brown drove to G. W. Carver, fearing the damage white students would do to his vehicle. Although white residents openly engaged in violent behavior, Black kids, in keeping with prevailing custom, were not allowed such privileges. Being angry was typically not a crime, but Black children of any gender or class status were rarely able to freely express their frustration without repercussion.[60] With the Ku Klux Klan spirit running high, white Bellmead residents, including La Vega ISD stakeholders, threatened to physically attack any Black student expressing that they felt wronged and asking that something constructive be done about it. This sense of agency runs through each version of the walkout origin narrative, including Michael Bass's.

### *Spontaneous Refusal: "Homeboy Went Off on Him" in the Boys' Bathroom*

Michael's story adds some spice to Marshall's. This origin account suggests that for some students, the walkout was not previously planned. The conditions, nevertheless, against which Black students were protesting held constant across all retellings. Black La Vega students were protesting how the district had stripped them of their sense of belonging to G. W. Carver and the identity that provided. Like Marshall's account, Michael's features the students' direct involvement in the protest, though it begins in a boy's bathroom the day of the walkout: "A white dude said something . . . called one of the [Black] guys a nigga or something because he was picking his hair out. He [the white boy] said something and the [Black] dude hit him in the throat with the pick [he was using to comb his hair]. And we [Black boys in the bathroom] threw him [the white boy] over the balcony."

Michael's description suggests there was a large, perhaps floor-to-ceiling, window in the bathroom that facilitated air circulation. Because many schools, including La Vega High, at the time lacked centralized heating and cooling systems and permitted smoking indoors, windows in school bathrooms were standard. Presumably, this window opened to the outside and, likely as a safety feature, was framed midway by a railing, which functioned as a balcony of sorts. Michael continued, "There was more than one [white boy], but the other ones, they just stayed in a corner. But he [the instigating white boy] was the aggress[or]; he was one of those big ol' redneck cowboys with boots and pants stuck [i.e., tucked] off in the boots with chewing tobacco in his back pocket. Talking 'bout 'I don't know why you niggras come out here to our school. This ain't y'all school.' [To which Michael responded,] 'We didn't want to come out here.'"

Michael underscored that Black students had not wanted to attend La Vega High; the school board—with the support of the federal and state government—had forced their hand. The assumption that African Americans wanted their school to be closed in order to attend a previously non-Black school is representative of popular erroneous presumptions on the part of white individuals across the country.[61] The white instigating student demonstrated white students' pronounced sense of privilege, ownership, and entitlement by expressing demands and giving instructions as to how the chaos of desegregation could be remedied: through the elimination of Black students and the reclamation of "his" high school. Such a declaration reifies whiteness as a valuable form of property, a point that underscores how spatial contestation was a central issue in school desegregation.[62]

Michael's description of the instigating white boy's attire contextualizes the demographics of La Vega ISD's student body. As illustrated earlier, these rural white students often occupied a lower socioeconomic status than residents of west Waco. Their position correlated with more and stronger threats of antiBlack violence amid school desegregation because, according to white supremacist thinking, African Americans threatened the social order given their new access to the same facilities and education that white students had. In challenging white folks' political and economic edge, even ever so slightly, Black students summoned economic insecurities that coalesced around deeply engrained antiBlack racism. It did not matter that most of the Black students also had a low socioeconomic status, because race converged with class to make them more vulnerable to injury.

Recounting the conversation that took place in the bathroom, Michael remembered the aggressive white boy saying, "'Well, I don't know what you're doing out here. You ain't got no business out here anyway. You should have stayed at your own school.' [Michael replied,] 'Hell, we wanted to stay at our own school,' and he [the white boy] said something to somebody, and homeboy [Black boy picking his hair] went off on him. After that, the fight was on. Trash cans were being thrown; people were flying off the balcony; girls were running and screaming. . . . [*Michael laughs*] It was wild."

According to this white student, white people felt Black students were encroaching on their territory, and this particular student, with no help from his friends, felt inclined to explain exactly how he saw the problem; he assumed Black students had wanted to attend La Vega High and was instructing them to return to where they came. Black students had no business at the district's white high school, according to this student, so they were to find another Black school to attend, notwithstanding the fact that the district had just closed G. W. Carver forever. In doing so, the district signaled its adherence to traditional, dominant beliefs that refute Black peoples' production of space and their capacity to act consequentially on it, even on spaces to which Jim Crow segregation had relegated them.[63] Not only did the white boy show himself to be mistaken about the reason for Black students' presence in "his" school (demonstrating that the district had failed to communicate important changes to both the Black students and the white students), but he was also making demands on implicated Black students that had no basis in reality.

The Black boys in the incident, flustered beyond reason by the accusations that they had wanted to attend La Vega High and leave behind their beloved G. W. Carver, took matters into their own hands. Michael could not recall whether the white boy sustained serious injuries, but he did remember more than one person falling over the railing. The bedlam that followed led directly to the walkout. Michael described the march from La Vega High to G. W. Carver: "Well, it was a big old thang [in the school] for a whole minute. Then, somehow everybody got together. Just walked out of class. Then we all walked straight down Bellmead Drive, blocked traffic, walked all the way up Bellmead Drive to Waco Drive. Went down that side road and come up straight up Faulkner Lane and went home [toward G. W. Carver]." As one of the only firsthand reports detailing the walkout's route to G. W. Carver, Michael's recollection reveals that students were intent on constructively and collectively conveying their ire. His comment that "somehow everybody got together" suggests that when Marshall's cadre had agreed to walk out and were following through with their plan, the ruckus in the bathroom was unfolding and fed into a partially planned walkout already underway. The palpable racial tension makes Michael's reference to G. W. Carver as "home" all the more meaningful given the duress the Black students were under in this new environment.

In this version, performances of male ego couched in toxic masculinity take center stage, both of which were expressed in physical force and magnified by racism.[64] Unable to back down after being challenged, the instigating white boy persisted in asserting himself, thus revealing he was not scared and conveying his refusal to be intimidated by the Black boys to whom he felt superior. In a similar vein, in this volatile, racist environment, it appears the Black boys strove to appear unafraid and willing to risk punishment, escalating the situation by retaliating against threats that had been leveled against them since day one at La Vega High. Both race and gender factored into this rendition, as racial power was amplified by the white boy's aggression, which could only be matched momentarily through the Black boys' revocation of said power, which they carried out by tossing white students out of the bathroom.

### *Black Girl Refusal: "She Slapped a White Teacher"*

Willie Brown's recollection of the walkout centers on Black girls and is distinct from both Marshall's and Michael's. This detail is important because, as historian Rachel Devlin has argued, Black girls often led many school desegregation struggles but have long gone underacknowledged.[65] In Willie's recollection, the catalyst of the walkout was "one of the Black students, a female . . . Ivy Branch. She slapped a white teacher." This quickly led to "all hell [breaking] out in the hallway. . . . Kids were coming out the classroom and . . . Erma Jean Smith . . . she organized us, and we walked from La Vega [High] back the Carver school, all the Black students."[66]

Ivy Branch and Erma Jean Smith were just two among many Black girls at La Vega High driving change in ways largely underappreciated. It is unknown what provoked Ivy to slap a white teacher. Reports from other La Vega High students, such as Michael and Marshall, indicate that the all-white teaching staff openly showed disdain toward Black students. This was customary in previously non-Black schools that viewed Black students, Black girls especially, as unintelligent interlopers. The perspectives of Black girls clarified most acutely an issue faced by Black students in general.[67] Some Black students like Ivy responded by striving to advocate for themselves—though, according to alumni, her response was atypical. Despite the pivotal role Black girls have historically played in a wide array of historical processes, including school desegregation, their experiences and contributions overall have been widely undervalued and disregarded. Sociologists such as Belinda Robnett have recognized, however, that Black women tend to tell more "holistic" stories of social movements, including the civil rights movement itself.[68] Thus, continuing to overlook Black girls' contributions to and experiences of school desegregation stands to compromise a wider, more comprehensive understanding of how this policy unfolded on the ground and what it meant to those involved.

Willie explained, "All the kids poured out of the school and 'fore you know, we was all out and was walking back to East Waco back to Carver." This deliberate action reveals the Black students' full sense of the issue. Perhaps Superintendent Cranfill, as he was quoted saying, was unsure and thought Black students were simply upset for the sake of being upset. Marching back to their community institution, however, served to clarify any remaining uncertainty about what Black students intended to repossess.

### *Synthetizing Origins and Demanding Dignity*

The written sources corroborate details in all three students' counterstories but also reflect their limitations as written records. Decades later, *Waco Tribune-Herald* reporter Terri Jo Ryan described how Erma Jean Laster (née Smith) "organiz[ed] an act of civil obedience in the 1970–71 school year" by "staging a walkout" and how the participating students "began a 5-mile march . . . [that] took them across the Brazos River to G. W. Carver High and on to Carver Park Baptist Church."[69] "[Rev.] R. T. Booker of Carver Park Baptist Church convinced the youths to leave the streets and meet at his church," where they, alongside Black adult community members, held planning meetings from which they barred media.[70] Ryan's insight on Erma Jean is important, but as noted in the previous chapter, because the Brazos River sits west of Bellmead, G. W. Carver, and East Waco, Ryan's account is likely mistaken given the area's physical geography and built environment. Nonetheless, with respect to other key details, Ryan's version does adhere closely to Willie's in that both pointed to Erma Jean's participation and her leadership role in the walkout. Though Marshall did not specify Erma Jean as an organizer, his retelling overlaps with Willie's in that it identifies the ten o'clock hour as the walkout's starting time and a specific group of Black students to have initiated the protest. Finally, Michael's account agrees with Willie's because he also noted a similar walkout route.

A significant detail, however, distinguishes Ryan's account from others and exemplifies the white-run media's misrepresentation of the motivation behind the walkout. In asserting that the walkout contested La Vega ISD's "plans to not renew the contracts of several popular Black teachers," using a comment by Erma Jean to support this claim, rather than focusing on the closing of G. W. Carver, Ryan's walkout narrative emphasized what was only a minor grievance of the protesters. Although Erma Jean had confirmed "that La Vega ISD renewed each [*sic*] coach Clarence Chase's contract for the next year," Black students felt slighted primarily by the district's refusal to consider reopening G. W. Carver.[71] It is true that La Vega ISD met the students' demand to rehire a teacher and coach, but the white-owned media's presentation of this small victory as an example of the walkout's overall success was misleading because the most important issue—G. W. Carver—stood unchanged.

Erma Jean's exclusion from most walkout renditions showcases how patriarchal norms pervaded Waco, as they did most of the country. A decade earlier in Mississippi, as historian V. P. Franklin documented, high schooler Brenda Travis's school suspended her for seeking service at a Mississippi Greyhound station. Her suspension sparked an organized walkout involving more than two hundred students.[72] Critiques of the civil rights and Black Power movements note how both movements nevertheless marginalized Black women and failed to recognize their essential contributions as a result of patriarchal systems of domination that routinely dismiss their contributions.[73] This issue regularly surfaced in Waco.[74] As the historiography of the civil rights movement makes clear, patriarchal views of prominent male figures in the movement are common, are more likely to credit Black male "natural" leaders with heading protests, and have hence routinely overshadowed Black girls' and women's involvement.[75] In the case of this walkout, evidence shows that a young Black woman, Erma Jean, served an important role, and the history of this event should reflect that. Underscoring the activism of Black girls alongside their peers' willingness to stand behind them is a vital step in establishing Black girls' contributions to the movement.

Erma Jean was in good company, as young Black women had led direct-action demonstrations in Waco's fight against racial segregation, events that reporters and historians deliberately underdocumented. In the 1960s, Paul Quinn College student Cherry Boggess and her classmates staged sit-ins at the downtown Pipkin Drug Store, which was happy to sell to Black customers while denying them seats and service in the store's restaurant. Having undergone sit-in training in Tennessee, Cherry was well versed in tactics that facilitated the desegregation of public spaces. According to a local newspaper, however, little was recorded about such shows of courage and activism in Waco, as newspaper editors and Black community activists entered into an unofficial agreement "to downplay news coverage of public protests in return for quiet, behind-the-scenes pressure for integration."[76]

A local news report published the day after the walkout, Tuesday, September 15, underlines significant details regarding the protest that complicate the narrative and humanize its actors.[77] Participating students delineated thirty-five grievances after their walkout and "vow[ed] not to return to La Vega High until the phased out Carver High [was] reopened."[78] Although the walkout may have been spontaneous, the students seemed well versed in potential strategies they could employ to have their demands addressed. Superintendent Cranfill's response, however, to their demands, which he labeled "impossible," suggests a reasonable reply was unlikely; it also revealed how he understood the racist dynamics of the situation, as he admitted that "they are just unhappy with integration, the loss of their symbolism, and the loss of their own identity with Carver High School."[79] In some ways, Cranfill's remarks reflect he was aware of the reasons Black students were upset; however, he was wrong in stating that they were unhappy with integration on the whole. They debunked some of Cranfill's assumptions by communicating a crucial aspiration for their former school: "They didn't care if Carver opened as a high school or junior high as long as it opened. . . . If Carver was converted to a junior high school then high school age students would willingly attend La Vega."[80] These students were thus capable of understanding the necessity of change, even if it meant G. W. Carver would no longer solely be a high school; what they could not accept, however, was its complete end. Social and political influences from media sources, for instance, spurred the Black students' recognition that racial change was inevitable, but that did not mean they had to willingly accept the disproportionate burden it placed on them and their community.

After the walkout on September 14, some Black students continued their protest by boycotting school for the rest of the week; this protracted protest exemplified how seriously Black students took La Vega ISD's antiBlack implementation of school desegregation and, going forward, what it meant in terms of restrictions they would face in creating an educational space for themselves to meet their needs. Few if any white La Vega ISD stakeholders saw Black students as belonging to the district's formerly non-Black schools; they treated Black students, as Michael's vignette poignantly demonstrates, as intruders. Drawing on the principle of self-determination, many Black La Vega ISD students, however, were committed to redefining their place in this new schooling space.[81] The rate of absenteeism was near 50 percent despite the urgent appeals from two Black-led community groups, the East Waco branch of the NAACP and Committee for Better Schools, headed by Robert E. Smith, that students return to La Vega High.[82] Nevertheless, La Vega High School Principal Donald Richardson declined to close La Vega High School, where La Vega ISD had reassigned many of G. W. Carver's students, while "hop[ing] no one g[ot] kill[ed]."[83] Richardson's lackluster wish squares with Cranfill's cries of bloodshed as part of his portrayal of Black students as overly violent troublemakers in need of control by any means necessary.

Regardless of the specific origin of the walkout and subsequent boycott, each version highlights the level of marginalization that Black students and many Black people in the community felt. As if their school being closed was not enough, the failure to notify them about the closure beforehand characterizes a particular form of negligence and contempt on the part of both La Vega ISD and the federal government. By not requiring the district to notify Black families long served by G. W. Carver, the federal government prioritized the process and execution of school desegregation over Black dignity. Overseeing the abolishment of a community institution that functioned not only as a school but also as a community center and beacon of hope, the federal government colluded with La Vega ISD to cast aside Black agency and the goals of Black community members unduly burdened by this consequential decision. Prioritizing process over dignity and decency, both the federal government and La Vega ISD showed the Black community they were unworthy of justice and respect, and the school year that followed only exacerbated these tensions.

## "TRYING TO FIGURE OUT WHAT TO DO WITH US": THE 1970–1971 SCHOOL YEAR

After haphazardly finding out G. W. Carver was no more, Black students prepared to face what they suspected would be an unrelenting school year. As Beverly Rickford, a seventh grader at the time, remarked, "I think they really were trying to figure out what to do with us. They were hoping we wouldn't rebel. They were hoping we wouldn't . . . be mad and be upset" about the school closure. This call for suppression motivated many Black students to convey just how much they did not want to be at formerly non-Black schools and how disregarded they felt. Although the walkout and boycott were dynamic and unifying shows of force, they did not reopen G. W. Carver. Therefore, Black students readied themselves for what they knew would be a trying year.

White students, along with their families, stood ready to express, often with firearms or physical violence, that they did not want Black students in "their" school. In essence, this spatial declaration charged Black students with trespassing on white-only grounds. The grassroots Council of Parents for Action provides one such example. "A group of more than 100 white persons . . . [who were] white parents in the La Vega district," reported the *Waco News-Tribune*, denounced the high number of Black students in the district and ultimately recommended that "the boundary lines should be shifted so some of the blacks would attend other districts, so the unhealthy conditions at La Vega can be eliminated."[84] This group urged fellow white residents in La Vega to join them and vote in upcoming elections to oust the district's Black students, saying they sought "equality with the Blacks" and insisting white Bellmead residents "take action . . . [and] band together."[85] Using white nationalist rhetoric, the group gave the district the solution it would soon take to eradicate Black students.

Knowing from the beginning that Black students did not want to go to non-Black La Vega schools because "we just felt like they didn't want us over there," Wanda James remembers the internal unrest she felt before the school year even began. The issue of spatial contestation arose again as the implementation of the school desegregation plan worked to displace and ostracize Black students. As a high school student, Wanda's premonitions proved to be accurate; she remarked on how this open rejection played out: "If you were at La Vega, they [teachers] may send you to the office [for so-called behavior issues] really fast." From Kentucky to Mississippi, Black students withstood white educators accusing them of cheating; slapping them in the face; relegating them to seats in the back of classrooms so white students could sit up front; ignoring them; limiting their interactions; and applying deodorant to them to chemically intervene on their supposedly innate foul odor.[86] "But if you were at Carver," Wanda explained, "they [teachers] tried to work with you and make you say [to yourself], 'Hey, I'm going to make it; I am going to get there.'" Being made to feel like "problems" in school likely persuaded Black students to yearn for their former segregated Black schools, where many had felt affirmed and supported. Black teachers had historically taught their students that teachers need not rely on administrative support to manage their classrooms.[87] But that external support was now the norm, and Black students were now seldom fortified as they had been before desegregation.[88]

Classroom observations help expose issues revealing important aspects of students' quotidian experiences. Wanda recalled, "I can remember in a classroom, as far as seating in the classroom, all the Blacks was on one side and the whites were on the other, even though they [teachers] tried to switch it up, it just didn't [work]." Although some white teachers tried to ease some of the racial tension, white and Black students still refused to sit next to each other. Given that the safety of African Americans was already compromised, being a Black student in a school where white persons openly conveyed their repulsion toward Black people only added to that sense of danger. In addition to Bellmead's pronounced KKK legacy, local white residents had already established themselves as threats by brandishing shotguns, for instance, as they had during the walkout, so it was impossible for Black students to take too many precautions regarding their safety. Detroit's school desegregation battle displayed similar themes, as "Black students . . . encountered not just community violence, but the racist attitudes of teachers and administrators as well as a racist curriculum."[89]

In some cases, teachers played into racist tensions and strove to undereducate and unfairly assess Black students' academic performance. Michael Bass recalled,

> It was just racism. Period. Because your people that were A students and B students [at G. W. Carver] were now C students [at La Vega High]. . . . You could tell what was going on. They [teachers] were teaching us one thing and teaching the white kids another thing. . . . You're being told one thing [by the teachers] and they're doing something else [to better teach the white students]. What you're doing [as a Black student] is wrong, but what they're doing [as white students] is right, but you're doing the same thing they doing.

Michael underscored the orchestrated undereducation and manufactured underachievement he suspected of white educators. A few years later two Black students, Sarah Johnson and Debora Wilkerson, experienced some of these same dynamics in Waco ISD.[90] It was clear, according to Michael, that white students' academic achievement mattered more to white teachers than that of Black students. With Black students receiving little intervention or assistance from teachers, the individuals whom many had come to know as advocates in their earlier educational lives were nowhere to be found. This marked shift in instructional approach may help explain why Michael could not "remember none of them teachers at La Vega, not one. I mean not one. I don't even remember if I had a Black teacher over there." Although records for the 1970–71 school year show that the school employed Black teachers and administrators in addition to several Black cafeteria and auxiliary staff persons, white faculty made up the majority.[91] In such an arrangement, it was possible that Michael was not assigned to a Black teacher's class, which helps shed light on the general disconnection he felt between himself and educators at La Vega High and that he, like other Black students around the country, may have blocked out catastrophic, traumatizing parts of his experience with school desegregation's implementation.[92] The psychological torment of feeling unwanted each day was difficult to manage on its own, but coupling that ordeal with the constant threat of physical assault and academic sabotage created an impossible climate many students would have done well to forget.

The fact that grade levels served by the respective Black and white La Vega ISD schools were incongruent added to the turbulence: La Vega High School included grades 10 to 12, while G. W. Carver had served grades 7 to 12. Therefore, when G. W. Carver closed, the district sent Black students who had been together at one campus to two different schools, La Vega Junior High and La Vega Senior High. Although the walkout and related events were largely limited to the high school, their influence was wide-reaching and affected the junior high. With many older students about to embark on their final—and arguably most significant—school years, the importance of these events at the high school was clear. Connie Sadler, a seventh grader at the time, remembered many of these issues pervading the atmosphere at La Vega Junior High, which she attended in the 1970–71 school year:

> While we were struggling at the intermediate [or junior high], you know, it was a constant clash over at the high school. . . . The intermediate students in junior high school, we had our fights. We had our disagreements. We [didn't] want to be here [at La Vega]. We had people that were disruptive, but it fed off of those things that were happening over at the high school because . . . they were constantly battling, fighting, not so much as physical, but the students were [constantly staging protests]. And rightly so, because you had seniors that were getting ready to graduate from Carver, and they can't graduate from Carver. They're having to graduate from La Vega.[93]

Connie described a hurt that cut deep, and many Black students felt the government and the school district had stolen their high school years from them, an act that landed like the ultimate blow in a series of unexpected and deeply disrespectful wrongs. As one might assume, older students set the tone for the younger ones, and this situation created an even more chaotic environment for school and district leaders to manage. No matter how the district attempted to separate G. W. Carver's Black students during the school day, they went back to the same neighborhoods that they had fraternized in before G. W. Carver's closing. This unity off school grounds fostered an overall climate of unrest that would remain charged in the absence of another drastic change to right the wrongs against the community.

During the 1970–71 school year, the nature of extracurricular activities also shifted for the former G. W. Carver students who were now at La Vega High School. Some students reported feeling a strong sense of disengagement from their new school, and in situations where Black students did join sports teams and participate as they had before, blatant racism curtailed their full participation. During his senior year, Marshall Baldwin remembered sacrificing his final football season in response to a deliberate act of gendered antiBlack racism. He shared that "some of us tried to go there and play football out at La Vega, but we didn't—the reason we walked off the football team is because we had more blacks at one time than the whites on the football team and you know, when it comes time to voting the sweetheart—the football sweetheart—we voted a black girl in. They gave it to a white girl, so we just didn't play. 'Y'all can have it.' So that's the way it was."[94]

Standing up for Black girls in this way was admirable. Although it did demonstrate the football players' strong moral character, it did not return their senior football season to them. Marshall's comments suggest the football sweetheart symbolized femininity and beauty, attributes that in the minds of most white folks at La Vega were presumably reserved exclusively for white girls.[95] Comparable episodes of protest happened within school desegregation contexts in New England, the mid-Atlantic, the Midwest, and the South, in Massachusetts, Illinois, North Carolina, and New York. In Massachusetts in 1970, Black male students refused to "participate in athletic events until the administration could guarantee the safety of students, particularly black females."[96] "The suspension of seventeen black football players who had skipped practice to protest that only one of the school's six varsity cheerleaders was black" spurred a thousand-student boycott in 1967 Illinois. The year 1969 saw a riot in one North Carolina town after the student body refused to elect a Black cheerleader, and the following year in New York "black students demanded that more blacks be placed on the cheerleading squad."[97] Unwilling to compromise on their (re)definition of what, to them, was beautiful and feminine, Black Waco boys, like other Black boys and Black students widely across the country, worked together to vote for the football sweetheart, and then again to expose and protest the school when it did not honor the election's results.

As the end of a long and tumultuous school year approached, seniors prepared for a graduation that many were reluctant at best and resentful at worst to attend. Indeed, feelings from the school year carried over into the graduation ceremony. The guest speaker, Marvin C. Griffin, a well-regarded Black former pastor of Waco's New Hope Baptist Church who had recently started pastoring Ebenezer Baptist Church in Austin, offered remarks; his prominent role in Waco's civil rights movement, community activism, and "unswerving emphasis on racial justice" made him a stark point of contrast to Superintendent Cranfill, from whom students were to receive their diplomas.[98] Marshall recalled the event:

> Because my [last] name started with a B, I was the first Black to go up there and get my diploma. So I didn't know if it was customary or what, I didn't know, I wasn't trying to start anything. I shook his [Pastor Marvin Griffin's] hand for speaking, and when I got my diploma, I went to shake Cranfill's hand, [but then] didn't. And every Black kid after me did the same thing, just got the diploma and walked off. And I wasn't—consciously, I wasn't trying to start nothing—but I remember what I had been through the past year, I remembered that. You [Cranfill] were one of those in power that could have made a difference, and you didn't. You turned your back to it. You turned a deaf ear to it. You just let things go the way they shouldn't. . . . When had you stood up and said, "Wait a minute, we can do better"? See, I would have had a lot more respect for him [if he did that]. But he didn't. So I didn't feel like I needed to shake his hand. And that was that. I got my diploma and walked on off the stage.[99]

Marshall underscored Cranfill's subpar character, reflecting the disregard and malevolence that he, other administrators, and white board members showed to Black students. Declining to shake the superintendent's hand was probably one of the more measured actions Marshall could have taken based on the year he had undergone. After being undermined in many ways, he and the Black students who followed were actually extending a courtesy to the school and superintendent by disengaging. Figuring they had nothing to shake Cranfill's hand for, Black students ended this year of turmoil much like they started it: with a feeling of righteous indignation.

Letters addressed to various law enforcement agencies from the La Vega ISD board speak to the hectic nature of the 1970–71 school year. These notes, signed by Cranfill, express appreciation "for the wonderful and efficient cooperation extended us during the troublesome school year we just ended." Cranfill and the La Vega ISD board specifically extended gratitude to the local police chief, Randall Kirk, as well as the Texas Department of Public Safety, the neighboring cities of Northcrest and Lacy Lakeview, the Waco Police Department, and the Texas Rangers.[100] These letters frame Black students as delinquents and implicate them as the source of such trouble, as there were no comparable letters in school board records from the 1950s to 1980. The unique focus on delinquency illustrates how deeply unwanted Black students likely felt throughout the entire school year. Unwilling to mask their disdain, Cranfill and white members of the La Vega ISD board hatched a plan to oust their newly relocated Black students.

The school year progressed and ended as it had begun—chaotically. The year's conclusion did not end the frenzy that defined it, however, as another furtive plan saw yet again the displacement of Black students. But few if any Black Texas students were spared humiliation in the school desegregation process.

## RESPATIALIZING BLACKNESS THROUGH BOUNDARIES AND TRADES

As the 1970s commenced, the push to desegregate was facilitated by key Black Waco actors. As was the case in many US school districts, this period of token desegregation produced little racial mixing, compelling the NAACP to sue the district again to comply with the federal desegregation mandate. In the fall of 1970, as the Black Power movement peaked and the Vietnam War waged on, Waco ISD was placed under court order again—this time to desegregate its faculty—a change that happened between the fall and spring semesters of the 1970–71 school year.[101] This process was prompted in part by Mrs. Jeffie Conner, a trailblazing middle-class education leader with a graduate degree from Prairie View A&M University, who was active in Waco's Black civic community.[102] Conner used her connections to the national NAACP to voice Black Waco residents' concerns about the unjust school desegregation process.[103] Her letters called attention to Waco ISD's ongoing postponement of desegregation and, after La Vega ISD closed G. W. Carver and J. Newton Jenkins, the termination of sixty-two Black teachers, just one instance of a widespread practice of firing teachers in the wake of *Brown*.[104] With her help, many of these teachers were able to secure new teaching positions. Financing the legal expenses associated with these lawsuits, Conner used her economic means as the wife of a physician and a federal home demonstration agent to amplify Black Wacoans' voices so that they could effectively instigate for educational justice. Such efforts, however, frustrated other African Americans involved in Black Waco's civic life, such as Robert Gilbert, Waco ISD's first Black male board member and Baylor University's first Black graduate, who criticized Black middle-class Wacoans' influence over the city's racial issues. Although class divides were salient and significantly shaped the lives of Black Wacoans, in some cases such criticism was unwarranted and sexist.[105]

The 1971 *United States v. Texas* case attempted to place the entire state under court order to desegregate its public K–12 schools, a legal effort that punctuated an already fraught political landscape.[106] At the behest of the federal Department of Health, Education, and Welfare, given its weak enforcement power, the US Department of Justice brought a suit against the state of Texas and the Texas Education Agency, the state's public school administrative arm, because of both entities' compliance with and perpetuation of ongoing segregation practices in small east Texas towns. The location of these violations was no accident, as Texas's history of enslavement and its high African American population were largely centered on this portion of the state. Ordering the swift desegregation of all the state's public schools, the presiding chief judge of the US District Court for the Eastern District of Texas, William Wayne Justice, a white, liberal Democrat from Texas appointed by President Lyndon B. Johnson, issued a series of desegregation orders that affected over one thousand school districts and millions of students. The following year, a ruling on an appeal of *United States v. Texas* limited the reach of what became Civil Order 5281, the desegregation enforcement mechanism emerging from the 1971 decision. A "modification by the Fifth Circuit Court of Appeals . . . placed those districts containing the most blatant remnants of a dual school system largely beyond [Civil Order 5281's] reach," and two of these districts were Waco and La Vega.[107] This order was significant nonetheless, because it resulted in arguably the largest series of school desegregation orders in US legal history. Moreover, Judge Justice had found the Texas Education Agency guilty of permitting school segregation across the state, yet he charged this agency with overseeing district compliance.[108] To be clear, entrusting this state agency to oversee desegregation meant that the organization that had previously failed to enforce school desegregation would now be required—under federal scrutiny—to see school desegregation through. To remedy violations found in east Texas, in which segregationists had been redrawing district lines to gerrymander their way out of fully complying with desegregation mandates, it was necessary to place the entire state under court order.[109] Consequences associated with violating the decision included losing accreditation, federal funding, and state funding, repercussions that would render districts virtually inoperable.

Waco ISD found itself embroiled in a boundary controversy that was linked to the faculty desegregation issue and that disproportionately harmed Black stakeholders. With the 1971 closing of A. J. Moore High School and the opening of Jefferson-Moore High School as its desegregated replacement, Waco ISD set out to reconfigure its boundaries. These changes related directly to the district presenting to the community its desegregation plan, which resulted from a court order issued in 1973 by US District Judge Jack Roberts that had derived from a 1971 lawsuit, *Arvizu v. Waco Independent School District*. This 1973 court order's origin was different from that obligating Waco ISD to desegregate its faculty, as discussed above; Waco ISD's faculty desegregation stemmed from the 1964 court order issued by US District Judge Homer Thornberry to accelerate the pace of desegregation as a result of the 1962 *McGrue v. Williams* lawsuit mentioned in the previous chapter. Attorneys from the Civil Rights Division of the US Justice Department, Craig Crenshaw and Jean Ollivierre, visited Waco ISD in November 1970 about the district's compliance with desegregation requirements, giving Waco ISD until February 1, 1971, to reassign faculty on an eighty-white/twenty-Black basis.[110] The district agreed as a sign of good faith that it would reassign students the next semester for the start of the 1971–72 school year. Both students and faculty would be reassigned based on the same eighty-white/twenty-Black basis.[111] This deadline was likely prompted by contemporaneous Supreme Court rulings in which the court insisted on desegregation compliance, 1969 verdicts including *Alexander v. Holmes County Board of Education* and *United States v. Montgomery County Board of Education*.[112] Unable to postpone faculty desegregation any longer, Waco ISD was forced to implement a plan at the beginning of the spring semester of the 1970–71 school year.

Redrawing district lines set many white Waco residents ablaze in fury, as attested by letters from two local professionals, one a dentist and the other a physician.[113] Waco ISD officials working to curb anxiety about this process appointed the biracial Waco Citizens Advisory Committee, whom Waco ISD tasked with redrawing district boundaries for the 1971–72 school year. Led by Dr. Raymond Biles, a white Baylor University professor, the Citizens Advisory Committee was distinct from the aforementioned citizens' councils that zealously fought school desegregation across the South in that it was designed to facilitate school desegregation. The committee's first duty was to determine which students would attend Jefferson-Moore High School, which ultimately replaced A. J. Moore High. A key function of the committee was to exonerate Waco ISD, as the committee was positioned to assume blame for impending issues sure to arise regarding the location of boundary lines.

Complaining in various ways, Waco ISD parents of different backgrounds took issue with having to change schools because of new boundary lines. Many mailed letters of protest and attended local meetings at which the committee and school board presented their plan and solicited community feedback.[114] This process was vital, as the Citizens Advisory Committee shared multiple drafts of boundary lines with the public before the board could officially approve and implement the redistricting plan. Although many of these complaints came from flustered white stakeholders, some came from people of Color, including an ethnic Mexican parent, Ramsey Muniz. He drew on legal knowledge of the recent 1968 *Green v. County School Board of New Kent County* and 1971 *Swann v. Charlotte-Mecklenburg Board of Education* cases to highlight the district's fixation on high schools to the detriment of elementary and junior high schools. Although people of Mexican heritage in Waco were legally considered white and therefore had historically attended non-Black segregated schools, Muniz argued that the underemphasis on the lower-level schools harmed Mexican-origin students because, as a result of systemic racism, they were unlikely to go beyond early levels in their schooling.[115]

Since closing its Black schools, La Vega ISD had been intent on finding a way to purge its Black students, and it did not take long for the board to achieve this objective. Following through with plans crafted seven months into the school year, "the [La Vega ISD] board authorize[d] school attorneys and the superintendent to prepare a request for District Judge Jack Roberts to 're-open the court case in regard to the present integration plan with a view toward the adjustment of boundary lines between this district and the Waco Independent School District in order to effect a reduction in the ratio of blacks to whites in the district.'"[116] The rationale—ratio reduction—was telling given that La Vega ISD's Black-to-white student ratio was a nearly perfect one-to-one. Although this was the first official mention of such a boundary change in school board records, related files suggest that board members, administrators, and white Bellmead residents had been looking to relocate Black students since the beginning of the school year.

A unanimous motion by the school board urged La Vega ISD's attorneys to "go back and bargain with the Waco School Attorneys in regard to the plans for boundary line changes."[117] The plan was to have the La Vega ISD attorneys go "with the Waco School Attorneys into the office of Judge Jack Roberts, with each side presenting the plans and facts to Support such plans and ask the Judge to set the boundary line for the two Districts."[118] A few days later, on July 22, La Vega ISD board member Tommy Herring shared the "agreed settlement of the boundary line change between La Vega and Waco School Districts. He stated Judge Jack Roberts had directed that an order be prepared and presented to him for signature on July 28, 1971, establishing the line."[119] Ultimately, this new boundary placed the Black neighborhoods of Carver Park, Hollywood, and Estella Maxey under Waco ISD jurisdiction. This flagrant show of antiBlackness revealed how school desegregation promoted the racialization of space and rendered the implementation process a site of acute spatial contestation. The urge to maintain white dominance drove La Vega ISD's decision to manipulate spatial markers—boundaries—to sustain a white majority.

Fretful about the ulterior motives of these boundary changes, on August 16, 1971, La Vega ISD attorney J. C. Hinsley sent a letter "respectfully request[ing that] the Board of Trustees of the La Vega Independent School District . . . agree to the termination of my employment by the school district and to agree that I may request the court to permit me to withdraw from the above case as an attorney for the La Vega Independent School District."[120] The board unanimously passed this motion the following day. Hinsley's reason for requesting termination is plainly stated in his letter and is tied directly to this boundary request and the change it facilitated. His resignation letter warrants quoting at length:

> You will recall that when the Board of Trustees decided earlier this year to request the United States District Court to rearrange the boundaries between the Waco Independent School District and the La Vega Independent School District, I advised that I was not in sympathy with these proceedings and requested that I be permitted to withdraw from that case because I could not conscientiously support that move. From news items appearing in local newspapers and from statements made to me by individuals in [the] Texas Education Agency I understand that La Vega Independent School District is now involved in other difficulties which may or may not have resulted directly or indirectly from the boundary changes mentioned above. In any event, I am of the opinion that these additional problems must of necessity have a direct bearing upon the case brought against the district by the East Waco Branch of the NAACP.[121] Under these circumstances, including the possibility that I might be called upon to attempt to defend actions growing out of the change in boundaries procedure to which I objected, and the seeming impossibility

of separating all of these actions from the NAACP case against the school district, I must respectfully request the Board of Trustees of La Vega Independent School District to agree to the termination of my employment by the school district and to agree that I may request the court to permit me to withdraw from the above case as an attorney for La Vega Independent School District.[122]

Hinsley's refusal to be associated with La Vega ISD's shamelessly antiBlack maleficence underscores the underhanded nature motivating this boundary change. La Vega's racist reputation gave Hinsley reason to believe the district was trying to undermine justice by literally eliminating its Black students.

Redrawing district boundaries left other assets in question. Reports attribute "the racial tensions at La Vega [to] le[ading] the federal courts to negotiate a plan with Waco ISD to take in East Waco. The courts agreed to place General Tire in Waco ISD's tax base to provide extra funding for the 1,300 new East Waco students who were to attend Waco schools in late summer 1971."[123] Thus, in the new district lines, General Tire, "Waco's largest private employer," was now within Waco ISD's jurisdiction; this reallocation totaled "$17 million in property, including [in addition to] General Tire, Texas Concrete Works, Pure Milk Co., and H&B Packing, [which] were transferred to Waco ISD."[124] Such reports, however, suggest that the federal government initiated this plan, a view that contradicts Hinsley's statements. Gaining these businesses eased the financial burden of taking on additional students and demonstrated the lack of altruism motivating the deal.[125]

Therefore, at the end of the 1970–71 school year, 1,300 Black students were forced out of La Vega ISD and into Waco ISD. With avid support from Superintendent Cranfill and white Bellmead residents, La Vega ISD and Waco ISD had colluded with the federal courts to dislocate Black Waco students. This reallocation of resources through La Vega ISD's payment to Waco ISD for taking on 1,300 Black students violated yet again the spatial agency of Black students while conveying that Black students were a costly and unwanted burden.[126] This handover sent them to majority-white schools in west Waco such as Parkdale Elementary School, Lake Air Junior High School, and Richfield High School.[127]

To facilitate the mass transfer of Black students from La Vega ISD to Waco ISD in 1971, Waco ISD implemented a busing plan, supported by the 1971 *Swann* case, "to fulfill the court-ordered rulings. This was the first time the Waco Public Schools used busing to achieve integration."[128] Debora Wilkerson noted that the new use of busing enabled her to transfer from the "very white"

Waco High School to Jefferson-Moore High, which had a much Blacker, less white student body.[129] Debora warmly welcomed this change given the racial hostility she faced at the previously non-Black school. Thus, busing effectively facilitated school desegregation in Waco ISD, but it was often at Black students' expense because they typically had the longest distances to travel.

Even after this mass transfer, Waco ISD continued to racially segregate students. While there were no longer any fully non-Black schools, three Waco schools in the early 1970s remained nearly all Black: J. H. Hines Elementary, Oakwood Elementary, and R. L. Smith Elementary.[130] Therefore, more action was needed from the Waco ISD board to fully desegregate. In 1973, Judge Jack Roberts approved a more aggressive plan, and after administrators implemented the plan, the district was legally considered desegregated—nearly two decades after the 1954 *Brown* decision. However, during public forums hosted by both Waco ISD and invested community members, Black Wacoans raised issues with the plan. Many felt Waco ISD was "misrepresenting its strategy for addressing" their "concerns about busing and student discipline" by unduly burdening African American and Latine students with, for example, longer bus rides.[131]

As La Vega ISD's Black students prepared to move schools yet again, Waco ISD scrambled to accommodate its 1,300 new Black students. Lacking sufficient space, the district requested funding from Model Cities, the federal urban renewal program that ran from 1966 to 1974 and aimed to ameliorate poverty as part of the Johnson administration's Great Society initiative. The request was for "26 temporary classroom [*sic*] to house the students at campuses that were over capacity for the main building," as part of "steps . . . to welcome the students from La Vega affected by the district boundary changes."[132] Waco ISD would add this support to regular state per-pupil funding.[133] Desperate to eradicate their Black students at any cost, La Vega ISD sacrificed its Model Cities funding as a result of the drastic decrease in its student population.[134] Although boundary finessing was a strategy school districts across the North and South, including those in Nashville, New Orleans, and Flint, deployed during school desegregation, this Waco-area case may be one of the only instances in which two school districts gerrymandered attendance zones with one essentially paying the other to take its Black students.[135] For its high schools, Waco ISD prepared to send "all new Negro and Mexican-American county transfers . . . to Richfield High, where most of the student body and faculty were white. All new white county transfers w[ould] attend Jefferson-Moore High," Waco ISD's high school with the largest Black population.[136]

So for the 1971–72 school year, the 1,300 Black students who had been transferred from G. W. Carver High School to La Vega High School were now headed across town to Waco ISD schools. That is, in three years, more than one thousand Black students had been forced to attend three different high schools. Many, like Willie Brown and Michael Bass, ended up at Richfield High in west Waco. Both boys attended G. W. Carver for tenth grade, La Vega for eleventh, and Richfield for their senior year, giving them a disjointed high school experience. Other students who were younger, like Connie Sadler and Willie Williams Jr., headed to Lake Air Junior High, which was half a mile from Richfield in west Waco, the white(st) part of town from which African Americans had historically been excluded.

Black Waco students' experiences in La Vega ISD immediately before and after the district carried out school desegregation in 1970 were patterned on the antiBlack nature of the wider process of school desegregation implementation. The Black students' race and low socioeconomic status converged to make them increasingly susceptible to harm, as their lack of racial, political, and financial capital impeded their efficacy and hindered their community from reopening G. W. Carver. The walkout Black students led to protest the abrupt and surreptitious closure of G. W. Carver, however, showcased their investment in repurposing their school based on their own conceptions of what the space ought to be. As districts displaced Black students time and time again, Black students strove to make their way in climates hostile to their presence.

# 3

# Made You Feel Less than Human

## MAMMIES, BUCKS, PROBLEMS, AND MASCOTS IN HOSTILE TERRITORY

*"They treat us like dogs," he said of his predominantly white high school.*

BETSY FANCHER, *VOICES FROM THE SOUTH*, 1970

Richfield High School's architecture featured two large, separate brick walls that served as the school's front-facing walls through which one passes to enter the school. Former Richfield High student Willie Brown vividly recalled that in 1971, on "the very first day [of school], in red paint somebody painted on those walls NIGGER DEPOT, NIGGER DEPOT."[1] Vandals ensured this epithet greeted Willie and hundreds of his Black peers, who, as this welcome sign broadcasted, were singly identified as NIGGERS—as trouble to be dealt with. This antiBlack slur overtly signaled to Black students that they belonged elsewhere—that they were displaced interlopers encroaching on white territory.[2] It also exposed the racial attitudes that informed Waco's white education stakeholders' commitment to stereotyping African Americans, and it amplified the crude manner in which the school district decided to dump hundreds of Black students off at the high school with the largest non-Black population in the district. Such expressions of contempt were troublingly common in previously non-Black contexts, as Mississippi's "white children . . . greeted the black children who entered their school . . . by cursing them, calling them names, and throwing rocks at them." As Willie soon discovered, Black children like himself were "constantly being called, 'nigger.' Constantly being made fun of."[3]

School districts' pointed disinterest in the well-being of Black Waco students demonstrated the popularity of controlling images that imagined African Americans as fungible, perpetually displaced, and lacking complex emotions. As one of the more than 1,300 students whose schooling trajectory was abruptly jolted by Black school closures in La Vega ISD, Willie started his senior year at Richfield after attending G. W. Carver from first to tenth grade and La Vega High School for his junior year. Black students, therefore, encountered turbulence at Richfield High in 1971 that reflected the little regard school districts or the federal government had for the continuity of Black students' schooling. Remembering the indecisive nature with which administrators handled his latter high school years, Willie observed, "They was figuring out what [they] was going to do with us the following year. . . . Of course . . . they shipped us across town to Richfield. . . . Now we [had] just left La Vega with this crap and get out here . . . and that's how they greeted us the first [day we] had there. . . . A lot of people [were] traumatized from all that moving" around to different schools.[4] According to commonly held racist beliefs, Waco's Black students were largely immune to such repeated dislocation and the emotional upset it induced.

Located in west Waco, Richfield High School was nestled in the historically white, wealthier part of the city and boasted the school district's newest high school, which opened in 1961. Willie, like other Black Waco students, understood the city's racial geography and how it implicated class; he remarked that his arrival at Richfield required he assume space next to "the rich . . . we used to call them the rich white folks out there." Racial covenants coupled with structural employment barriers, as discussed in chapter 1, historically prevented Black Wacoans from residing in west Waco; thus, the five-mile-plus distance between Richfield and La Vega ISD's Black students' homes in East Waco essentially guaranteed many would arrive to school by bus and that they would carry the stigma associated with living far from the school.[5] Many white residents in the district had fought to maintain Richfield's moniker as "Whitefield" by resisting school desegregation for decades. Five years after opening, Richfield "had an all white student body of 1530," according to a federal statistical report. When Willie and other Black Waco students arrived in the spring of 1970 en masse, "only eight minority students, one Negro, ha[d] [to that point] enrolled in the dominantly [*sic*] white student body of 1638 students."[6]

Racial tropes played incredibly powerful roles in the lives of Black Waco students during school desegregation. Regularly encountering ideas about who (all) Black people were or what (all) Black people did, Black students like Willie confronted long-standing antiBlack caricatures that robbed them of their individualism. For Willie, the NIGGER DEPOT graffito represented the ways that white stakeholders were marking their territory to ensure African Americans knew they did not belong in white Waco and never would, regardless of what the school district or federal government had decided. The racist act mapped onto a long and sordid history of white racial violence with which Waco as a city and its Black residents in particular were familiar.[7]

Although stereotypes are not inherently negative, white society has regularly employed them to hamper Black progress in the United States.[8] They were relevant to school desegregation discourses because prevailing assumptions about Black students literally met them at the schoolhouse door in their transition to new schools. White folks already had ideas about Black students' capabilities and behaviors, particularly in a Southern context that was still socially segregated in many respects. White Southern lore often characterized Black people as objects that required management and control, and Black students who had to directly confront such presumptions learned firsthand how poorly many white people felt about them.

Black students encountered new racial contexts that required them to reconfigure their extant sense of the racial world. Some Black students, however, internalized the stereotypes—or what Black feminist sociologist Patricia Hill Collins calls controlling images—of them, further texturing the mosaic of Black thought and action in desegregated Waco schools.[9] This chapter asserts that these stereotypes—specifically, the Black Buck, the Mascot, the Mammy, and the Problem—showed white supremacy's inherent depravity and how it felt for Black personhood to be systematically undermined, sometimes through paternalistic praise, with nonchalant regularity. The long history of antiBlack tropes exemplifies how white actors used them to justify, for instance, Black Codes, lynching, and de jure segregation. Rooted largely in enslavement, these misconstructions were still prominent more than a century later, reflecting the longevity of slavery's afterlife in US schools and other institutions well into the twentieth century.[10] Although Black students had every right to assume victimhood, this chapter demonstrates that many refused to do so, instead crafting analyses of whiteness and racial power based on their experiential knowledge, their agency, and their capacity to critically read their new social world.

This account is far from the first to critique these antiBlack controlling images. Scholars have written little, however, about how the time and place—the when and where—of Blackness, alongside its gendered and classed dimensions, gave new meaning to dominant tropes that shaped Black students' experiences as a result of school desegregation. Bringing Black students face-to-face with racism and heightening their vulnerability, school desegregation created an opportunity for gendered and classed Blackness to take on new meaning in places different from those it had previously occupied. Black boys and Black girls, then, withstood subjugation via stereotyping that reflected the contextual temporality of oppression; that is, they were subject to an antiBlackness that differed along gendered and at times classed lines, reflecting the importance of time and place in constructions and manifestations of Blackness in the white imagination.[11]

## THE BLACK BUCK UNRAVELED

Priding himself on his appearance and independence, high school junior Willie Brown reluctantly found himself a La Vega High School student during the 1970–71 school year. This change in schooling did little to curb Willie's dedication to maintaining a job, which gave him the means to afford a car and his stylish wardrobe. After district administrators that summer abruptly closed his segregated Black high school, G. W. Carver, Willie found himself witness to the prevalence and sturdiness of the Black Buck stereotype, which, as he experienced firsthand, presumed a Black male of any age to be a primitive subhuman with an insatiable penchant for white females, a penchant that required violent correction.[12] Willie underscored the thick racial animus that defined the single year he spent at La Vega High: "I remember at La Vega, it was still so tense that whole year." Much of this tension centered on controlling images of Black male sexuality. As Willie recalled,

> It was my junior year and I had me a little job. I was into clothes, and of course, back in school, you know, you had your best-dressed this and your best-dressed that. Well, my junior year, they voted me Best-Dressed Junior [Boy]. The Best-Dressed Girl was a white girl. So, we gone take pictures for the annual . . . [at] Cameron Park. . . . Of course . . . I remember driving my own car, and the little white kids drove they car. When we got out there, we was taking pictures [on] the

park benches. . . . They wouldn't let us sit side by side. She sat on one side of the park bench, and I was on the other side of the park bench behind her.

To preserve an image of white female purity and Black male depravity, La Vega High School relegated Willie—a barbaric savage whose brute strength required violent quelling—to the back of the yearbook photograph.[13] Widely synonymous with depictions of the Black Brute stereotype, the depictions of the Black Buck feature his awareness and willful defiance of the existing social order, highlighting his eagerness to incite violent terror in white populations, ravaging white women in particular.[14] This baseless construction implicates Black males of all ages, as scholar-activist Angela Davis clarifies, and is rooted in "the myth of the black rapist [which] has been methodically conjured up when recurrent waves of violence and terror against the black community required a convincing explanation" throughout history.[15] Journalist, educator, and activist Ida B. Wells-Barnett brought attention to this practice in the late nineteenth century to expose the lethal power of white supremacy and vindicate Black men and boys.[16]

School personnel constructed Willie as the primitive, subhuman Black savage unable to manage his yearning for what they took to be the pinnacle of femininity, so they took care not to "tempt" him or to leave photographic evidence that they had. In doing so, they adhered to Southern mores that contemptuously viewed interracial romantic relationships featuring Black partners. Years into Mississippi's implementation of school desegregation, Black boy students continued to confront manufactured attempts to remove them from mixed-race schools. In one case, "white female teachers in Jackson [were] offered $500 'to . . . [facilitate] the permanent elimination of Black males from our Public Schools' . . . [by] 'maneuver[ing] a black male into a compromising position'" and subsequently reporting it.[17] The work of racialized gender in Willie's instance demonstrates how time and place played major roles in the manifestation of oppression, for Willie's gender, in its convergence with his race, made him uniquely vulnerable to the application of this controlling image and the white violence that had long accompanied it.

In Willie's case, the literal place, a park bench, and occasion, a photography session for class superlatives, opened him up to insidious attack. Such subjugation, however, also implicated Black girls, who were physically separated from their white boy peers in some of the same superlative, full-body photographs as Willie. In lieu of the park bench in Willie's case, floor-to-ceiling partitions performed this separation, insertions that bolstered depictions of

Black girls as incompatible with and unappealing to white males. In contrast, school administrators inserted no such partitions in photographs of white boys and white girls together. Several years after the Supreme Court passed the 1967 *Loving v. Virginia* verdict, which permitted interracial marriage, the arrangement of these photographs reflects the separation that white school personnel manufactured to communicate their stance on interracial relationships between Black and white students. These portrayals and the ideologies underlying them indicated white people's selective belief that Black females possessed little virtue or femininity, a perception that in some ways contradicted another construction—that of the lascivious Black Jezebel whom white males were incapable of resisting.[18] Black girls' "dearth of femininity," therefore, worked to reinforce Black boys' "hypermasculinity."

In clarifying that he had no remote desire to know, remember, or be intimate with this white girl student, Willie inverted stereotypical assumptions about himself as a Black Buck. Almost five decades later, he underscored that "to this day, I don't even know that [La Vega's Best-Dressed Junior] girl name. I don't even know how her face looked. [I don't] remember; like, all these people had no faces to me." Part of his strategy involved maintaining distance from the white people he knew were disinterested in humanizing him. This tactic offered Willie a layer of protection. Compelled to not register white people as individuals, given the gendered antiBlack treatment to which they subjected him, Willie instead elected to view them as a group that was averse to his personhood and well-being.

The multiple shifts in school assignment that Black Waco students like Willie underwent were certainly challenging as well as eye-opening in giving Black students different racial economic contexts with which they could make comparisons. The common practice of school districts shuttering segregated Black schools to comply with federal school desegregation orders made many Black students' schooling experiences disjointed, forcing them into environments marked by gendered antiBlack racial animus.[19] Much of the tension Willie felt that shaped the treatment of him as a Black Buck was related to socioeconomic differences between white students in Waco and those in La Vega schools.[20] Astutely, he sensed that the higher-class status of white Wacoans helped provide them with an enhanced economic security that was not dependent on job competition with African Americans in the city. This dependence was a central factor because the disdain that low-income white residents in Bellmead expressed for Black pupils was rooted in the dynamics of racial capitalism.[21] These socioeconomic differences influenced Black students' impression of Waco schools as slightly more hospitable given the adverse racial climate many had just left in La Vega schools, and their perceptions aligned with research, which showed that "low-status whites may have little with which to differentiate themselves from blacks other than the rights and privileges accorded their race but denied blacks. School desegregation and other changes which undermine the myth of white superiority might leave lower-status whites on a par with blacks. Thus, lower-income whites are more likely to experience a sense of relative deprivation when blacks' conditions improve."[22]

School desegregation threw Black communities' anxieties into sharp relief given the new proximity white girls had to Black boys, which stood to enhance the latter's vulnerability to harm. For good reason, the caretakers of Black boys were especially concerned for the boys' safety in desegregated schools. This generational perspective reflected many of the lessons Black communities took from the all-too-common lynchings that were founded on unsubstantiated claims about Black boys' hypersexuality and the threat it posed to white girls. This new arrangement also exposed spurious beliefs about Black boys adamantly pursuing white girls in desegregated schools, offering evidence that the reverse was often true.

When Russell Livingston entered Waco High School in 1970 as a tenth grader, just as the Congressional Black Caucus was established, he quickly found himself favored by many of his white classmates. This favored status afforded Russell invitations to exclusive white-only outings, which he accepted despite the apprehension it provoked in his father. One winter break "while I was at an integrated . . . school," Russell reported, "I went skiing. But I was the only Black that went on the trip. I came back, and I was showing my dad some of the pictures [in which] I'm standing with the white girls, and it scared him to death. . . . He didn't want me to go back to school. He said, 'They're gonna kill you!'"[23] Although Russell dismissed his father's fear, it was well founded. Mr. Livingston knew that close contact with white girls could easily have led to unwarranted persecution of his son given the strength and ubiquity of the Black Buck trope. Fearing for Russell's life, literally, Mr. Livingston cautioned his son, who, as illustrated in the subsequent Mascot section, relished the preferential treatment he received from his white classmates. "Always leery of what could happen" because history had taught him to be "afraid of . . . mixing" and to maintain a safe distance from white people in general, especially white women, Mr. Livingston, according to his son, interacted with white people only when necessary—for instance "with some on his job, at General Tire." The fact that the concern came from Russell's father rather than his mother conveyed a specific form of trepidation unique to their shared identity as Black males reared in a Southern context where the Black Buck construction was prominent. Such unease was routinely communicated in desegregated schooling contexts, as Ernest Green of the Little Rock Nine in Arkansas was similarly reminded by his grandfather of the danger close contact with white women or girls portended.[24]

This generational anxiety crossed ethnic lines, influencing whom Black boys envisioned as viable romantic partners. Among the families of Black boys, the anxieties about white people's views on interracial dating included concerns that Black boys should date neither Latinas nor members of other white-adjacent groups. Darrick Bledsoe, part of Jefferson-Moore High's graduating class of 1986, for instance, recollected how his uncle "was dating a Hispanic female that he was obviously in love with. Well, his mother, my maternal grandmother, was not having it."[25] Darrick's grandmother was deeply "upset" by her son's dating choice, making Darrick feel strongly about "not dating outside [his] race." Motivated to be extra careful about his interactions with white and white-adjacent women, Darrick heeded his grandmother's warning, which acknowledged the legacy of racial violence against Black males who were deemed a threat to white females.

Both Russell's father and Darrick's grandmother deeply understood how white society viewed Black boys and white girls sharing educational spaces. Nine days after school segregation was ruled illegal in US schools, "the University of Texas's registrar and dean of admissions—a man named Henry Y. McCown—wrote to University of Texas President Logan Wilson with a plan to 'keep Negroes [boys] out of most classes where there are a large number of girls.'"[26] This chorus of baseless opposition reflected the attitude of fear that confronted Black boys in newly desegregated schools. In addition to this fear, African Americans had fears of their own, many that revolved around white retribution for trumped-up charges of Black male sexual impropriety.[27]

Cultural views about interracial dating between Black boys and white girls of any ethnicity were confusing even to Texans familiar with the state's ethnoracial context. Working to make sense of the issue, Darrick asked himself rhetorically, "'What's wrong with him dating a Hispanic girl? She not a white girl.' . . . At least he didn't bring a white girl home." Darrick's distinction between "Hispanic" girls and white girls (i.e., Anglo girls without "Hispanic" ethnicity) speaks to the spatial context of desegregated Waco schools, where Black, white, and Latine students closely interacted. As was the case in Texas for most of its history, particularly before widescale school desegregation, Mexican Americans were considered white, and this category informed how Black residents viewed them, given that in Waco, Mexican American students had attended non-Black schools since at least the early twentieth century.[28] Through this episode with his uncle and grandmother, Darrick learned that white girls, regardless of their ethnicity, were off-limits. He captured the way he came to understand the cultural expectation with this slogan: "If they can't use your comb, don't bring 'em home."

As one of the most ubiquitous racial constructions, the Black Buck controlling image stood at the forefront of Black Waco students' minds throughout their school desegregation experiences, something many, if not most, Black boys like Darrick and Willie came to understand.[29] Their awareness was crucial given the strong messages white society disseminated. Across various political and educational discourses at the national level, for instance, leaders echoed this oppressive mythology. Dwight Eisenhower, "the Commander in Chief refer[red] to Black boys as [either] overgrown Negroes . . . or big Black bucks," indicating that his "sympathy for and identification with white southern segregationists tended to be more the rule than the exception. The implications of either description speak to incredibly durable ideas about Black bodies as subhuman."[30]

White girls' palpable interest in Black boys—to which they had more direct access in desegregated schools than in segregated ones—represents one of the most underappreciated contradictions of the Black Buck controlling image, and contrary to popular belief it placed Black boys in precarious circumstances. White girls' overt pursuit of Black boys challenged multiple myths about Black male and white female sexuality. First, it challenged the presumption that Black males lusted unidirectionally after white females. Second, it destabilized constructions that depict white female sexuality and desire as compatible exclusively with white males. Third, it cast white female sexuality as assertive—if not aggressive—in much the same way that the Black Buck was characterized. Last, it exposed the erroneous claim that white girls needed to be protected from Black boys who were unable to control their sexual appetite for white females. That said, Black boys in Waco schools reported consistently that white girls vocalized and acted on their interest in them through active pursuit, seeking sexual experiences. As Calvin Jones, a University High School student in the class of 1976, recalled, "White girls were crazy about those Black guys." White girls were responding to prevailing stereotypes about Black males and their heightened sexual prowess. Athletes, according both to Calvin and to Connie Oliver, a Waco High School student from the class of 1971, were especially enticing, as both Black boys reported being highly sought after as high school jocks.[31] This trend was evident across the South decades earlier. According to an observing teacher, a white girl student in the desegregated Little Rock Central High School, for instance, "paraded to and fro past Ernest Green [her Black boy classmate] four times, staring hard at him each of the eight times she passed his table. Ernest never raised his eyes." That same white girl also sat in Ernest's lap.[32] Neither the passage of time nor the change in location did much to alter white girls' lust for Black boys in either 1950s Arkansas or 1970s Texas. Black boys, therefore, represented uncharted territory for many white girls, who were enthusiastic about conquering this new and forbidden challenge.[33]

In such a context, not only were consensual interracial relationships perceived as improper; they were considered immoral and sacrilegious. Although these ideas were certainly not limited to Texas or Waco, they clarify the ahistorical beliefs of many white Wacoans who conveniently forgot that white actors, both male and female, had historically initiated many interracial pairings.[34] As school desegregation scholarship has shown, "prevailing white norms regarding beauty and culture drove the dating dynamic in favor of white girls," leaving Black girls insulted and Black boys with more, albeit perilous, dating options.[35] Developed in the minstrel-show era and portrayed in white supremacist propaganda films such as *The Birth of a Nation*, the Black Buck was called on as one of the most pressing reasons why schools should stay segregated, lest innocent white girls risk their purity and safety.[36] What white girls' adamant pursuit of Black boys in desegregated schools showed was the grave fallaciousness of this construction.

## UNPACKING THE MASCOT

Richard Jenkins entered Waco High School "expecting to have [it] happen," to be one of the school's first successful Black athletes and, relatedly, for the racism other Black students endured to elude him.[37] The white coaches who successfully recruited Richard fed his already pronounced ego, encouraging him with statements like "I want you to be my [star athlete]." Richard's healthy sense of self-worth was typical for boys generally and Black boys in particular.[38] This invitation fed Richard's high self-confidence, which reached beyond the playing field, for Richard above all viewed himself as "a leader" and "an exceptional student." Initially optimistic about beginning high school, despite warnings from older Black students he knew who were the first African Americans to desegregate Waco High, Richard stated that he "tr[ied] to brush those [warnings] off because they were getting in the way of the hope that you had that was ahead of you." His father's decades-long military career had given him regular "racial contact with other white kids on base," an experience he felt made him widely impervious to white supremacy and gave him an advantage over his older Black peers, who tried to caution him about antiBlackness at Waco High. Like Malcolm Little (later known as Malcolm X and then as El-Hajj Malik El-Shabazz), Richard exceeded the expectations for both white and Black boys, only to be relegated to the Mascot role. "Malcolm Little believed his mimicry of the successful white man had lifted him out of the category of 'nigger' and enfranchised him in an American meritocracy," only to be shown that it, in fact, had not.[39]

Richard's actual experience did not meet his expectations, as his first year of high school, which was his tenth-grade year, was, as he explained, "the year that I was just in a daze"; that is, he was in denial about antiBlackness's unforgiving ubiquity, which would not spare him. Having been "so caught up into high school, I thought I was on an accelerated course" that might permit racism to bypass him, Richard explained. "I didn't really start to feel discriminated against until . . . about my junior year." Despite his hopeful outlook, Richard confronted "a whole lot of emotions" and ultimately resolved that his older peers were right, as "some of the things that were undeniable by the third year were things that you heard about the first year." As Richard progressed in school and experienced racism firsthand, he was pushed to refuse to serve as the exceptional Black student in his majority-white high school. Getting "in touch with other people," his Black classmates in particular, made "some things . . . clear to us all," things that pivoted on the racism his self-importance had previously obscured. Later, when he left Waco "to pursue my future," Richard described himself as "bitter" as a result of the antiBlack experiences that plagued his high school years. Navigating a desegregated high school had taught him that none of the attributes that made him special could safeguard him from racism—not his middle-class status, not his intelligence, not his athleticism, and not his familiarity with white peers. Excelling academically was common for Mascots like Richard; in many cases, exceeding expectations helped solidify their place in the social order of desegregated schools. High school taught Richard a sobering truth that lies at the heart of racial realism. "I had already determined," Richard said, "that not only was I as capable . . . I was more capable than a lot of my so-called white counterparts, but that it didn't matter. No matter what, somehow, they were going to always slight my efforts."[40]

Not all Black boys labeled as exceptional in Waco schools came to such conclusions, however. Learning early on that he thrived on popular acclaim and a full schedule, Russell Livingston, who graduated from Waco High in 1973, grew so invested in his majority-white, desegregated high school that he prioritized extracurricular activities over his academics. The school initially placed him in advanced classes, Russell recalled, and, somewhat regrettably and unbeknownst to his parents, "I took myself out because . . . those classes were taking up too much of my extra time." He also shared, akin to Willie Brown at La Vega High, that "the very first year I was there [at Waco High], I was voted by the student body as the best dressed of the students, so that . . . [signaled] they know me, they respected me." As the white majority's symbol of racial acceptance, Russell prided himself on "wear[ing] a suit at least once a week."[41] Paramount to looking the part were his friendships with his white classmates, which he perceived as being largely responsible for his ability to deftly navigate a new social milieu as an outgoing, agreeable Black student.

Russell's niceness, as he explained, enabled him to build friendships that permitted him entry into social spaces previously exclusive to white people—namely Young Life, a white Christian organization geared toward ministering to youth in school. Texas's firm place in the Bible Belt, a "part of the nation in which theologically conservative Protestant churchgoing thrives," made Young Life a popular evangelical pastime.[42] "I would say at any of the Young Life meetings, there'll be maybe twenty, twenty-five whites and maybe three Blacks," Russell said, "and the meeting was always after school. It'd be at night at someone's house. So, I remember going to these real nice homes I ain't even know existed, and forage my way home from where we lived, and . . . everyone [loved me,] I guess because [of] my personality." Traveling across the city to affluent, white west Waco for these meetings, Russell found himself surrounded by markers of wealth and privilege nonexistent in his Black East Waco neighborhood. Despite being a lifelong Waco resident, Russell was surprised to learn firsthand of the grave class disparities in Waco's racial geography. The housing discrimination coupled with the economic subjugation that precluded Black middle-class families like Russell's from residing in west Waco, however, was apparently not a conversation topic.[43] Grateful for the opportunity to be included, Russell attributed his good fortune to his affable demeanor and interest in blending in with wealthy white Wacoans to whatever extent possible.

After one of Russell's Young Life visits to a white classmate's house in wealthy west Waco, the parents of this white peer contacted Russell's parents to express how much his behavior impressed them and to extend a standing invitation to visit.[44] "Those parents loved me," he recalled, "and matter of fact, some of the parents ended up calling my mother [and father], telling them, 'Hey, we really enjoyed Russell coming over . . . and you're welcome to come over anytime.'" The exceptional nature of such comments illustrated how white figures avoided race by focusing on how "normal" they considered Russell. These remarks suggest these wealthy white parents wanted Black people to know they positively perceived of Russell, in a way that exposed their nonracism. That is, Russell served as their Mascot.

Russell's experiences largely parallel those of Malcolm X, whose childhood had showed him firsthand what it meant to endure extensive white patronization. The Mascot, as Malcolm X viewed it, closely aligned with the notion of a token individual, often an "exceptional" one, chosen by white actors to serve as automatic defense against any accusations of racism against those white actors.[45] As a Black male in majority-white educational spaces, Malcolm X eventually came to realize how white actors in his life used him as an instrument of white supremacy. A notable phenomenon in the treatment of Mascots is that, as Malcolm X observed, white actors will often retract their support once these stereotypical Black figures develop "the sense of being a real part of a mass of [their] own kind," meaning they exhibit autonomy and self-determination that undercuts white supremacy.[46] In a condescending and paternalistic manner, white people positioned certain African Americans, often males, as Mascots, holding them at a distance that othered them while affording them superficial advancement opportunities.

Frequenting not only white religious meetings but also exclusive weekend parties at Lake Waco, Russell declined few invitations to see whiteness up close.

> The whites would have a party out at the lake at night. There was some of the Blacks, which I was one of them, that they would invite to their parties. . . . They were out there drinking and smoking, which I didn't do either one of them; they just liked to have . . . some fun. . . . It was a real secluded place out by the lake. We'd go out there . . . we'd do that like maybe twice a month or so. . . . I can only remember one Hispanic that . . . would be there.

Russell relished the opportunity to navigate these prohibitive spaces, where he could be among the white group but not of it. A component of this approach meant abstaining from illicit substance use, which suggests Russell's awareness of the harsher penalties for African Americans who did engage in illegal substances.[47] Russell's loyalty to whiteness bolstered his ascent up the social ladder at Waco High.

Unlike Malcolm X, who upon reflection realized that he had served as a Mascot for the white individuals in his life, Russell proved unable to see how white supremacy shaped his perception of his high school experiences as overly and uncharacteristically positive. Stated differently, he enabled white Wacoans "to produce just one [token Black student]: enough to gratify those concerned with black achievement that these students were being treated equitably, but not so many that white community residents and school administrators felt threatened by a radical reorganization of status arrangements," a trend sociologists have observed in other school desegregation contexts.[48] Eventually coming to terms with the way he had been used by white supremacy, Malcolm X described the Mascot role in terms of white people being incapable of, as he explained, "understand[ing] . . . that I wasn't a pet, but a human being. They couldn't give me credit for having the same sensitivity, intellect, and understanding that they would have been ready and willing to recognize in a white boy in my position. But it has historically been the case with white people, in their regard for black people, that even though we might be with them, we weren't considered of them. Even though they appeared to have opened the door, it was still closed. Thus they never really did see me."[49]

Coming to a different conclusion, Russell credited his upbringing with providing him a tool—race-evasive niceness—that facilitated his success in breaking racial barriers in high school. He stated:

> I think a lot of it was my upbringing. . . . I was just being myself. I was always taught to treat people nice. . . . I continued to do that. . . . I just treated people . . . the way they should be treated. . . . I wasn't mean to anyone, and I guess one of the things that they [whites] admired about me [was that] I treat[ed] them like they were just friends, all of them, Black or white, Hispanic, all, and I was nice to all of them. I think what happened was that since my parents did not teach color [i.e., race] to me, I didn't go in [to the desegregated school] with any preconceived notions. So, I just treated everyone, you know, the same.

This view contended that because of the good nature his upbringing gave him, white actors could look past Russell's race to see him as a full person. In other words, Russell was socially successful in a desegregated school because his white peers and their parents accepted him. The foil to the Black Buck, Mascots assuaged white fears about dangerous, menacing figures eager to destroy their quaint white school community. "The mascot," however, "wasn't supposed to dance with any of the white girls."[50] Contrasting the Black Buck trope La Vega ISD administrators imposed on Willie, Waco ISD school officials permitted Russell to pose often and comfortably next to his white girl classmates.[51] The Mascot construction undoubtedly aided in this allowance because white power holders assumed Russell knew and accepted his inferior place in the social hierarchy.

As a reward for the Mascot staying in his place, white figures often selected him for leadership positions in school government. Russell explained, "I was the first Black mayor of the student government at Waco High, and I was the first Black senior class president. So quite naturally, a lot of them [whites] knew me and were very accepting of me."[52] Explaining that in high school and adulthood the majority of his friends were white, Russell reiterated that it was his personality—not his race—that suited him to these roles. Feeling like the equal of his white peers, Russell explained this acceptance as mutual: "They [whites] were very accepting of me, and I was accepting of them, and we all got along. . . . I have more white friends from high school than I do African American friends from high school." In part because of the untimely deaths of many of his Black friends, his "long-lasting relationships [were] more [with] the whites than the African Americans." Feeling fully seen by white Wacoans as their equal, Russell embodied the Mascot stereotype and assumed a race-evasive stance that bolstered the argument that inequity existed as a result of individual failing and not structural flaws in society as a whole. However, Black girls in desegregated Waco schools who enjoyed a comparable level of popularity, such as Pamela James, Katherine Sanford, and Connie Sadler—some of the school districts' first Black cheerleaders and homecoming queens, elected by student vote—never mistook their ability to garner white votes as a sign of their full acceptance into white society or of racism's irrelevance in their lives.[53]

Russell's Mascot role rendered his racial consciousness subdued but not totally absent. Despite his flourishing social life in school, he realized upon reflection that his high school counselor had not once discussed with him the possibility of college, which he would go on to attend. His experiences track with other Black students navigating newly desegregated schools. Louis Mudd, a Black Kentucky student, recalled his desegregated high school having "an office staff with a female counselor and a male counselor that were totally insensitive to black kids."[54] Tellingly, like Michael Bass at La Vega High, Russell could remember only the names of the personnel from his segregated Black schools; nevertheless, he went to great lengths to build excellent rapport with his peers of all races in high school.

In the school community, white people's normal gendered antiBlack acts toward a Black boy like Russell were slightly alleviated by his middle-class status. He was an only child who came from a dual-parent home where both parents worked full-time jobs—one of which required higher education and was salaried—and was raised as a morally upstanding churchgoer. Economically more secure than many of his Black counterparts, Russell was familiar with middle-class sensibilities and Protestantism, two factors that made him even more suitable for the Mascot role, particularly in the South. His male privilege may have given him some confidence to assert himself and to believe he could assume leadership positions, and he also benefited from the fact that white peers were in search of a Black individual who could attest to their nonracism. His father's concerns regarding his close interactions with white girls failed to dissuade Russell from embarking on platonic interactions with white females, and his parents' general skepticism of whiteness largely eluded him because white folks made him feel special as their Mascot.

Mascots walked the halls of other high schools in Waco. Calvin Jones, who thoroughly enjoyed his experiences in majority-white schools, attended University High School from 1973 to 1976. Although Calvin's working-class Black boyhood could have made him more susceptible to harm, his outgoing and optimistic perspective likely helped him look past daily instances of racism. Calvin reported that his white teachers in particular were excellent and treated all students equally. "We had two English teachers," he explained, "that were real good, both of them white. . . . They treated us all the same."[55] Calvin also credited what he considered fair treatment in the high school's course placement practices, as he recalled several names of Black students, excluding himself, who were enrolled in advanced classes. Treating all students the same, however, could often lead to the perpetuation of racism in the classroom, critical race theorists argue, because it was shown to "prevent the teachers from reflecting on their own practices and their role in the production of the underachievement of their students of colour."[56]

In desegregated Waco schools, Mascots, who in this context were exclusively Black males, enjoyed marked popularity, which was linked to and facilitated by their pronounced self-esteem.[57] Because student voting was a key metric that signified one's popularity among the student body—a student body that in Calvin's case was majority white—the distinctions he won by popular vote meant that, in his view, racism was largely a nonissue. Louisville's Black desegregating students endured white sabotage in the early 1960s when trying to assume such leadership positions for the first time, as school administrators "took names from my [a Black boy's] petition to put on a white kid's petition . . . to make sure that it [senior class office] was lily white."[58] Voted Citizen of the Year and Best-All-Around in his senior year, Calvin felt he had no reason to question or look unfavorably on his desegregated schooling experience.[59] Compelled to take on a leadership role, Calvin recalled, "I ran for . . . president [of] the Student Union. I didn't win it. I won vice president" instead. Although the yearbook lists Calvin as a part of the student council's executive board, a leadership position falling just below the named officers but above the rank-and-file members, votes were required for him to occupy this post.[60] Not all Black University High School students could say the same, however, as Calvin's classmate Carol Haliburton remembered a host of negative racist experiences in the same school and at the same time.[61]

Elected to leadership roles such as class president and offered jobs as a young teenager, Malcolm X, much like Calvin, Russell, and Richard, had initially relished these experiences in his school and home, until he considered the underlying logic that white people employed in their treatment of him. Any time African Americans attempted to move outside the prescribed boundaries associated with their Mascot role, as Malcolm X did when he told his teacher he wanted to be a lawyer, white people reminded them of their constrained life options. Such reminders obligated Black folks to adjust their aspirations according to what white people decided they were best suited for; Malcolm X's teacher, for example, reminded him of his lowly "nigger" status and redirected him to carpentry as a more realistic career goal.[62] To not make such an adjustment placed African Americans in a precarious position.

As a Black working-class boy that whites had positioned as a Mascot, Calvin seemed aware of white supremacy but to a lesser extent than most of his Black peers. Nonetheless, his sustained interest in politics throughout his life raises questions about how his high school experiences affected him in the long term. His motivation for joining the student council was deeply racialized: "I wanted to try to be a part of student council . . . [to] make sure things were done right, [so] no one was left out. . . . I just didn't want all the white kids making all the decisions." This perspective illustrates the agency even selectively race-conscious Black boys displayed to produce spaces that could foster racial justice.[63] It is unclear, however, the extent to which Calvin, in his capacity as a student council executive member, advocated for Black students or their success, given that, as he reflected, "we didn't have no problems" related to race in high school.

It is difficult to divorce Calvin's contemporary political views from his role as a Mascot in desegregated Waco schools; his example illustrates Black people's heterogeneity, making the case that no one has to have any particular view or set of experiences. Pointing to the fallacies he believed pervade the contemporary Black Lives Matter movement, Calvin explained, "I always hear people talk about Black Lives Matter. Okay. I say, 'All Life Matters, Black, white, or whatever, all of them.' Not just Black; we killing each other. . . . All

Lives Matter."[64] Further conveying his racial perspective, Calvin added that he continues to take an unconventional approach to political issues: "A lot of people [get] down on me because I don't just vote Democrat or Republican. I vote both. Well, I vote for the person." Decades before, in his desegregated high school, Calvin applied similar logic to insist that Black students were treated fairly and there were no racial problems, essentially dismissing the racism other Black students suffered. His peer Elaine Mosley, a classmate of Russell's who graduated in 1973 from Waco High, also recounted her high school years as largely uneventful in terms of race and racism.[65]

Calvin, Russell, and Richard, all Black boys, embodied the Mascot controlling image in that all received high praise, advancement, and, as they perceived it, positive treatment from their schools' white stakeholders. Mascots were distinct from the other stereotypes to which white gendered supremacy subjected Black students in majority-white desegregated schools, because Mascots tended to embrace their role—sometimes temporarily—if not by name, then certainly in form. White people's favorable treatment of them resulted in each assuming leadership positions within their respective high schools. As some of the few Black students in such roles, Calvin, Russell, and Richard understood their positions as reflective of their ability to get along well with their white classmates and effectively garner a positive image despite, not because of, their race. As in other desegregated school contexts, these three Black boys represented "superstars [or] . . . tokens . . . [who] provid[ed] protection for teachers and administrators against charges of racism or ineffectiveness in educating blacks, but also deflect[ed] attention away from the school's poorer record with most black males."[66]

It is not a coincidence that the students most suited to the Mascot role were male. As has been the case historically, the overlap of racism and misogyny created avenues for Black boys to leverage their gender privilege.[67] Although racism was alive and well in these spaces, some Black boy students operated in social spheres that made it appealing to be whites' "chosen" one for a range of reasons that coalesced around propping up white supremacy.[68] Wrestling with W. E. B. Du Bois's notion of double consciousness, viewing one's self as situated within an uneasy dualism of Black and American, exposed how psychologically treacherous such close contact with white society could be for vulnerable Black adolescents developing their self-perception.[69] Outside Waco, Black desegregating students wrestled with a similar sentiment. In South Carolina, one student reported being scared by the taunts white students hurled at her because they made her feel "caught between white and black worlds."[70] This sense of "living in two worlds," as one Black youth in

Atlanta described, was representative of a reoccurring process that rendered them largely unable to reconcile their Blackness with their Americanness.[71] Overwhelmingly, Calvin, Russell, and Richard understood—when operating in their Mascot frame of mind—school desegregation to be an advantageous affair that benefited them and left few negative aftereffects. For Calvin and Russell, their engagement with white persons left them after their high school years with little to no skepticism regarding race relations in the United States. For Richard, however, this contentment quickly turned to bitterness. Treating certain, seemingly exceptional Black students in favorable ways often helped white people feel better about themselves and deny their own racist views and actions. It also enabled them to reject ideas that such students were part of a larger mass of African Americans whose interests in racial equality conflicted with white people's.

## THE MAMMY DETANGLED

Charlotte Adams and her classmates desegregated Waco High School in 1969, a year before the district more fully implemented the mandate, and the relationship she cultivated with one of her white teachers exposed the prevalence of the Mammy controlling image. In part, this trope suggested that any interaction involving Black females in whites' homes was strictly for labor purposes. Broadly speaking, the Mammy construction portrayed the Black woman as an asexual, dark-skinned, overweight enslaved house laborer, though it implicated Black females of virtually any age. The trope grew out of enslavement, as the Mammy was often portrayed and perceived in white lore as a loyal, reliable, exceptional enslaved woman.[72]

Arriving a year early afforded Charlotte the opportunity to have the school pair her with a faculty mentor, white home economics teacher Ruth Nolte, who was tasked with helping ease Charlotte's transition into a formerly non-Black high school.[73] Although this practice was defunct by the start of the next school year when greater numbers of Black students started attending, Charlotte was thankful for and spoke fondly of the arrangement and of Nolte, recalling how the teacher took her on outings around the city, gave her (unsolicited) etiquette lessons, and even invited her to her home in west Waco to socialize with her children, who were around Charlotte's age. These journeys to white west Waco were a type of geographic exercise for the Black students who made them, nuancing their racialized conceptions of place. Coming from an East Waco middle-class home, Charlotte, like Russell Livingston, observed up close the significant differences between Black middle-class life and white middle-class life.[74] Importantly, Charlotte's relationship with Nolte had no parallel to those she had with her other high school teachers, which she described as transactional and existing on a surface level. Charlotte viewed her connection with Nolte as more meaningful and humanizing, indicating it was an exception, not the rule.

As history attested, it was quite difficult for white educational stakeholders to see Black females of all ages in complex ways that exceeded or invalidated trite controlling images such as the Mammy. Mrs. Minnie Washington, the first Black (and Black woman) teacher at Viking Hills Elementary School in white west Waco, for example, encountered white parents who openly challenged her authority by assuming she was part of the custodial staff, not their child's teacher.[75] In high school, Charlotte faced much of the same, as she recalled, "She [Nolte] would take me to her neighborhood and people will look at us like, 'Oh, that little girl is cleaning up for her.' And they might would say that [to us,] and she [Nolte] said, 'No, she's not cleaning up for me; I am bringing her home for the weekend to be with my girls.' So, her neighbors were kind of like, 'Oh, so is she your maid? Does she clean or does she iron clothes?' And she was like, 'No! She don't iron clothes!'"[76]

Without naming race specifically, Charlotte, Nolte, and Nolte's white neighbors referred to it by engaging a racial signifier—the Mammy—namely in the questions neighbors asked. These questions asserted white superiority and Black inferiority, as they casually applied a hierarchical understanding of society to register a seemingly familiar relationship between a white woman and a Black girl. On closer examination, however, this relationship diverged starkly from their expectations. School desegregation prompted this instance of cognitive dissonance, putting in close contact Black girl students and white women teachers who could try to rewrite social narratives about the terms of their engagement. First, however, they had to be filtered through a white racial frame.[77] Nolte's fondness for Charlotte contrasted with accounts from other Black girl students from working-class families, such as Waco High student Pamela James, who recounted an incident involving a group project in which Nolte, Pamela's home economics teacher, lowered the grades of a group of Black students that included Pamela and raised the grades of a group of white students.[78] This inconsistency between Pamela's experience and Charlotte's suggests that Charlotte's middle-class standing may have influenced Nolte's inclination toward her, and it also sheds light on a particular form of social education Nolte tried to impart on Charlotte—specifically uninvited lessons in "proper" decorum. Seen through this lens, Nolte's efforts appear not only patronizing but also contrived in the sense that she was presumably striving to give Charlotte social knowledge about white decorum norms that might help Charlotte capitalize on her middle-class status. This white social knowledge could help Charlotte disassociate herself from negative stereotypes like Mammy. Nolte's neighbors' repeated remarks appear even more insulting, then, given Nolte's pointed investment in altering Charlotte's comportment.

That so many neighbors mistook the purpose of Charlotte's visits to Nolte's home suggests that white Wacoans were nearly incapable of understanding that Black girls could serve in any capacity other than that of a maid and that African Americans and white people were hard pressed to interact on equal social terms. Mainstream white society did not expect Black girls to socialize with other children—either those of their race or another race—because white folks were less inclined to extend girlhood privileges to them. This disassociation between Blackness and girlhood assumed Black girls existed solely to labor (for white households) and thus discounted Black girls' ability to enjoy typical adolescent pleasantries such as visiting a friend's home. Charlotte, rightfully, expressed annoyance about these careless insults. This account and the numerous others that echo it suggest that in Black students' day-to-day lives, they confronted white figures who held disparaging ideas about them. No matter which school Black girls like Charlotte attended, in the view of many white Wacoans, they would always be "the help." Charlotte was, as a result, tasked with overriding these white-dominant beliefs about who she was and what she was capable of—something she seemed to have managed quite well into adulthood.[79] Pigeonholing a Black girl in this way speaks to the broader notions white folks held for them in terms of their place in society that were at odds with Black females' social, economic, and political advancement.

The social status of Black women in the South in part explained why Nolte's neighbors did not entertain the idea that Charlotte could be visiting her home for reasons unrelated to paid labor. In the 1970s, there were far fewer employment opportunities for African Americans across the country, particularly in the South, than those available to white people.[80] One of the jobs most commonly available to Black women was as a domestic laborer working for affluent white people in their homes. Connected to vestiges of enslavement, this position was held by several students' caretakers, including the caretakers of Debora Wilkerson, Willie Brown, Connie Sadler, Anslum Hudlin, and Katherine Sanford.

When a white family living in west Waco asked Katherine Sanford, a Waco High student, to babysit for them, she expected just that—to provide childcare and interact professionally as needed with the child's parents. Coming from a middle-class family where her father served in the military and her mother worked intermittently as a domestic laborer, she had some familiarity with what such work entailed. Shortly after starting the job, however, Katherine sensed that "something wasn't right. And I kept telling my mom—I haven't quite figured out why he [the father] talks to me just any kind of way, but I was young, so I had to respect what he was saying."[81] Katherine explained how she "and his little girl got along fine. It was him that seemed to have had a problem." Although the Mammy caricature was manufactured, Black girls in desegregated schools regularly confronted idealized expectations associated with it. Mammy was believed to diligently care not only for the "big house" and her owners but also for her enslavers' children to the detriment of her own family.[82] Her faithful devotion to the plantation household, especially to the rearing of its white children, made her dependable and revealed her strong maternal instincts. This construction stressed her contentedness, compliance, and model behavior because her enslavers did not have to question her loyalty.

The white patriarch who employed Katherine meted out his demanding and rather arbitrary orders in a deeply subhumanizing way. Describing how he routinely spoke to her, Katherine noted, "Before he went to work, he would eat his breakfast. He would fix it up like . . . I can just see eggs and ketchup and something else. And that would look so bad [unappetizing] to me. I would just walk out of the room, [and he would say,] 'What's the matter? You too good to sit here and watch me eat?' [Katherine rhetorically responded,] 'Why do I want to watch you eat? I'm not hungry.'"

It seems the social or domestic arrangements this white male patriarch was used to involved Black females' total capitulation to white people's commands and their adherence to the racial hierarchy that demanded such capitulation. Katherine's assertion of her personhood thus violated multiple aspects of the father's world view. To his chagrin, times were indeed changing.

The white male patriarch's expectation for Katherine's submission went unmet. Eating in the dining room, he was careful not to defy the Southern custom that required "Black Southerners . . . to dine inside the kitchens where they labored" rather than in the dining room where white Southerners often ate, demanding Katherine comply with his order that she remain in his physical presence.[83] The sexual undertones in this interaction are difficult to overlook. Refusing to grant him better access to her body, Katherine subverted not only the Mammy role she was supposed to play but also expectations associated with the Jezebel controlling image, the promiscuous Black female who incessantly tempts (white) men; Jezebel, as popular lore imagined, was undeniable and unrapeable.[84] Black Mississippi girls encountered similar circumstances. In 1965 with spitballs being hurled at them, they were "constantly [made to] walk . . . through [the] hall surrounded by white men" who threatened Black girls' sense of safety. One Black girl student "remember[ed] going up a flight of . . . stairs [that] were crowded . . . and somebody coming up behind me grabbing my hips, and I really felt violated."[85] Because the Mammy construction was largely fabricated to assuage white Southern disappointment about losing the Civil War, assumptions about her and her role at times drew on ideologies related to Black female sexuality. White Southerners erected the Mammy trope in an effort to romanticize and reestablish the power relations that structured Southern forced labor camps (i.e., plantations), arrangements upended by the Civil War. Although, as noted, the Mammy figure was typically imagined as unattractive (i.e., defying white feminine beauty standards) and thus asexual, the expectation that she satisfy her domestic and maternal duties sometimes veered toward expectations of satisfying white male's carnal desires. Additionally, it was widely understood in Black communities that "private white homes were often sites of physical violence, psychological terrorism, and sexual predation against black female workers," making Katherine's refusal even more important.[86]

As the harassment intensified, Katherine's mother supported her in crafting an exit plan on her own terms, demonstrating the crucial role Black mothers played in helping their daughters navigate difficult gendered-racist issues. This man would remind Katherine that she "need[ed] to keep on being on time because if [she did] not, [the white family would] need to get somebody else." By threatening to terminate her if she arrived late, he prompted Katherine to recognize and cower to the control he sought to exert over her economic well-being, a show of power that revealed his white toxic masculinity. "Every time he would say some stuff like that," Katherine explained, "I'd go home and tell my mom and she'd say, at one point, it was time for me to go," that "if it [got] bad, just go ahead and tell them you leaving, and they can find somebody else to do the job." Black Kentucky student Deanna Tinsley was similarly guided by her mother after her white teacher at her desegregated school invited her to her home; Deanna quickly learned, however, that this teacher hoped to employ her to do "housekeeping work," something Deanna's mother predicted but let play out so that her daughter could see for herself.[87] Ultimately, Katherine heeded her mother's advice to "be nice [but] don't try to change who you are." After the white man verbally harassed Katherine again, Katherine's mother advocated for her child by telling his wife, the wife and mother of the household, that he was harassing her child. A few days later, the wife said to Katherine while she was babysitting at their house, "You don't have to stay here. I understand what's happening." Despite the duress the wife could have been under in her own home with such a man, the wife's complicity is worth consideration. Admitting to Katherine and her mother that she knew her husband was mistreating their babysitter, the white woman gave Katherine permission to leave. These attempts may indicate her understanding and compassion, but she had permitted his verbal abuse before that conversation.[88] Only after Katherine's mother raised the issue did the white woman speak with Katherine about leaving. With this blessing, as Katherine explained, "I just left. I had to go and catch a bus to get home. . . . I had to walk so far, but I didn't care about it. I just left." Emboldened to modify her situation rather than subjecting herself to something she did not deserve, Katherine departed with her dignity intact.

Katherine left on her own terms. The great distance she had to travel to get home is indicative of Waco's racial geography, which even in the era of desegregation continued to maintain vast distances between middle-class Black families like hers who owned their homes and wealthier white Wacoans like the ones for whom she worked. This illustration of Black spatial agency is complicated because Katherine had to endure harassment for it to reveal itself, yet it is empowering because she was able to leave when she felt she needed to. Nevertheless, as she explained years later, "my feelings were really hurt," largely because she knew what it was to be humanized and had learned firsthand how it felt for one's humanity to be denied.

## DECODING THE PROBLEM

Problems warrant solutions, and being labeled and treated as problems by virtue of their Blackness was one of the most ubiquitous issues Black Waco students confronted in their newly desegregated schools. In this respect, white educational stakeholders viewed Black students as entities that needed to be handled or managed rather than humanized. Although this misconstruction was indiscriminate in terms of gender or class status, casting Blackness as synonymous with trouble in ways that proved largely inescapable for Black students in majority-non-Black school contexts, some of the most illustrative examples involved working-class Black pupils. Given the prevalence of this mischaracterization, examples abounded. Most Black students were cognizant and critical of their "innate" problem status, which, in terms of how such "problems" were handled, manifested as physical, verbal, and structural abuses across Waco schools.

West Junior High School saw its first Black students in 1966, and the previously non-Black school made sure Black students knew just how unwanted they were.[89] Anslum Hudlin and Connie Oliver were two of the school's seven total Black students, all of whom were boys entering the eighth grade. Their gender is striking because, in many cases, the first students selected to desegregate in communities across the South were girls.[90] It was immediately apparent to Anslum that the district imposed the Black students' arrival onto the school, seeking to comply with federal mandates to desegregate. The intolerance was incessant and violent. Both on their walk to school and during the school day, these boys routinely faced verbal and physical attacks. Within days of the school year starting, Anslum knew "there was going to be a fight. One of us was going to have to present ourselves as a token of being able to fight. Every day. It was an everyday thing. One of us" would be selected for battle.[91] This looming assurance of violence damaged his psyche and presented itself as "a constant taunt," according to Anslum, who explained, "You could be in school, and something hit you in the back of the head. BAM! A pencil, a hand," any number of objects could strike one of these Black boys, forewarning them of the physical violence they would soon face later on their journey home from school.

The school's and district's negligence, which facilitated this abuse, was overt and rested squarely on a disregard for Blackness. Anslum learned quickly that protection was not something his new school was willing to provide its Black students. The daily fights happened, as he recalled, "maybe a block away from school. It wasn't like it was way down the road. It was a couple of steps across the street." Within sight of West Junior High, Anslum and his Black boy peers fought for their lives each day while traveling to and from school. It was something he could not "see them [school leadership] not knowing." Much the same occurred up north; in Detroit, Black students traveling to desegregated schools "oftentimes had to run home to escape being attacked," unable to rely on their school for protection. After school, Black students "had to run to catch the bus because" whites were known to "grab the kids and beat them up. They'd get out . . . with slings and belts and things scaring you half to death," reported one Black student. Like Anslum and his Black peers, Black Detroit youth "had to walk through a hostile white neighborhood before they reached safety."[92] Raised by his grandmother, Anslum was shown that white Waco held little respect for Black perspectives in part because Waco ISD, as he remembered, had declined to solicit his grandmother's permission for Anslum to attend West Junior at all. This oversight taught Anslum that Black consent meant little to school administrators or the broader white power structure that ordered their lives, a view consistent with G. W. Carver High's closure covered in this chapter. Despite visible physical evidence of his daily battles, Anslum "never complained . . . the whole time about it" to his grandmother. As he came to view it, the abuse "just became a way of our life" that did not merit discussion.

Anslum and the other Black boys risked their safety each day to travel to school. Seeking to protect their Black children's lives to whatever extent possible, the boys' caretakers instructed them to spend as little time as possible in the areas where any group of Black pedestrians invited violent correction. This well-warranted concern stemmed from the numerous occasions in which Black people walking in areas white people claimed as their property saw their lives end because, as human geography scholar Mona Domosh explains, "a black body out of place was assumed a criminal, a runaway, subject to immediate arrest or, worse, torture and death."[93] It rarely occurred to white Wacoans that they themselves might be more representative of the trouble they so often assumed Black people to be.

Alongside the mere presence of Black bodies in previously non-Black school spaces, specific features of Blackness sparked widespread controversy, and few examples show this more clearly than Black hair.[94] In Edwin James's case, his tenure at Waco High from 1967 to 1969 was truncated because he grew his hair out into an Afro, after which the school administration, as he recollected, "told me I couldn't come back unless my hair was cut."[95] Messages exposing the haphazard, unfounded association of Blackness with problems were common. Anslum received the same message from his Waco High basketball coach, and Black students at La Vega High challenged this issue the next year.[96] Adamant that "I'm not hurting nobody. I'm not creating no problem," Edwin resolved, "I'm not cutting my hair." And he didn't. He knew he was being arbitrarily villainized for embracing his Blackness in such a visually striking way, and he followed through in his resistance by transferring to a different high school.[97] As he stated, "I love the Afro, and I like my hair to be long. . . . I didn't want [to] have my heritage dimmed or lost." Connecting his hair to his African ancestry and his "slavery ancestors," Edwin reasoned that his hair was not something the school should have the power to control. Labeled a troublemaker because he refused to comply with a white supremacist grooming policy, Edwin reassigned blame to the true source of the problem.

When W. E. B. Du Bois asked more than a century ago how it feels "to be a problem," he was querying how African Americans grapple with the weight of their problematic existence, a feat marked by the afterlife of their enslavement and the "wake work" they perform to resist annihilation.[98] These ideas show how the mischaracterization of African Americans was rooted in dominant geographical beliefs about their innate placelessness.[99] More than sixty years later, analogous questions loomed as Southern schools desegregated and white Wacoans treated Black students like the problems they believed them to be. White educators rarely gave Black students the opportunity to thrive or be evaluated on their own merit, pushing them to languish in unfamiliar spaces that contrasted with their former segregated environment where, as all alumni in this study reported, they were deeply cared for and fortified as capable and complex persons.[100]

At La Vega schools in 1970, the climate was tumultuous. La Vega ISD had just clandestinely closed its only Black high school, G. W. Carver, without duly notifying Black residents in the area or the school's student body, which included sophomore Wanda James. During that year, Black students fought back against the district's constant affronts. They witnessed, as Wanda recalled, white "parents withdr[a]w their kids from school [because they] did not want them to go to school with Blacks."[101] The way white families repelled Black students was emblematic of their problem status in newly desegregated schools. Such disdain was communicated openly throughout the Bellmead community, where local shops instituted new policies that limited the number of Black students who could enter during students' lunch hour. According to one news report, "At least three nearby businesses, including a grocery store, and café, have started closing during the school lunch periods because of the number of students who congregate there midday. 'Sure there has been some stealing going on, but I close my store now mainly because I can't wait on my regular customers and keep an eye on the students at the same time,' said one merchant."[102] What these articles omitted was that, according to Black students who were there at the time, these new prohibitive policies were specific to Black students and did not apply to their white peers. Given that these closures happened alongside the pronounced rise in the Black population of La Vega Junior and Senior High Schools, the merchant's implicit reference to the Black thief, a criminal stereotype, was hard to miss and indicated prevalent racist ideas that shaped Black students' experiences.[103]

It was evident to La Vega High's new Black students that these lunchtime closures were deeply racialized—and racist—decisions on the part of store owners. Wanda recalled that "it was really bad during lunch because there was a lot of fights; places where you used to go, like across the street to get something to eat, they [white store owners] would not let you in." In search of a brief respite from the lunchroom chaos and combating what they saw as draconian lunch policies that gave them neither sufficient time to eat nor space to sit during their lunch period, Black La Vega students sought to rectify these issues by going off campus, only to be humiliated by being denied entry to local establishments.[104] These rejections occurred once they started attending desegregated, majority non-Black schools. The Black Waco community was unwilling to tolerate local cafés' wholesale ban on Black students, however. Their objections influenced the creation of a new policy. As Wanda recollected, "After they got a lot of complaints about it . . . they put [a sign up saying that] maybe only one [Black student could] come in the store at a time." This minor shift from allowing no Black students in to allowing one at a time did little to convince the students that the store owners' attitudes had changed. Each revision to the lunch hour policies reminded Black students that their mere presence merited them being targeted and demeaned.

Affixing the Problem tag to Black La Vega students ensured they had to contend with the psychological toll of their less-than-human status. Reflecting on these circumstances, Wanda poignantly concluded, "It made you feel like less than a person because you felt like, 'Why can't I go, and they can go in?' . . . And a lot of them didn't even know us because they didn't know anything about us. . . . And [it was] . . . just because of the color of our skin." Manufacturing a policy that forced Black students to confront their second-class citizenship amid an educational shift ostensibly intended to advance racial equality reveals how school desegregation drew on geographic ideas about spatial inclusion and exclusion that extended beyond the schoolhouse. Blackness, as Black La Vega students were coming to learn, invited and permitted such insulting treatment for which they found little redress.

As Wanda's experience attested, white society has long treated Black folk like problems in need of a more severe set of rules. In both his 1899 landmark study *The Philadelphia Negro* and his 1903 book *The Souls of Black Folk*, Du Bois analyzed how the dominant white society prevented African Americans from achieving progress socially, economically, or politically by deeming them a social nuisance.[105] In his book, Du Bois posed a provocative question: "How does it feel to be a problem?"[106] Identifying a core issue in early twentieth-century US life, this query exposed how the United States' treatment of African Americans manifested itself in their psyche. The desegregation experiences of Black Waco students illustrate this question's resonance as they negotiated their personhood in the very schools civil rights activists had fought for them to have access to.

Racial disparities in school discipline and punishment were common during the switch from racially homogeneous schools to mixed ones.

Designing discipline policies in favor of white, middle-class norms, most schools managed the enforcement of student behavior with the preconceived idea that Black students were troublemakers who incessantly misbehaved. In cases where white students and Black students committed the same infractions, punishments were often greater for Black students.[107] Multiple students, including Michael Bass and Sarah Johnson, described the drastic contrast they noticed in how white teachers managed their classrooms and attempted to administer discipline compared with their former segregated schools.[108] Alumni reported that in those schools, discipline was firm but administered in a spirit of love and genuine care for their well-being, with behavioral corrections coming from compassionate, dedicated educators who had relationships with students' families.[109]

As a University High School student in the mid-1970s, Carol Haliburton faced repeated disciplinary issues that exposed systemic unfairness. During high school one afternoon, she and two white girl classmates decided to take a smoke break in the girls' bathroom. Just a few years earlier, white students could openly smoke cigarettes in school. Some of Waco High's first Black students in majority-white schools were quite surprised to learn that teachers and students at that time shared a common smoke room and smoke breaks during the school day. This practice diametrically contrasted with typical student-teacher interactions at Black segregated A. J. Moore High School, where Black students said they could have never dreamed of smoking alongside their educators.[110] By the mid-1970s, however, smoking in the bathroom was a punishable offense—at least for Black students, it seemed. "I'll never forget the incident," Carol recalled. "Myself and two white girls . . . we were in the bathroom smoking. . . . And then the teacher came in, and I was going to be the only one who got expelled," by which she meant suspended. This discipline disparity occurred in other desegregated school contexts. In Mississippi, for instance, "a black girl . . . got into a fight in the lunchroom with two white girls in the fall of 1970, [and] only the black girl was suspended." White educators justified their actions by claiming Black students needed harsher discipline to help them "adjust to this more orderly environment."[111] School desegregation exposed such tensions and provided little to no support in helping negatively affected stakeholders manage them.

Carol's father was notified, and once he arrived, school leaders informed him that Carol, as she reported, "was gonna be the only one who got [suspended]." Carol was aggrieved about her racially discriminatory punishment. Underlining that "they didn't [suspend] the other two girls, but they [suspended] me," Carol reported that this situation "built up more and more resentment for that school"—resentment that, as I explore in chapter 5, resulted in the school ultimately pushing her out before graduation. This deliberate move by Carol to disassociate with her school represented one way to resist the heightened vulnerability she endured there, a lack of protection exacerbated by her father's stance, which isolated her misdeed from the context in which it occurred. Carol remembered him saying, "You know you wrong [for] smoking in the bathroom," which failed to acknowledge the discriminatory way she was disciplined. Such unjust targeting had long characterized how schools and other institutions dealt with Black girls, who were often "pushed out, overpoliced, and underprotected," a trend that tragically has persisted into the present day.[112]

Although neither Carol's name nor her case was highlighted specifically in school board minutes, her punishment is consistent with the scores of Black Waco ISD students who in the 1970s found themselves before the school board for either suspension or expulsion. Minutes suggest that an appearance before the school board was reserved for more egregious infractions involving physical violence, including the use of a knife or a pistol, and that each school likely handled less serious offenses as it saw fit, as in Carol's case.[113] The significant attention paid at school board meetings to discipline issues in the 1970s sharply contrasted with the pre-desegregation decades of the 1950s and 1960s, before school desegregation unfolded in earnest in Waco; in September 1972, the Waco ISD school board appointed a Discipline Committee "charged with the duty of suggesting appropriate rules and regulations that would hold promise for student behavior improvement where needed," based on "numerous parent complaints and petitions, as well as expressions of concern from teachers." The report produced in February 1973 by this committee informed the seven-page "Policy on Student Behavior" that it unveiled in January 1974.[114] Not only did this strident policy and the process that manifested it coincide with a pronounced increase of Black students in formerly non-Black Waco schools, but the fact that no such policy existed before suggested it was designed to specifically target Black children like Carol.

The myth of the Black menace informed Carol's punishment, as it did too many other Black Waco students'. Showing remarkable maturity, she was more than willing to accept the terms of her punishment for smoking in the bathroom. Her frustration, however, stemmed from receiving a penalty that targeted her personhood—her Blackness—not from her breaking a rule. This penalization indicated there was something fundamentally wrong with her, not her actions, something she could not change. Black organizations like

Waco's Black Federation and the local NAACP branches were vocal opponents of Waco ISD's racist discipline practices and showed themselves more broadly to be advocates for Black education in Waco. The actions of these Black groups echoed the advocacy efforts of the national Black women's club movement, which had advocated for juvenile and criminal justice reform in the early twentieth century.[115] Although there are no records indicating that these organizations came to Carol's defense, it was not uncommon for them to stand on behalf of aggrieved Black students or to ask the board to reopen a Black school.[116] More to the point, throughout the 1970s these active community members repeatedly requested that the board consider forming a discipline committee to examine the school district's student penalization practices. These requests, even when made by (Black) members of the school board, went unmet, however.[117]

Despite being cast as problems of different sorts, virtually all Black Waco students found and created a variety of ways to subvert white supremacist domination. From simply refusing to comply with racist policy to maintaining an acute perception of their racialized circumstances, they often recognized the enduring schemes that exposed why Waco's white education stakeholders viewed them as they did and, therefore, treated them as they did.[118] Fortunately, most Black Waco students understood that little of this treatment reflected who they actually were; rather, it echoed the long-standing antiBlackness on which society was founded. This theme of contempt responds to Du Bois's provocative question, "Does the Negro need separate schools?"[119] It reveals that such a query is perhaps misguided and that focus is better placed on the atmosphere of the schools Black students attend. Are they nurturing and affirming places that promote academic achievement and holistic well-being, or are they scornful beds of hostility incompatible with learning and thriving? Shedding light on these considerations, the different battles Black Waco students had to fight in newly desegregated schools pushed them to renegotiate their relationship to schooling and broader community spaces that were shifting as the 1970s unfolded. What most held on to, however, was their Blackness, which gave Black girls in particular a special stage on which to perform an endarkened femininity they crafted in their new schooling context.

# 4

# I'm Black, and I Can Do This

## TENACIOUS, AUDACIOUS BLACK GIRL VISIONARIES REDEFINING FEMININITY

*The students contended that black students could never prove themselves in integrated classrooms because they could never win the vote for student council, cheer leader and other offices. The black student who did win an office, they said, was invariably the one with the straightest hair.*

BETSY FANCHER, *VOICES FROM THE SOUTH*, 1970

In 1970, the only—and the first—Black girl on Waco High School's homecoming court had hazelnut-hued skin that naturally distinguished her from all other nominees. It was not a special desire to be distinctive, however, that influenced the hairstyle Kay Williams chose for this signature event or for her senior class photograph. Uncommitted to any particular hairstyle, Kay noted that she "would change my hair every other day if it suited me," and it just so happened that a neat, round Afro felt most fitting for homecoming in 1970.[1] Growing the Afro was far from a simple feat, as Kay undertook a complex, multistep process to manipulate the various textures that grew from her head. She reflected that to achieve the "natural" Afro look, "I had to go through a process of shampooing my hair, putting setting solutions [in it] that I made up myself, rolling my hair in . . . sponge rollers, letting it dry fully, and then fluffing it out. I couldn't just wash my hair [and] pick it out." Destabilizing the white beauty standards that had historically reserved prettiness exclusively for white girls, Kay made a series of decisions that elevated and elegantly punctuated her Blackness, invoking one of the most iconic, menacing political symbols of the era (at least in the eyes of many conservative white people).

Kay's quiet audacity was not the only instance of a Black girl in a newly desegregated school striking a chord vis-à-vis a racialized beauty aesthetic that reimagined Black girlhood. Just two years later at Waco High, Darlene Lewis, one of the school's first Black cheerleaders, would stand out in yearbook photographs with her sizable halo of gravity-defying coils.[2] And a few years later across town, Constance "Connie" Sadler would take defiance to an even higher—and louder—level. Poised to make her visual mark on the whitest school in the district, Connie brought Blackness to bear on nearly every event in which she participated as Richfield High School's first Black cheerleader. Like Kay's decision, Connie's required of this lightly melanated history-maker significant labor. As Connie described, "The texture of my hair was different from others'," meaning it was straighter and therefore less kinky compared with that of many Black students.[3] Thus, "it was an all-day feat for me to get my hair to have the bushy effect" that most closely resembled the quintessential Afro. Since Connie "couldn't wear it often," she strategized about when she did, including at football games, where she could be easily "identified . . . since I was the sole Black cheerleader on my squad."

Recognizing the posterity of the printed photograph, both Kay and Connie went to great lengths to style their hair in an Afro for their class pictures as well.[4] Indeed, Black girls like Kay, Darlene, and Connie were embracing bold trends set forth by their Black girl peers, such as Saundra Williams, who in 1968 was crowned atop a roundly shaped "natural" as the first to hold the Miss Black America title. A Black nationalist demonstration held in protest against the racially exclusive Miss America contest, this counterpageant celebrated—in the same city and on the same day, no less—the Black female beauty repeatedly refuted by mainstream white entities like the Miss America Organization.[5] During the era of school desegregation in the 1960s and 1970s, daring to wear an Afro for someone in a highly visible role like a cheerleader or a homecoming court honoree was a bold statement of refusal and a political act of spatial reclamation. "Many blacks" and icons such as Angela Davis,

Diana Ross, and the Jackson 5 "chose to wear 'natural' or Afro hairstyles as a celebration of self-esteem, a rejection of the shackles of racist oppression, or a claim to cultural identity [risking] . . . stiff opposition."[6] When Black girls like Kay and Connie styled their hair in such a way, they made a choice that resonated with other African Americans in majority-white settings to directly confront their historically fraught, contentious relationship to their hair and to publicly undercut white beauty standards by deliberately fashioning a look distinct from their white girl peers.[7] These insights rang especially true in Waco for these audacious, tenacious Black girls.

But what about the Black girls who proved unable to occupy these roles? What other attributes did Black girls—on different ends of the class status spectrum—share in Waco's majority-white desegregating schools? Who were they, how did they view themselves, what did their bodies symbolize, and how did they see their place in the social world? Although the written record has left little in the way of answers to these questions, oral histories thankfully supply some of the only insight available into these topics. Crucially, in one sense, Black girls with seemingly incompatible experiences had far more in common than one might expect. The experiential knowledge of Black homecoming nominees, cheerleaders, young mothers, and pregnant students spotlights the marked determination of Black cis-heterosexual girls in newly desegregated schools. This chapter posits they were visionaries who expanded white notions of femininity and capability, employing tenacity to achieve their goals and audacity in believing they could hold titles routinely reserved for their white girl counterparts. Their visionary acumen helped redefine and expand traditional, hegemonic notions of femininity and capability, making their new schools, the South, and the nation more inclusive and representative of their dynamic experiences. Few roles connote ideas about femininity or morality as do homecoming nominees, cheerleaders, young mothers, and pregnant students, and the Black girls' experiences in such contexts highlight extraordinary acts of bravery, audacity, and tenacity in the face of adversity. Furthermore, extracurricular activities and girls' transitions into parenthood are sites of largely underexamined cultural innovation in the history of education. The emerging field of Black girlhood history, however, is exposing the intricate, delicate social and inner lives of Black girls as subjects, not objects, of history and the peculiar constraints and imaginaries that have historically ordered their lives.[8] This small but growing body of work makes the compelling case that Black girls have historically been subject to a unique vulnerability distinct from that faced by other racial-gender groups. Ideals of femininity and morality, notions that a leading scholar in this area,

LaKisha Simmons, contextualizes as deeply classed, sought to restrict how Black girls navigated the world and expressed themselves as whole, sufficient, and unique on their own terms.[9]

A focus on several Black Waco girls exemplifies the rich mosaic of Black girlhood at that time, the threads that held it together, and the choreography that facilitated it. This planned movement, as Black girlhood scholar Aimee Cox argues, "can disrupt and discredit normative reading practices that assess young Black women's bodies as undesirable, dangerous, captive, or out of place."[10] Such reading practices became especially crucial as they unfolded on and through Black girls' bodies, sites revealing "that there is a map of movement or plan for how the body interacts with its environment" that "suggests that by the body's placement in a space, the nature of the space changes."[11] In this instance, the spatial shifts prompted by Black girls' bodies happened through the desegregation of Waco's schools and in response to the hegemonic conceptions of Black girls' place therein, spaces forever changed as a result of Black girls' audacity and tenacity. Using a life-history lens, which clarifies how sociohistorical contexts, changes, and processes shift humans' lives, illuminates their perspective on their primary school years to contextualize their junior high and high school days, during which they transformed schooling spaces to meet their needs and pursue their interests.[12] This sequential perspective highlights the salient role socioeconomic status plays in informing Black girls' preparation for and disposition toward certain roles, some coveted and others dishonorable according to social mores. Such a lens acknowledges the different pathways Black girls charted to achieve at high levels, disprove negative tropes, contend with the antiBlack sexist standards against which Black girls were judged, and—in loud and quiet ways—cleared hurdles for acceptance and success on their terms.

## PRIMARY SCHOOL YEARS

Despite the landmark *Brown v. Board of Education* case of 1954, most Waco students in the 1960s still attended racially separate schools. For many Black children and their families, however, this was a cherished time, as it was in many other Black settings in light of the strong community fabric that nurtured Black Waco children and prepared them for a range of experiences.[13]

Pamela James, one of Waco High School's first Black cheerleaders and a homecoming queen nominee, attended J. Newton Jenkins Elementary School, a segregated Black school in La Vega ISD, in the early 1960s. By her own admission, she "was really quiet, and I tried to be like a sponge, just absorb everything that I could. So, I didn't talk a lot, but I just tried to soak in everything."[14] Through this practice, Pamela was able to carefully study her environment and adapt as necessary to any situation. Starting school, however, presented race- and class-based challenges for her:

> Starting out in the first grade, I realized the [other] kids were a lot smarter than me. [For example, while reading] I would get stuck on a word, and I couldn't remember what the word was, and I asked my mother, "Why are they [the other students] so smart? How did they learn all of that?" I found out they learned through kindergarten. I didn't go to kindergarten, and I asked [my mother], "Why didn't we call [i.e., go to] the kindergarten?" She said, "Because we didn't have the money." I had a stay-at-home mother, so we couldn't afford to go to kindergarten. But I decided [from] that day on I was going to be, or learn, just as much as everybody else because I was going to study harder.

Class disparities between Black families played out materially in segregated schools. As in other Texas cities through the 1970s, Waco's primary schools started in the first grade, making kindergarten programs largely inaccessible for those unable to pay for an early private or parochial education. In both the Lone Star State's capital city and in Waco, kindergarten programs outside of Head Start remained unfunded from 1970 until the end of the decade.[15] For those with access, advanced literacy skills, from Pamela's view, set them apart. Afraid of being labeled "stupid," Pamela demonstrated awareness of the stigma this label could confer well before high school; doing so signaled the tangible consequences of class position for Black children and the link to perceived intelligence. In addition to explaining why circumstances were what they were, as Pamela's mother did, Black mothers found ways to stand in the economic gap. Beverly Rickford, who became a mother during high school before graduating on time from Richfield High School in the mid-1970s, journeyed through school as a working-class Black girl aided by her mother, a "neighborhood beautician," who at times bartered her services to ensure her children had nice clothes to wear to school.[16] Looking back, Beverly deeply appreciated her mother's sacrifice to ensure her children's needs were met. This class-based awareness evolved into a strong work ethic and determination that would serve as a hallmark of Pamela's and Beverly's entire school tenure. Examining their social world and adapting their actions accordingly, both Black girls identified ways to achieve at high levels given, not in spite of, their race and income level.

For Connie Sadler, the salience of race, gender, and color (i.e., skin hue), started to emerge quite early. In the late 1960s at her segregated Black elementary school, Dripping Springs, Connie's light complexion and finely textured hair became a subject of focus for her classmates. She explained, "I kind of got a little slack. Of course, being of a lighter complexion and my hair being long [and relatively straight], I got ridiculed for being a white girl. [*Connie laughs*] . . . That pretty much went through . . . high school. [*Connie laughs*]" Incessant teasing aside, Connie's Black peers were acutely aware of the hegemonic beauty standards through which her appearance was lauded, with colorism often manifesting as a social preference for lighter-colored skin.[17] In tandem with her presumably middle-class position, Connie withstood typecasting long before high school. These messages had long tracked in African American communities. Connie's classmates understood what the upbringing of Texas's own Barbara Jordan had taught her: That "for a girl-child, the degree of melanin pigmentation in [her] skin and the tone of [her] features mattered. The shape of [her] nose or the texture of [her] hair determined acceptance, opportunity, and status."[18] Speaking from experience, Jordan was a pathbreaking politician born in Houston in 1936. A queer, dark-brown-skinned, thickly statured Black girl with short, kinky hair, Jordan was bestowed with an unfavorable aesthetic that contrasted that of Connie. Jordan, nevertheless, went on to make history in multiple ways. In 1966, she became Texas's first Black state senator since 1883 and six years later served in the US House of Representatives. In 1976, Jordan delivered a keynote address at the Democratic National Convention—the first Black woman to do so.

Although a Black family's ability to own a home set it apart from those unable to do so, middle-class status rarely offered the same level of financial security that it did to middle-class white families. In Waco, many of the Black families precluded from homeownership lived in an East Waco housing project, Estella Maxey Place, where Pamela's family resided for a time. Other Black East Waco neighborhoods nearby, such as Carver Park, Hollywood, and Sharondale, housed more economically secure Black families. This entire area, as discussed in chapter 1, once bustled with Black-run businesses, churches, and schools, including the historically Black college Paul Quinn, all of which gave the community purpose and distinction. An analysis of the city as a whole, however, reveals that the economic advantage of Black home-owning families was slight. At this same time, west Waco, an almost exclusively white area of the city, boasted Waco's most affluent homes and families. There, home values were triple or quadruple that of Black-owned homes on the other side of the city.[19] By the late 1960s, Connie's family had relocated from the Estella Maxey Place housing project to a home in the adjacent Carver Park neighborhood of East Waco, illustrating how Black families' economic status remained fluid. Connie's supposedly "middle-class" nuclear family had "just enough [food] for us." Whenever they hosted a visitor for a meal, the family's fixed provisions constrained how much they could eat. Despite people's willingness to be hospitable and share what they had, the material resources of Black "middle-class" families proved precarious.[20]

Nevertheless, for Connie, class stood as a contentious site of social learning. In the mid-1960s, she nonchalantly described to her elementary school teacher and classmates how her family had spent their summer, only to find the experience set her further apart from many of her Black peers. She remembered, "The teacher said, okay, [write and share with the class] what you did this summer. . . . [So I explained,] 'We drove to New York and dah, dah, dah, dah.' And I would get the side-eyes from my classmates, 'You think you something; you just a white girl.' You know, this kind of stuff. 'No, I'm not!' I'd say. 'I'm Black just like you are.' [*Connie laughs*] And I did find myself—I won't say struggling to fit in. But I did find myself wanting to fit in, you know. I wanted to be accepted by my classmates."

It did not matter to Connie's peers that her mother, a New York native, had family who still lived there. Given the economic oppression Black communities were still facing in the 1960s, it was reasonable for her classmates to make associations between white racial identity and a Black family's capacity to travel out of state on vacation. Connie's classmates assumed that summer vacations, certainly ones as far as New York, were reserved for wealthy Anglos and not their Black classmates. Such accusations of whiteness exposed the complicated intersection of race and class position and sought to distance Connie from her Blackness. Such pursuits were generally beyond the reach of most working-class Black families in and beyond Waco, and the children unable to have these experiences pointedly contested their marginalization.[21] Indeed, varied stereotypes take hold and develop early on in children's education, certainly earlier than high school. This class-based criticism served to challenge Connie's racial identity. Although her middle-class upbringing would in time furnish myriad points of connection with her majority-white peers, Connie's progression in school saw her class status shift as a result of the premature death of her father. This change caused her mother to seek employment as a domestic laborer, underscoring yet again the precarity of the Black middle class. Rather than making her doubt the salience of her Blackness or develop resentment, the breadth of Connie's experiences motivated her to concentrate on the broader systems of racial oppression she knew to be at the heart of her classmates' comments.

Black grandmothers have historically played an integral part in rearing their grandchildren, and in Waco their influence on their granddaughters from an early age is evident in the girls' work ethic, ambition, and healthy self-worth.[22] Wanda James, who became a mother in 1971 and graduated on time with her class from Jefferson-Moore High School in 1973, gained appreciation of her grandmother by watching her "work so hard . . . and [she] didn't have a lot, but . . . kept going." Like several other Black Waco students, Wanda noted she was impoverished but "didn't even know we were poor. We didn't have a lot. But . . . you make the most of what you have."[23] Going with her grandmother Ms. Laura Mack "to work . . . [where] she used to clean the houses" for white homeowners in west and north Waco showed Wanda what it meant to work hard and subsequently "save my money," working to disprove negative controlling images about Black people as shiftless.[24] Many Black Waco students' caretakers labored as domestics, including Debora Wilkerson's grandmother; Debora also entered motherhood in 1971 during high school and graduated as part of the first graduating class of the newly constructed Jefferson-Moore High School in 1972. Debora recalled her grandmother Ms. Quincy Wilkerson telling her, "I want you to have a better job than I do. I want you to do better than I have."[25] Debora's superior view of her grandmother had given her the impression that the woman was wealthier than she was, something Debora realized later in life. Coaching her to present herself proudly and speak with confidence to white teachers and students, Debora's grandmother bolstered her self-esteem. Describing her own grandmother as "phenomenal," Wanda manifested the appreciation for all her grandmother taught and showed her through her dedication to her own advancement, by "push[ing] beyond that spot," or a particular limitation that sought to diminish her life, a perspective Debora's grandmother similarly implanted in her.

## JUNIOR HIGH SCHOOL DAYS

The 1970s represented a time of significant social change in US Southern schools. Such places had historically upheld the region's regressive and rigid sociopolitical traditions that, for example, as late as 1970 expected girls to become homemakers, as indicated by the large number of girls in Waco High School's Future Homemakers of America Club. As a complement, the Personality Development Club was committed to "polishing [girls'] personality";

the club's members were expected to "learn grooming [and] manners" and adhere to advice "on hair care, make-up and clothing."[26] According to the Waco High School yearbook, however, the 1969–70 school year marked the first year female students were permitted to wear pants to school, and that year the school also changed the name of its former "Future Secretaries Club" to "Nike Club," which was sponsored by the Business and Professional Women's Club of Waco.[27] These departures from conventional gender roles and expressions took place as Black girls were rearranging their relationship to their educational environment in a pre–Title IX setting.[28] The culmination of such events portended continued cultural and racial change—whether Waco was ready or not.[29]

As the racial tide started to shift, Black Waco girls cherished events that would ultimately serve as some of their final memories of the Black segregated schools they so loved. As a G. L. Wiley Junior High School student in the late 1960s, future homecoming queen nominee Elaine Mosley remembered her time "in the Host and Hostesses Club. . . . I [also] remember being a hall monitor, so we would have to stand out in the hall when the students would be going from lunch or passing from class to class."[30] Her "eighth-and-ninth-grade prom" was also a highlight of these years, as photographs captured her standing to the right of her first cousin Debora, both wearing ivory dresses with their hair coiffed neatly atop their heads and bearing grins indicative of a Black girlhood they relished in the safety of their own community's care.[31]

When Black girls left this familiar context, they entered a racial atmosphere that their gender further complicated. Specific extracurricular activities, including cheerleading and being a homecoming court honoree, served as some of "the most important student activities in terms of prestige" and "positions of high status or authority," hypervisible positions over which Black students were willing to stage protests if they were underrepresented.[32] Scholars writing about cheerleading specifically found that it "is said to embody the qualities associated with 'emphasized femininity' . . . notably supportiveness, enthusiasm, and sexual attractiveness. . . . Cheerleading has served as an icon of normative—meaning white, heterosexual, middle class, and American—girlhood, as well as a ready target for those contesting that ideal."[33] Such a title proved so significant in some cases that one Missouri school district saw Black students protest the absence of Black girls on the cheerleading squad by staging a walkout, not unlike the demonstration Black Waco students waged in 1970, as described in chapter 2.[34] Unlike the process in many contemporary schools, making the cheerleading squad in the early

1970s in various high schools, including some in Texas and Missouri, involved a student body election. In another case, "a demonstration of black students at South Iredell High School in North Carolina protest[ed] the absence of black students from the 15-girl homecoming court."[35] Black students across the country understood the significance of assuming these titles and showed themselves willing to fight for the representation they deserved.

The phenomenon of Black girls participating in sport as bona fide athletes has historically ebbed and flowed. Before the 1940s, according to historian Linda Perkins, society expressed little issue with this group developing their athleticism. Near the middle of the twentieth century, however, both Black and white educational institutions at the lower and higher education levels started to rescind opportunities for girls to participate in organized sport. Schools acted on growing concerns about the supposed threats girls' athleticism posed to their femininity given the sweating and running required.[36] By the late 1960s, cheerleading, however, was beginning to represent a hotbed issue in newly desegregated schools, one indeed tied to conceptions of sport and athleticism with a more feminine twist. Black student activism, as Mary Hanson shows, was responsible for increasing Black girls' representation on squads across the country in places as diverse as Indiana, Illinois, North Carolina, and New York.[37] The antiBlack sexism Black girls confronted in newly desegregated schools in terms of gaining spots on cheer squads was demonstrated in white stakeholders' preference for what one collegiate cheerleader called "traditional . . . straight-arm motions," which contrasted Black schools' style "of a stomp-clap, soul-swing thing."[38] By and large, the previous masculine stereotypes girls encountered as athletes in school found a more balanced home in cheerleading, which society viewed as more feminine. This site of sport, nonetheless, suffered from the same racialized-gendered oppression as most other facets of desegregated schools, rendering Black girls who dared to try to participate especially visible and vulnerable.

Waco schools saw social transformation and assertions of Black agency run parallel to gendered antiBlack racism. For junior high schooler Beverly Rickford, a darker-skinned, robustly framed, working-class girl, the end of junior high marked a harrowing turning point in her schooling. The previous year at her segregated school, G. W. Carver Junior and Senior High in La Vega ISD, Beverly had been selected for cheerleader. But, as detailed in chapter 2, federally mandated desegregation abruptly shuttered G. W. Carver, forcing her

> to move to [La Vega Junior High School,] a school where you have all races, and then [the white cheerleading sponsors there] say things

> to you [like] "Well, we don't have a uniform to fit you because your behind is too big or your breasts are too large." And I remember some friends and I crying because we [had] just made [it onto the squad] at [Carver]. Why now as we come together with . . . whites [do] I . . . have to be [a] skinny white girl [to keep my spot]? Why does it have to not be us? . . . Because we just [qualified for the squad at our previous school] and . . . now we're being infiltrated into other schools, mixed schools. But why were those [body type expectations] the standard criteria for us? If you [had said] we couldn't make it because of our grades or . . . because [of] some other [reasonable] standards, [that's one thing] . . . but our physical . . . we all thought that was just very derogatory to say to us.[39]

Beverly's account underlines that both Black girls and "Black women bear the brunt of racist intimidation resulting from western standards of physical beauty. This intimidation begins early in the lives of black female children."[40] This event negatively altered Beverly, curtailing her school involvement thereafter. Black females who lacked "skinny white girl" bodies suffered ridicule, exclusion, and ostracization.[41] This painful reminder that she was lacking in hegemonic femininity serves as an important illustration of how Beverly was treated in school. The conceptualization of hegemonic femininity offered by sociologist Patricia Hill Collins asserts that "hegemonic, marginalized, and subordinated femininities" represent an "ideology [that] proscribes behavior for all women based on . . . standards that only some women (including many White ones) may be able to achieve." This "ideology . . . deems middleclass, heterosexual, White femininity as normative," positioning "Black femininity as a subordinated gender identity . . . [in which] . . . hegemonic (White) femininity . . . becomes a normative yardstick for all femininities in which Black women typically are relegated to the bottom of the gender hierarchy."[42] As with Barbara Jordan, school taught Beverly that "her color, her size, her hair texture, and her features would determine and limit her choices."[43]

As shown in Beverly's case, hegemonic femininity is applicable to Black girls and Black women alike. Society thus defines femininity as something largely inherent to white, cisgender, heterosexual, middle-class females. The dominant racial group regarded the Black female body as irreconcilable with notions of femininity, virtue, purity, or frailty. This hierarchy reached back to the period of enslavement (and even after it), when "the actual or attempted rape of an enslaved woman was an offense neither recognized nor legislated by law."[44] Furthermore, scholars have shown that historically, the

Black female body has contended with virtually unmitigated, uninvited, and violent patriarchal abuse.[45] With breasts and behinds white society found both threatening and tempting, Black girls like Beverly threatened the social order by occupying bodies that hegemonic femininity deemed aberrant. Unlike many of the Black girls who would go on to become cheerleaders or sit on the homecoming court, Beverly languished in desegregated schools with little recourse to ameliorate her plight. Her salient junior high experiences exemplify which Black girls did not—or rather, could not—become a cheerleader or homecoming queen.

Moreover, Beverly's battle with hegemonic femininity confirmed the way that "historically, in the American context, young women with milky White skin, long blond hair, and slim figures were deemed to be the most beautiful and therefore the most feminine women. Within this interpretive context, skin color, body type, hair texture, and facial features become important dimensions of femininity. . . . These standards of female beauty have no meaning without the visible presence of Black women and others who fail to measure up. Under these feminine norms, African American women can never be as beautiful as White women because they never become White."[46] Some Black girls, it seems, stood too far outside this hegemonic frame to burrow their way in, for they had to vie head-on with ideologies in desegregated schools—and in society at large—that positioned them as oppositional to the hegemonic norm. Many students insisted that possessing light-colored skin, a thin build, finely textured straight hair, and a thin nose and lips made a Black girl more likely to be able to become a cheerleader or homecoming queen.[47] Carol Haliburton at University High School, in fact, received so many messages from different sources that her body was too shapely for the cheerleading squad that she never bothered to consider trying out.[48] With aspirations to join the dance team, Sarah Johnson at Jefferson-Moore High watched white school personnel prohibit Black girls with more curvaceous bodies from joining the team, as detailed in chapter 5.[49] Thus, the Black girls eligible to become cheerleaders or sit on homecoming court possessed some features that aligned with hegemonic femininity, exhibited middle-class sensibilities, and were lucky enough to avoid an unintended pregnancy.

Even Black girls who ascended to the cheerleader role or sat on the homecoming court attested to these problematic expectations. Pamela James, for example, speculated that she would have lost out on the opportunity to become a cheerleader or sit on the homecoming court "if I had gone to [A. J.] Moore [High School]," attesting that "I think I would've been [physically] inadequate there. I really do." As she recognized, "I didn't have the body that the other girls at this segregated Black school had. . . . They had boobs; they had everything. Legs and all that." Admiring her voluptuous peers, she remembered asking her mother, "When am I going to get some breasts like that?" Admitting she "never did," Pamela concluded that her slight physique enabled her to hold these roles at a majority-white school, where white beauty standards diverged dramatically from the beauty standards at an all-Black high school. She acknowledged that these experiences were available to her chiefly because of school desegregation.

Although some lacked the statuesque figures of their peers, these particular Black Waco girls had since childhood yearned to be a part of a Black dance tradition that celebrated curvy Black female bodies and motivated Black girls to be part of the halftime action. This appreciation for a Black aesthetic, featuring clear markers of Black racial identity that society has historically rendered antithetical to white perceptions of beauty, reflects one of the many ways Black communities situated the body as a racialized site to advance a value system that opposed hegemonic notions of beauty.[50] Part of Black segregated G. W. Carver's drill team in junior high from 1968 to 1970, Wanda James characterized the school as "popular" largely because of that team: It was "fascinating to me to see . . . [an] all-Black . . . drill team. Everybody was [moving] together and it was hard to get on [i.e., make the team]. You had to go to the practices; you ha[d] to make sure you got the routine down." Clearly, Wanda relished her time on the team. In a similar vein, Debora Wilkerson recalled being "just excited to be with my friends and go to [segregated A. J.] Moore High and be a fire twirler." Although Debora did not matriculate at A. J. Moore High, she was mesmerized by these majorettes, as they were often known, a staple in Black high school and music culture. Along with a school's widely entertaining band, these dancers were showstoppers and continue to be, engaging the crowd in some cases more than the football team.[51] Someone whom Pamela in her childhood considered a paragon of beauty was a Black girl a few years her senior. Walda Kennedy, a Waco High student in the late 1960s, was part of the school district's first crop of Black students to desegregate.[52] Before entering high school, Pamela vividly remembered watching Walda, whom she described as "so pretty" and "so sharp," perform at local Black events. "I really thought a whole lot of her." The inspiration Pamela drew from seeing Walda perform motivated her to believe that "I could do that, too."

Because requirements for femininity were predicated on whiteness and its associated beauty standards, many Black girls stood outside its boundaries. This marginalization meant femininity was largely unachievable for many Black girls in newly desegregated high schools given that the onset of puberty accentuated one's proximity to or distance from the hegemonic norm. Thus, hegemonic feminine appearance, traits, demeanor, and traditional gender role ideology constituted a femininity that did not, and effectively could not, absorb or make room for all Black girls.[53] Regardless, many Black girls managed to "stay in their bodies to rewrite the socially constructed meanings shackled to them," assuming titles many considered incompatible with Black girlhood.[54] Society has historically constructed Black women and girls in contradictory ways that simultaneously degender and oversexualize them. Insights from cultural studies scholar Patricia Davis bolster literary scholar Hortense Spillers's claims about enslavement stripping Black females of their gender, a tendency that has shaped femininity since that era and denied Black females womanhood, girlhood, and femininity by labeling them pathological matriarchs responsible for the moral, economic, and cultural failures of the Black race.[55] This enduring perspective was founded on scientific and medical literature that supported enslavement, according to Davis, ideas that "transcribed the masculine onto the black female body, thus positioning black women as the embodiments of racial and sexual alterity. . . . These discourses ensured that black women were perceived as lacking the feminine virtues expected of women, such as passivity, frailty, and purity," while also underlining their "licentiousness" and innate propensity to withstand hard labor, including that required for breeding and child-rearing, as in the Mammy role.[56] Mapping onto social constructions aimed at denigrating Black females of all stripes, "these images were and are critical to the construction of normalized white femininity," and they took hold in desegregating Waco schools.[57]

### *The Collective*

A deep sense of duty to the collective—in both a racial sense and school pride sense—motivated Black girls to boldly face their insecurities and embark on new experiences. Claiming Waco High in the early 1970s as hers, Pamela James, as the school's first Black cheerleader, declared, "I could represent my school" as a cheerleader despite doubts about her dancing skills. Largely responsible for her confidence, her Black classmates encouraged her by affirming they wanted her to be a cheerleader at Waco High. "I knew I wasn't the best," Pamela admitted, but "we [as cheerleaders] were supporting our team. And once . . . they announced [that I had been elected a cheerleader], I knew I had to do it. I had to be responsible. . . . I had to do this because everybody was supporting me, and I felt like it was a necessary thing to do. I didn't want to let anybody down." Pamela's feelings of social obligation reflected the sense of many "Black women [who] believed their role was to ameliorate the effects of racism, seeing the future of the race as residing squarely in the role of women," which often extended to Black girls.[58] Pamela explained that "[because] they nominated me," she felt compelled to view "this as something I had to do to stand up for the people that were behind me," both Black people and white people.

Beyond their immediate school communities, Black girls who occupied these symbolic roles understood that such an endeavor was much bigger than them as individuals, that their selection and concomitant visibility represented their larger communities and families. "For me," Kay Williams, Waco High's first Black homecoming queen nominee, shared, "the recognition . . . the opportunity builds your self-confidence [in] all the lessons that you were taught, the preaching of your parents and your grandparents and your neighbors, the neighborhood, the teachers that you were exposed to before [desegregation]." This long list of the groups entwined in Kay's history-making reinforced her conviction that she came from excellent folk and speaks to her awareness that, as scholars have observed, "parents and the community prepared Black women to take a position of 'socially responsible individualism.'"[59] Being the traditional "standard bearers," many Black females in educational contexts in particular possessed "faith in their own ability to succeed" while recognizing that "their decisions as individuals needed to be firmly rooted in community considerations and expectations."[60] Having been "prepared . . . to know how to conduct myself . . . at home generationally," Kay prized the outsize part her community had played in her upbringing and in getting her to a point where she could confidently assert herself.

Pride in the accomplishments of these Black girls emanated across the school, highlighted Black students' investment in traditional social values, and indicated how unlikely many Black students believed Black girls' chances at securing such spots were. Having attended Waco High with Katherine Sanford, Anslum Hudlin, a Black working-class boy, "was so surprised" that Katherine was elected by a majority-white student body at Waco High.[61] His doubts about how his white peers would value Black girls reflected his perception of the new social world and its racial dynamics. Anslum remembered

Katherine as "a real pretty girl . . . [who was] . . . real soft-mannered . . . [and] came from the east side of town. Her family name was reputable in the Black community . . . [and] she had both parents in the home." Framing Katherine's life as "a picture-perfect, TV-type setting," Anslum venerated her family because it was, according to him, "something I always wanted. I would see people with a two-parent household . . . [and think] that's the dream. That was big for me." Anslum's desire for a nuclear family was rooted in the humiliation to which he was subjected given the conditions surrounding his birth. As detailed in chapter 5, Anslum never knew his father and was raised in north Waco by his maternal grandmother, a domestic laborer in white homes. He underscored "how embarrassing it is when you take your birth certificate to your school, then you don't have a father's name on it." Leaving the space blank on a birth certificate was common throughout the 1970s in McLennan County, where many Waco students were born. Anslum, like other students, felt Katherine's election helped Black students assert their racial pride, something both complicated by and symbolized in an otherwise conventional Black girl claiming certain key markers of respectability.

Like his classmate Anslum, Richard Jenkins dismissed the possibility that the school would actually elect a Black girl to such a highly visible role. School officials announced the voting results after the nominees and their escorts had walked onto the football field. Because he felt certain Katherine, his friend, would not win, Richard wanted to spare her and himself the public disappointment of watching the crown go to one of their white girl classmates, of not hearing Katherine's name. This motivated Richard to decline an invitation to escort Katherine onto the football field to accept her victory.[62] This mindset was typical, as Black students expected the results of any type of popular vote to be marred by racism. In fact, Black male athletes across the country expressed dismay that majority-white high schools seldom featured Black girls in high-status roles.[63] Richard recalled that his white teammate who ended up escorting Katherine appeared less than enthused; co-captain Johnny Dodd, according to Richard, "was standing there like he didn't want to be holding her, stiff as a board with his elbow pointing [out] almost like he was poking her arm, poking her in her rib."[64] In retrospect, Richard resolved that he had "made the wrong decision" in not escorting her.

Interracial alliances helped weave the larger student body together and stood as one of several indicators that Black girls were electable—even to their own surprise—by a majority-white student body. In the early 1970s, Pamela and Katherine considered themselves friends with some of their white girl peers. Although interaction with these peers outside school was limited, Connie Sadler identified that the cheerleading camp she went to in the mid-1970s gave her deeper insight into white people's grooming and living habits. Black hair, for instance, presented many white educators with a cultural puzzle they lacked the necessary tools to solve. In Louisville during school desegregation, a student recalled how her physical education teacher made class especially difficult for her Black girl students because "no black girl wanted to shower and wash [their] hair because hair, for black girls, is an issue. It's just too much work and you can't just brush it back and make a ponytail. I mean, you've got major work to do."[65] This major work was beyond the frame of reference for many white educators, who had spent little if any time around Black people to understand their grooming practices. Better prepared than many of her white educators, Connie gained at cheer camp firsthand perspective on how white girls went about taking care of themselves. Debora Wilkerson, who was also light-skinned and whose eyes were green, recognized how skin color facilitated her friendship with a white woman coworker at an upper-end department store in Waco. Playing a key part in her election process, Katherine's white friend Andrea "was really nice. . . . She helped me out doing some of my campaigning, but she was Caucasian. Andrea was really a good person." This unexpected support presented some level of cognitive dissonance for Katherine, making it difficult for her to believe "I would win [the election] . . . because I was at [a] school . . . [that] was more white than it was Black," a view her classmates Anslum and Richard shared. After clearing a hurdle no other Black girl at Waco High had before her, some of her white girl peers encouraged Katherine to enter the Waco Junior Miss Pageant, a school tradition. Competing against a slew of mostly white contestants, Katherine won first runner-up, gently nudging hegemonic femininity to embrace a Blacker aesthetic.[66]

Some lighter-skinned Black girls recognized how they benefited from colorism, but doing so did not mean they welcomed reminders that negatively implicated them in school desegregation's unmeritocratic reward structure. Katherine's stint in Waco High's theater department in the early 1970s showed her that in "some of the plays, we [Black girls with less melanin] did [get preferential treatment; there] might've been a difference as to complexion. If you were lighter, you [were] able to [get cast in better roles]." Like Connie's Black peers in elementary school, Katherine's classmates reminded her of the advantages lighter-skinned Black students enjoyed; "people would tease [that you're] brighter, so that's why you're getting this grade or some crap like that." Along these lines, one Black girl student in Charleston, South Carolina, during school desegregation developed a "feeling that she was a token, a nonentity, and that some whites accepted her because she was light-skinned and a good student."[67] As Barbara Jordan learned at her all-Black schools in Houston, "The kids who were the leaders were usually slim and pretty, with nice, long hair and pretty brown [not black] skin."[68] It seems of little surprise, then, that some of Waco's most visible and popular Black girl students possessed a lighter skin hue that facilitated cross-racial connections and, hence, the positive outcome of their elections. In contrast, Katherine observed that for boys "on the football field, I don't think [skin color] made a difference. Basketball either. They just wanted your skills." Lending merit to her claim, Richard, for example, was a deep shade of mahogany that made him easily identifiable in many yearbook photographs.[69] For Black girls, however, this type of athletic meritocracy was rare.

### *Discourses Around Sex*

Sex education has historically been a fraught issue involving central questions of morality, which grew increasingly more complex as sex education intersected with race, gender, and class. Interestingly, in New York and other Northern states, schools were well into the 1960s before they approved sex education, a comparably contentious matter bound up in race, desegregation, and rising teenage pregnancy rates.[70] Education historian Jonathan Zimmerman points out that as a result of the Southern zeal that sought to prohibit sex education in Louisiana, the state had completely banned it from its lower education curriculum by 1970, and "in a narrow two-year span, hundreds of school districts and nineteen states considered measures to ban or limit sex education" altogether.[71]

Waco saw much of the same. "Lackluster" is a generous characterization of the school-based health education available to Black Waco girls in the 1970s, which attempted at least nominally to address sex. Debora recalled health class in the early 1970s as the only place where students were presented with educational content about sex in high school. "Ms. Linda Mathis Davis was our PE teacher, and she was . . . a very outspoken, blunt . . . teacher" who corrected her students' use of "unofficial words" to describe sexual acts, using instead more formal terminology like "sperm." "Show[ing] us those old videos" about the mechanics of sexual intercourse and fertilization, Davis gave Debora some of the most direct, technical sex education she ever received, even though it was delivered in an impersonal manner and ultimately insufficient. The conversation centered on "what the end result [of sex] could be, but it . . . was like a curriculum [that only devoted] . . . six weeks . . . to talk to the girls and boys [separately] about the sperm and the egg. And then the next six weeks, you're going to talk to them about whatever else." Giving this topic short shrift could have life-altering consequences. Local newspapers in the early 1970s were reticent about and paid limited attention to sex education or motherhood, though by the mid- and late 1970s they raised alarm over rising teenage birth rates, focusing most information about reproduction on those who were already pregnant.[72] Some young Black mothers, like Wanda, were unable to recall getting any sex education at all, stating, "We had health [class], but we didn't have sex education. I don't remember having that." This undereducation contributed to Wanda being unable, as she remembered, to tell her mother she was expecting, "because I didn't know I was pregnant"; all she knew was that she "was sick and wasn't feeling good." When it came to preventing unwanted conception, little if any of this so-called sex education proved helpful to Black girl students.

To add to this problem, gender norms discouraged Black women and girls from having candid conversations about sex that might otherwise arm them with critical information about their bodies, health, and reproduction. Wanda underlined that in the early 1970s, "you wouldn't dare [talk about sex with anyone] because you wouldn't want them to know you were even interested in it." Historians investigating Black women's sexuality have demonstrated that "Black women have had to learn to cover up all public suggestions of [their] sexuality."[73] Shielding this aspect of themselves—regardless of whether their sexuality comported with heterosexual social norms or defied them—Black girls and women were reticent to openly discuss their sexual desires. Even as an adult, Barbara Jordan refrained from publicly admitting or discussing her queerness despite residing with her romantic partner in the 1970s until her death two decades later. Although Debora could recall that "some girls, same age, same class with me . . . told me about [how they had] these kind of conversations [about sex] . . . with . . . their mother, and that they were on birth control," she was unable to imagine doing so herself. It was outside the realm of possibility for her to, she explained, "say to my mother, 'Can you take me to Planned Parenthood to get some birth control?' I thought I was going to die [if I ever asked] because she'd kill me." In Waco, the Planned Parenthood clinic was located in south Waco and made, according to reporting in 1975, "reproductive autonomy" accessible to more than five thousand area residents, but Debora was not one of them.[74]

Conversations with their mothers and other women caretakers about sexual activity or contraception felt completely out of reach for both Debora and Wanda, certainly before they discovered they were pregnant. Ever astute,

Debora pondered how much that was the case for her own mother, asking "whether it was the generational thing, that those things just weren't talked about" in the era when her mother grew up. "Black women," historians note, "have learned to present a public image that never reveal[ed] their sexuality" in order to comport with respectable behavior, which "would not guarantee one's protection from sexual assault, but the absence of such was certain to reinforce racist notions of Black women's greater sexuality, availability, or immorality."[75] Additionally, the politics of respectability emphasized "sexual repression" particularly "among the poor," who may have been more sexually liberated and whom middle-class African Americans believed were too sexually expressive, beliefs that discouraged Black females from admitting they had sexual desires or were sexual beings.[76] The generational component of this culturally sanctioned sexual silence, then, rippled through Black girls' experiences during school desegregation, dramatically altering their lives.

Black working-class girls felt significant apprehension about how pregnancy might invite even greater stigma against them than already existed, because they knew that "race and class further inscribe . . . Black teen mothers . . . [as] inherently deficient, morally and culturally."[77] Apparently, one "almost never . . . s[aw] a white girl pregnant" in school, according to Debora, who used the same descriptor as Wanda—*taboo*—to describe pregnancy in high school in the early 1970s.[78] Prince Edward County, Virginia, responded to the school desegregation mandate by shutting down its public schools for five years, sparking reproduction-related consequences for Black youth. During this widescale shutdown, "At least two teenage mothers expressed an interest in returning to school." One affected Black teenager reflected on the fact that his "return to school [once it reopened] hinged upon whether or not he would be able to make arrangements for the support of his newborn child. . . . He observed that 'plenty of girls would not be pregnant' if the schools had remained open." For Black girls intent on continuing their education once the option returned to them, motherhood stood as a barrier. [79]

Relying solely on what one could see, however, obscured actual trends. The year 1970 saw birth rates for fifteen-to-nineteen-year-olds hover near 7 percent, with the rate for white teens at 6 percent and for Black teens near 14 percent.[80] To this point, as Wanda recognized, "it was not just Blacks; it was whites [too]. . . . They would go off somewhere and come back next semester [with] no baby . . . or be shipped off to [a] relative's house, or ha[ve] an abortion, where we [low-income Black girls] couldn't afford it." This practice created a situation in which "the majority of us that were pregnant were Black girls," Debora underscored. Racial differences in visible pregnancies exposed the reality that those with the financial means to address their circumstance in privacy could maintain a sense of personal decency that was out of reach for many Black girls from low-wealth families. Moreover, an education policy perspective highlights how schools systematically contributed to this pattern by discriminating against expecting students of Color, "plac[ing] teen mothers into different programs by race, with White girls most often being served in the regular public school or offered at-home tutoring until the birth of their child at which point they return to school."[81]

Debora expressed not wanting her pregnancy "to create the embarrassment for my family . . . [or for] the other Black girls," a desire many Black girls shared. In the midst of their personal strife, Black working-class girls' enduring concern for their wider race corroborates Black girlhood historian Marcia Chatelain's contention that "through their self-presentation and success, [they] . . . also carr[ied] the weighty responsibilities of race progress."[82] An unmarried, pregnant Black body, especially that of a low-income high schooler, invited scorn and ridicule, something of which Black girls were acutely aware.[83] Both Wanda and Debora gave birth in 1971, two years before the Supreme Court legalized abortion with *Roe v. Wade*. This unfavorable timing made the voluntary termination of their respective pregnancies less likely, less accessible, and far more dangerous.[84]

## *"We Had Made History"*

The homecoming court represents a particular site where Black girls remade the racialized-gendered landscape of desegregated schools by audaciously refashioning titles and roles historically reserved for their white girl counterparts. Annually, teens in Texas, as elsewhere, looked forward to homecoming, and the election of a homecoming court was a highlight of these events. To be elected to this role at Waco High, alumni described how one had to qualify by first being officially nominated (self-nominations, according to Pamela, were not accepted). Then, those elected had to garner a threshold of votes from the student body. A subsequent round of voting occurred later, usually immediately before the homecoming football game, to decide who would be crowned queen from the nominees.

No stranger to pageantry or modeling, Kay Williams in the fall of 1969 became Waco High's first Black homecoming queen nominee, an experience of which she thought little. Graduating the following spring in 1970, Kay described herself as "tall," "skinny," and fond of "wear[ing] cute clothes and shoes," so the chance to stand on homecoming court, as she viewed it, was "just something fun to do." In fact, she noted, "I didn't advocate [i.e., campaign] for it [homecoming queen], because I really could [not] have cared less." It was "a surprise" for her when she learned she had received enough votes from the majority-white student body to become an official nominee. With low expectations for her classmates, Kay proceeded to continue living a typical high schooler's life. At the time, the racial significance of Kay's seat on the homecoming court was unapparent to her and remained so until some five decades later, "when," as she relayed, "I looked at the yearbook at the [class] reunion . . . and I saw that I was the only dark spot on that page with that group. . . . It actually occurred to me . . . 'I [was] the first Black girl at homecoming court.'"

That Kay did not feel she was making history at the time, being unable to "recall that it was [of] any particular significance," suggests that not everything Black girls did was intended to resist or subvert oppression, even if that is what their actions signified to others. Literary scholar Kevin Quashie lends merit to this claim through an analysis that unsettles what he considers the overused paradigm of resistance in African American life and for African American females especially. He champions the concept of "oneness," which maintains that to be legible or relatable, Black females do not need to be compared to other persons or subjects.[85] Their assertion of this subject position constitutes his frame of "audacity," which works in tandem with "quiet," a disposition devoted largely to one's inner mind, an "interiority . . . a quality of being inward, a 'metaphor' for life and creativity beyond the public face of stereotype and limited imagination."[86]

In applying this sense of oneness and audacity, Kay paved the way for subsequent Black girls to break barriers at Waco High School.[87] One year Kay's junior, Katherine was Kay's peer and close friend.[88] Describing their relationship as "like sisters" who had "known each other for years," Kay recalled being "very proud of her" for her accomplishments. Kay, however, "never put it [Katherine's achievement] in a racial context." Viewing her friend on her own terms and, therefore, qualified and deserving of the title she earned in her own right, Kay rationalized Katherine's accomplishment as based on her being "charming . . . attractive . . . smart . . . [and] never really associat[ing] it with race or breaking a racial barrier" at the time. Reflecting on it decades later, Kay reasoned, "I don't even know when it really hit me that in our own way, we had made history, but you don't think about that at the time."

Even when they were not present in a literal sense, Black women guided youth in their family in desegregated schools. Katherine's loss of a close maternal figure during her senior year of high school colored her memories about breaking a color barrier during school desegregation, making her question whether she was elected out of pity. This important woman had been elected to a high-status position in the 1940s at segregated A. J. Moore High School. This legacy granted Katherine's relative the confidence to know she could also assume this title, should conditions prove favorable. Katherine, however, was preceptive and understood what a predominantly white student body meant for her chances of being elected to such a high-status position, as she, like many of her Black peers, held limited confidence in her white peers' ability to see her as feminine and deserving of the crown.

As the first Black girl to attain a specific, coveted title at Waco High, Katherine grappled with what her holding this designation signified. She viewed herself as both a role model for younger children and as someone whom white people saw as "an individual. That I did look nice and that I did carry myself correctly. I was respectful. You could respect me as the queen of Waco High. I was proud."[89] These blows to hegemonic femininity represented subtle shifts in what femininity now meant in racially mixed schools. As Black girls helped steer spaces that were previously earmarked exclusively for white girls into spaces of belonging for more girls of Color, they commanded respect and recognition as feminine and exceptional individuals—two attributes rarely bestowed on Black girls. In doing so, however, they also reinscribed middle-class ideals that deemed unrespectable behavior inferior and embraced a false sense of security.[90] Black girls who sat on the homecoming court drew on a complicated web of respectability politics to make meaning of their accomplishments, which unfolded within an environment that disassociated the Black female body from respect. This popular political strategy crystallized in the early twentieth century and promoted personal responsibility, modesty, and the engagement of seemingly white middle-class comportment, values, and practices.[91] Despite its limitations, the politics of respectability was a staple of prominent political organizations such as the NAACP and significantly shaped the social lives and views of many Black working- and middle-class communities. Even with the rise of the feminist movement during the 1970s, which largely excluded women of Color, respectability in Black Southern communities was highly valued.[92] This emphasis was apparent in Waco, where one of its only Black newspapers, the *Waco Messenger*, promoted such views.[93] Recalling some of the sources of guidance that had led her to become Waco High's first Black homecoming queen nominee, Kay credited her "Black teachers, they were always well put together; they were always reminding you that you were a young lady and to act like a young lady." This etiquette training disseminated notions of respectability that influenced how such Black girls and women carried themselves and, arguably, what made them electable to a majority-white student body.

Over the course of making history, Black girls rewrote the gendered-racial scripts across various spatial sectors in desegregated schools, including the academic sector. In Waco, this process saw many Black girls "shapeshift," to use Black girlhood scholar Aimee Cox's term, as they performed Black girlhood, disrupting dominant ideas that a cheerleader, certainly an academically successful Black one, had to come from a middle-income home. Cox describes the shapeshifting process as one in which "young Black women living in the United States engage with, confront, challenge, invert, unsettle, and expose the material impact of systemic oppression," a practice indeed evident in 1970s Waco.[94] Attending desegregated schools gave Black Waco students firsthand knowledge of, according to Pamela, "how dumb white people were," an insight that disrupted prevailing ideas about white intellectual superiority.[95] Her commentary echoed that of a Black student in Mississippi who was motivated to desegregate in part because she "simply wanted to show people that black students were not dumb."[96] In tenth grade, during her 1969–70 school year at Waco High, Pamela, whose family was working class, paid close attention to which racial groups earned which grades. Crucially, she wanted to know if her learning environment proved or disproved extant associations linking whiteness to affluence and academic proficiency and Blackness to impoverishment and academic deficiency.[97] Initially adhering to these beliefs herself, Pamela soon realized that "[the white students were] not really [better], and I don't know if we [as Black students] just tried harder" than they did. Pamela recounted watching teachers pass back graded assignments and seeing that Black students would earn "a 98, and [white students would] get their paper back and they might have a 60." These grade differences also applied to herself and the white cheerleaders, who "didn't make straight A's" as she did. Like other Black girls who led school desegregation battles—in Texas, no less—Pamela did not shy "away from challenging subjects . . . [despite the possibility that] academic ambition would be noted by the white community and perceived as a threat."[98] Having developed her competitive disposition throughout her segregated elementary school years, Pamela was poised to excel both academically and socially as a working-class Black girl. Such a positive self-perception motivated Pamela's participation in several other school activities, including her place on homecoming court and in choir.[99]

Black girls had a shrewd consciousness and subverted the tacit curriculum of Black intellectual ineptitude that was embedded within the school desegregation process.[100] Shapeshifting in this sense meant that Black girls would perform a middle-class status despite occupying, in material terms, a less economically viable group. Both in their social dexterity and in their intelligence, Black working-class girls demonstrated "the instability and flexibility of identity in variously configured locations" such as classrooms, choral risers, and playing-field sidelines.[101] In paying close attention to the mechanisms of oppression intended to limit their possibilities, they were able to reject dominant paradigms intent on undermining their capabilities.

### *Unfettered Determination*

The life circumstances of some Black girls required them to navigate especially treacherous obstacles and to practice more tenacity than their peers. Through their unrelenting resolve, these wondrous Black girls were able to graduate from high school, a remarkable feat especially for those who found themselves expecting a child. "Because I had a baby" and "had failed myself," Wanda explained, "I wanted to do better, and I knew I could." Wanda's baby was born in August 1971 during her junior year in high school, when she was seventeen. Initially, she had felt an excessive sense of personal culpability, failing to also see how the system had failed her. Proudly, Wanda disproved those who said, "Oh, you had a baby. You can't do this; you can't do that." "It was important that I graduate," Debora echoed, "after seeing that there was an effort to hinder my progress . . . [by] this [white] lady [counselor] that was telling me that I couldn't . . . graduate because of choices that I've made." Her sense of personal liability seemed only to inspire her. In Debora's case, this naysayer was her guidance counselor, Grace Hamilton, who barred her from finishing her coursework at Waco High; instead, Debora would have to transfer to another high school to graduate on time. Hamilton's justification was that Debora had missed the first few weeks of her senior school year to give birth to her child in September 1971.[102] At seventeen, Debora had effectively concealed her pregnancy during the previous school year, which further angered her counselor.[103] Unwilling to view her life as being limited by her motherhood, Wanda wrestled with being her "own worst enemy as far as being down on myself . . . [for] having a baby young in school." But she pressed on, showing a steadfast "determination . . . to . . . focus on . . . graduating and going forward." Wanda understood that accomplishing this goal would illustrate to her child that "no matter what happens, if you are determined to do something, [if] you want better for yourself, that you can do it." The ambition and persistence of these Black girls paved their way to graduation. Debora described it as both "self-determination" and "self-motivation that . . .

in spite of where I was . . . I wasn't going to stop." Clearing this hurdle, both Debora and Wanda graduated from Jefferson-Moore High on time with their respective classes. To do so, however, both had to transfer from Waco High to Jefferson-Moore High after facing sustained opposition to their graduating as young mothers, a process detailed in chapter 5.

Waco's Black girls were visionaries. Although Connie did not make the cheerleading squad at predominantly white Lake Air Junior High, she remained determined. Connie entered tenth grade at Richfield High School, the whitest high school in the district, in 1973, which meant that she saw mainstream fashion magazines during this time begin to feature African American women. In 1974, Beverly Johnson made history as the first Black woman to grace *Vogue*'s cover, three years after she had done the same on the cover of *Glamour*.[104] As Connie started this new chapter, she declared to her friends, "I'm going to be a cheerleader my senior year." Despite "barely [being able to] find me in school" in tenth grade because she skipped school so often, Connie reported "always fe[eling] good about my grades" and made sure they did not suffer too much. By her own admission, "I did as much as I could get away with" early on in high school, telling herself, "You get this all out of your system 'cause in eleventh grade you got to buckle down so that you can be this citizen of the year . . . and . . . a possible candidate for cheerleader. So again, like I said, tenth grade, rebellious. Eleventh grade, buckle down. You know, I'm doing everything, I'm participating in all kinds of stuff. And so, I'm trying out for cheerleader, along with several other Black, white, and Hispanic classmates."

Employing a level of intentionality and forethought uncharacteristic of most high schoolers, Connie strategized to become a cheerleader while fitting in time for childhood mischief. As she progressed in high school, Connie worked "to prove myself: that I'm Black and I can do this." Her efforts panned out just as she had envisioned. In the years between Pamela's time as Waco High's first Black cheerleader during the 1971–72 school year and Connie's time during the 1975–76 school year at Richfield, the selection process had shifted from a nomination and popular vote to include a performance (i.e., tryout) in front of the student body. In the 1960s and early 1970s, schools across the country were using one or both selection methods.[105] In Waco, the change from solely a popular vote to the addition of a tryout alongside an election happened shortly after the start of school desegregation when Black students began, rightfully, taking up more educational space. Outgoing Black girls like Connie welcomed and excelled at this public performance. The new racial elements Connie brought to bear on cheerleading embodied the spirit of an expansive femininity that some but not all Black girls could inhabit. Because Blackness had historically been omitted from hegemonic femininity, Connie dared to dream into existence a reality she had never known. Some of the strongest evidence of such Black girls' effectiveness was in their election by predominantly white student bodies.

The ambition, dedication, and persistence young Black mothers marshaled to accomplish goals they deemed meaningful allowed them to exceed society's standards of them. Entering motherhood with the birth of her daughter at the beginning of high school, Beverly refused to allow early parenthood to prevent her from earning her high school diploma in the 1970s at Richfield High School. Like Debora and Wanda, she managed to graduate on time, but unlike them, Beverly did not have to transfer to do so.[106] It is unclear whether there were additional supports that facilitated Beverly in this endeavor, but nonetheless, she was able to make history as a young Black mother high school graduate. Such a predisposition was evident in many young Black mothers who simultaneously navigated pregnancy, early motherhood, and high school. What motivated Wanda was that "I've always been such a go-getter. . . . I was just real strong-willed," she remarked. Her family understood her "outgoing" nature, which helped convince them to "never worry about [her] because [she] was going to make it." For Wanda, the role of the strong Black woman, despite its connection to negative health outcomes, was something she prided herself on playing, especially in the face of adversity.[107] Similarly, Debora said, "If my mind says that it can be done, I'm going to work to figure it out," especially if "you . . . tell me that it can't be done." This attitude also applied to Black girls' sense of failure, on which Wanda commented, "If I fail at something, I'm going to get up and try it again . . . [in] a different way. That's just me. I just don't give up easy."

Black girls who navigated pregnancy as high schoolers were planners who proved able to adapt to their fluid circumstances, a critical life skill that was often born out of their engagement with gendered racism. As high schoolers, Debora and Wanda both married the fathers of their children, who were servicemen; being married, however, did little to shift social views of their purported immorality as young Black mothers. The choice to marry was in part a romantic one, but it was also a practical decision that reflected the intentionality required to meet the material demands of a young family. For Wanda, marriage meant "I could travel with him [her husband], and he could get . . . an allotment [of money] for us." She began receiving this financial support after getting married in 1973. In the interim between the birth of her child in 1971 and her marriage in 1973, Wanda, as she explained, "worked because they [Waco ISD] had a program where if I went out to MCC [McLennan Community College] and took up a nursing aide program and . . . graduated from [it], they would hire you at Hillcrest [Hospital]." Finding opportunities to stand in the gap while parenting a young child and finishing high school was par for the course in Wanda's case. Her unwillingness to let motherhood take her further off course reveals much about Black girls' agency and self-determination.

The cheerleader role rendered Black girls vulnerable to attacks from resentful white mothers, hostility that served only as further motivation for some girls. The mother of one of Pamela's cheer mates, for example, asked her, "What does your mother think about you being a cheerleader?" and "You sure you want to do this?" Noting that these questions surprised her by "just knock[ing] me for a loop," Pamela felt this hostile white mother was essentially asking her, What are you, a Black girl, doing being a cheerleader? This probe represents one of the tactics white mothers deployed to defend a crucial site of white girlhood—cheerleading—which they felt Black girls and, more broadly, school desegregation, were threatening.[108] Routinely viewing Black females antagonistically, white women stakeholders during school desegregation reaffirmed their commitment to such subtle forms of violence, shown most clearly in the mass resistance efforts against school desegregation by white mothers, who were some of the policy's most egregious opposition.[109] Repeatedly characterizing this white mother as "just nasty," Pamela underlined the extreme discomfort this white mother stirred in her through not only the questions she posed but the contemptuous tone in which she conveyed them. "She's talking down to me," Pamela explained. The mother sought to sow seeds of doubt and inadequacy—to no avail—in this young Black girl's psyche.

White women educators in desegregated schools also singled out Black girls for daring to take up spaces traditionally reserved for white girls, in particular subjecting them to elevated scrutiny of their attire. Remembering that she and many of her Black girl classmates "got our dresses measured to make sure they were long enough" by white women school counselors, Kay sensed "some of the counselors . . . might've been a little more judgmental for the Black girls." Black women historians have worked to unsettle the prominent notion that white women possessed an inherently kind, generous, compassionate disposition that benefited all those fortunate enough to interact with them.[110] Ideas about the Black female body as deviant and immoral informed standards that equated all Black girls with unrestrained sexuality.[111] In many cases, Black girls, to Kay's mind, knew better and were less willing to "conform" to what they viewed as arbitrary standards of dress that were unrelated to their hygiene or presentation. As someone who was "always clean, well-dressed," Kay was unclear what these white women administrators expected of Black girls, especially those like her who upheld respectability politics in their appearance and comportment. Echoing Debora's sentiments about the questionable treatment to which white women counselors subjected Black students, Kay learned to view such harassment as groundless because, as she explained, "my mom sent me to school in this outfit, and she thought it was okay."[112] Placing more value on her mother's expectations than she did on her white school counselor's, Kay moved through school unbothered.

The stigma attached to young motherhood for Black girls was shaped largely by the publicity of their pregnancy, and it only snowballed once their children were born. Some Black girls like Debora were able to hide their pregnancies, enabling them to forgo much of the humiliation suffered by others unable to do so. Despite gaining thirty-plus pounds, Debora kept her pregnancy a secret through a careful choreography.[113] This movement involved Debora planning her maneuvers and mapping her pathways to, through, and from school in ways that helped her veil her pregnancy, working to avoid certain individuals who might disclose her secret. A sense of dishonor still colored virtually all young Black mothers' sense of self, however, particularly once their children were born and it became public knowledge that they were mothers. Debora managed this sense of disgrace by seeking redemption: "Despite getting pregnant at sixteen and giving birth at seventeen . . . [and going] off track . . . [I] made it" by graduating on time.

Unable to conceal her pregnancy for reasons beyond her control, Wanda was banished to the new special school for pregnant girls, the one Debora was determined to circumvent. According to a local newspaper, "Waco recognized the need for pregnant girls' continued education and initiated the Prenatal Continuing Education (PCE) Program at the beginning of the 1970–1971 school year," making Wanda one of its first students.[114] As scholar Monica Stamm explains, "The treatment of pregnancy schools is likely a consequence of society's discomfort with pregnancy and females."[115] Disdain for Black single mothers who were ostensibly on welfare also motivated the effort to disappear pregnant Black girls from desegregated schools.[116] Alternative schools were created with the intention of preventing these students from dropping out and, in Waco specifically, building their sense of self-worth, but it was hard not to notice the racial disparities across the county in these schools' student populations. A local Waco article observed at the time that "African American and Latina teens are overrepresented in separate school placements."[117] Of the experience, Wanda remembered, "You were . . . shunned . . . it was like a taboo if you had a baby." The ostracization she faced aligns with scholarly observations of "a societal aversion to [the] image of the unwed pregnant girl" and a "universal fear of teenage female sexuality."[118] Graduating from high school, Wanda recalled, amplified her "self-esteem" and reassured her that the problem was not her but society's judgmental attitudes. Adamant that she "was going to get through this . . . we [she and her child] were going to be okay," Wanda actualized this very adage: that she and her child were, in fact, okay; some might argue they ended up better than okay.

Evidence suggests that rather than allowing the space to diminish or distort them, these Black Waco girls transformed the educational spaces they traversed. Employing a special "choreography . . . young Black women read their location in social contexts with consequences that may lead to shifts in those spaces, themselves, and the processes through which they are seen and assessed."[119] Making history in such a way, as these Black Waco girls illustrated, was no small feat. Although elitism, white supremacy, and patriarchy continued to pervade desegregating Waco schools, Black girls, buoyed by a wide variety of experiential knowledge, created avenues to subvert this matrix of domination.[120] Their maneuvers demonstrate that resistance comes in many different forms, loud and quiet. With audacity and tenacity, Black girls in Waco carved out room for themselves to exist within frameworks meant to exclude them. Recognizing that some Black girls had more favorable experiences than others, and that such was predicated on hegemonic ideals of femininity, it is undeniable that Black girls' mere existence in desegregated schools posed a threat to the prevailing social order. And what they accomplished in both high- and low-status roles was little short of extraordinary.

# 5

# Crafting the Care We Deserve

## UNITING, TRANSFERRING, AND (DIS)ENGAGING IN THE PURSUIT OF BLACK DIGNITY

*The Court speaks eloquently of the damage segregation does to Negro children's hearts and minds, but the equating of constitutional and educational harm without cognizance of the sources of that harm will worsen the plight of black children for decades to come. By its silent assumption that segregation is an obsolete artifact of a bygone age, the Court sets the stage not for compliance, but for levels of defiance that will prove the antithesis of the equal educational opportunity the petitioners'* [sic] *seek.*

DERRICK BELL, "DISSENTING," 2001

The year 1971 marked the first time Carol Haliburton, an eighth grader at South Junior High School, attended school with non-Black students, a shift that transformed her relationship to school. From this point forward, poverty suffused virtually all aspects of her life, including her parents' ability to be present in and active at her school.[1] Before 1971, however, one of the only places where her socioeconomic status felt less foreboding had been school. Reflecting on this difference, she noted that by high school in 1973, she had come to deeply miss "the closeness [she and her friends had] felt at the Black school. I didn't feel that at University [High School]." Accounting for these new issues and experiencing confrontations with racial animus took a grave physical toll on Carol. Confronting circumstances daily that "was so bad that it manifest in pain," Carol described how her mother, Jessie Mae, had to miss work, and therefore wages, to "tak[e] me back and forth to the doctor because I was having actual stomach pains, and it wasn't no [medical] explanation for it." Carol's physician made the connection between her school and her physical anguish: "It was my doctor that realized that I didn't like the school. He said, 'How are things going at school? You like your school?' And I said, 'No! I hate it!'"[2] Several decades earlier, Black school desegregation pioneers suffered a similar fate. Heman Marion Sweatt, one of the University of Texas's first Black students, had a corporeal response to racial trauma in the form of chronic stomach ulcers.[3] In South Carolina, Millicent Brown obeyed her parents' directive to refrain from retaliating to or retreating from white hostility in her newly desegregated school, a response that led to her hospitalization during her junior year.[4] Carol, with no other schooling options available to her, had to continue languishing in a hostile environment with little recourse, illustrating how such consequences continued to reverberate as racially mixed, yet white supremacist schools became the norm.

Carol's experiences link the physical toll school desegregation took on some Black students with issues around school discipline practices that were new to students. Her pain was likely the result of the ostensible oppression she suffered at the hands of white school administrators, who suspended her for three days for smoking in the bathroom with two white girl students.[5] These classmates had handed Carol the cigarette that administrators had caught her smoking, yet no evidence suggests the two received a comparable punishment—or any at all. As Carol observed, "We [Black students] got harder discipline than sometimes what they [white students] did . . . because of [our] race." This situation is one of many instances in which Black Waco students, like too many others across the country, faced disproportionate punishment for infractions committed regularly by students in general.[6] One

Waco ISD school board trustee, Robert Gilbert, fought hard to address this trend; his efforts, however, failed owing to the white supremacist majority on the school board.[7]

One high school administrator, however, showed Carol kindness and encouragement, illustrating the power of compassionate guidance in the midst of structural racism. Carol's counselor, a white man named Jay McCullough, intervened when, according to Carol, "I just got to the point where I didn't really care about going to school anymore." As her emotional state worsened and she began to, as she remembered, "act out and skip school, my counselor, Mr. McCullough, he was awesome. He was really awesome; he really was. He worked with me and encouraged me. . . . That man worked with me."[8] While wrestling with the psychological torment she faced each day, Carol benefited from McCullough's affirmation, though it ultimately failed to steer her back onto a path through high school to reach graduation.

Because University High as a whole showed little to no care for her, Carol had little reason to demonstrate anything other than disinterest in school. She explained that "I definitely had singing skills, but I wasn't in the choir, wasn't in the band. . . . I really wasn't in anything." Her experiences had sullied her perception of and relationship to education, which explained why she "definitely struggled . . . in high school and never wanted to go to college." These dynamics contributed to Carol being pushed out of high school before graduating.[9] Autonomously framing her relationship to education in such a way, Carol redefined what school meant to her by limiting the power a place that showed her little to no concern could wield over her in the future.

Carol's story illuminates how the communal ethic of care that had animated Black Southern communities during the Jim Crow era was significantly undermined by the implementation of school desegregation. It also illustrates the importance of support from school personnel (even if it was ultimately inadequate in Carol's case), particularly when that support represents the only reinforcement a Black student receives. Indeed, the wide-scale elimination of Black schools was a significant blow to the project of Black community building and the vital role of care in that process.[10] Carol's account illustrates why it is crucial to consider what many Black students lost with the disappearance of Black schools and how they responded to the removal of interpersonal care by crafting diverse strategies to meet their needs in their new schools. Historian Vanessa Siddle Walker defines interpersonal care as "the direct attention an individual gives to meet the psychological, sociological, and academic needs of another individual or individuals."[11] In seeking this care, Black students like Carol were attempting to fill a new gap in their schooling, given that the educational milieu into which they were placed was largely at odds with the one they had previously known in segregated Black schools. Because their new educational setting was no longer integrated into their life outside school or invested in the whole Black child, Black students had to find ways to compensate for this void. For Carol, this meant withdrawing from school because it refused to demonstrate meaningful, holistic care for her.

Carol's battle with chronic pain sheds light on what it meant for Black students to be forced from the educational home they knew and for them to subsequently negotiate, along with their caretakers, a new relationship to school writ large. Like too many other Black Southern students, Black Waco pupils' daily lives shifted dramatically with the elimination of segregated Black schools as they watched white schools carry on essentially as they had before.[12] When their expectations for care went unmet, this chapter contends, Black Waco students like Carol devised strategies to manifest the care they understood to be an integral part of the educative process. Disinterested in playing the victim role, they responded in ways that were remarkably self-conscious and autonomous—reactions that reflected the importance they had learned to place on communal care. Despite encountering new learning environments that made every effort to strip Black students and the Black community more broadly of their personhood, Black students worked to preserve their psyches—which for Carol meant disassociating largely from school. Critical race theorist Derrick Bell identifies such an act as crucial for the survival and well-being of racially oppressed groups like African Americans and as one that required them to renegotiate how they practiced, sought, and mirrored the care they felt across desegregated schools.[13]

## "WE MADE A CONSCIOUS DECISION THAT WE WERE GOING TO GET ALONG"

To re-create the key elements of the communal education at their former schools, Black Waco students changed the way they cared for one another. In doing so, they reoriented the racial dynamics of place at play in desegregating schools, dynamics that were rooted in Black students' growing concern for one another according to the Blackness they shared, an identity that was heightened in these new sites. This process, however, required conscious effort. Perhaps for the first time, many started to grasp the salience of their race and how, in this new racial context, it trumped any class divisions among them. Black Waco students felt increased pressure to rely more on themselves collectively to navigate the perils of antiBlackness at school. Like their contemporaries in Boston and Virginia who formed Black student unions in high schools, these expressions of self-reliance served to "fill the vacuum of caring Black educators and to deal with racist and discriminatory treatment by White teachers and administrators."[14] Turning to one another, they took matters into their own hands to construct a learning environment where they could be more fully themselves, more fully human.

Although the violence Black Southern students widely faced in this context was multifaceted, the deliberate actions of Black Waco students illuminate how Black students engaged in solidarity to challenge their stereotypical treatment and combat the pervasive racism, white supremacy, and antiBlackness they struggled against each day. Importantly, unifying across class status served as a safeguard against racial violence and repelled breakdowns in racial unity that white teachers or students, for instance, might try to exploit. This strategy provided them a level of social protection. Additionally, although their class differences were rather slight in comparison to those between them and white students, they grew increasingly aware of what their socioeconomic level meant in these new schools.[15] Determined not to let these relative disparities be the cause of their demise, several Black students intentionally strategized to survive in their new, racially adverse school settings.

As a student at Waco High School from 1967 to 1969 for his sophomore and junior years, Edwin James and his Black peers encountered white resistance for simply being Black and taking up space, motivating them to craft a plan to preserve their safety. This intentional expression of care for one another compensated for that which their new school failed to grant. The planning required for the maintenance of their safety was a delicate matter and necessitated a level of privacy that the school itself did not offer. Thus, with a deft understanding of the context in which they were now placed, Edwin noted, "we made a pact . . . away from school . . . at one of the classmates' houses." As a student from a working-class background, Edwin spoke to the way Black students undertook such tasks by minimizing their socioeconomic differences in these new schooling spaces, highlighting how they learned to racially unify themselves given the incredible stakes at their new school.[16] He explained, "We all made a plot with ourselves. Whatever we do, let [nothing bad happen to] one of us . . . at least [let's] be in numbers. And we tried to do that. Even going to the bathroom. If one [of us] was going . . . [another of us] would go. Because there had been a couple of instances where stuff like that had kicked off. And I said, 'Well, it may have happened then, but we ain't going to let it happen no more.'"

Black desegregating students were prudent to practice extreme caution as they moved about their schools. A decade earlier, Melba Pattillo Beals, one of the nine Black students who desegregated Central High School in Little Rock, Arkansas, was visiting the restroom alone when white girl students tried to set her on fire by trapping her inside a stall and dropping burning paper on her head.[17] After trading these harrowing accounts with one another, Black students weighed what they risked in traveling alone. Edwin recounted that "somebody [had] went to the bathroom by themselves, and he had got harmed . . . jumped on by a couple of them [white students]. And then [the white students] threatened [the Black student, saying] that if he said anything . . . something would happen to him and the rest of his friends." Edwin insisted that this occasion prompted Black students to travel in groups of "at least three to four. And if [the group was] not [able to go] in there [the bathroom, they vowed to stand] at least right at the door," to monitor movement in and out.

The agreement Edwin and his socioeconomically diverse peer group made was influenced by the media's representation of the wider civil rights struggle across the South. Edwin recalled specifically that "the person that did it [made the suggestion that Black students travel in groups], had seen more of this [white racial violence against Black people] on TV than we had. It wasn't too far [i.e., long] after that bombing of the girls in Mississippi, [or when] those three boys . . . come up missing . . . right around that area" in the state. The bombing Edwin refers to is the September 1963 tragedy in which Ku Klux Klan members planted bombs in the basement of Sixteenth Street Baptist Church, a regular meeting place for civil rights groups, in Birmingham, Alabama, killing four Black girls: Addie Mae Collins, Cynthia Morris Wesley, Denise McNair, and Carole Robertson.[18] Not much later, in June 1964, James Chaney, Michael Schwerner, and Andrew Goodman—a Black man and two white men, respectively—were tortured and murdered by KKK members in Mississippi for their open support of civil rights.[19] Knowledge of these pivotal civil rights events speaks to Black Waco students' sociocultural awareness and the legitimacy of their group preservation concerns. Having access to a television at home to learn about these events was one way that middle-class Black students could leverage their material privilege for the broader benefit of their race.

In the coming years, solidarity remained strong, as Black students remained vigilant about presenting a united front against antiBlackness in desegregated schools. Alongside their high school counterparts, Black students in higher education in the 1960s and 1970s were navigating many of the same dynamics, forming Black student associations on historically non-Black campuses to foster a sense of racial cohesion and belonging otherwise unavailable to them.[20] Connie Sadler and Willie Williams Jr. both attended Lake Air Junior High School during the mid-1970s, when their awareness of socioeconomic differences and Waco's racial geography grew to more precisely shape their daily lives, alongside Black collective care practices that evolved to assume new meaning.[21] Connie had lived in two different sections of the east part of the city that reflected the socioeconomic diversity of Waco's Black community: first in the Estella Maxey Place housing projects and then in a single-family home a few blocks away.[22] Willie also recognized the stark socioeconomic divide that typified East Waco, where his family owned a home in the Sharondale neighborhood. Connie emphasized that in her experience going to racially mixed schools, it did not "matter how dysfunctional we [were] or separate we [were] within ourselves [as a Black community]; I still [had] to rely on them [other Black students] because I [didn't] know these other [white] people" at school. She continued, "We were one cohesive unit. We were still bound by one common theme" of Blackness. Students somehow managed to achieve this unity despite a clearly delineated class hierarchy that was palpable to junior high students. As Willie noted, "[At] Lake Air . . . [it was] us, who lived in Sharondale," alongside the lower-wealth Black East Waco residents whose families did not own their homes. The latter group, according to Willie and Connie, viewed the former antagonistically, pushing middle-class Black students like Willie to believe that working-class "Blacks . . . thought we [middle-class African Americans] thought we were better than them." In 1974, this contentious terrain grew further complicated with the addition of "the dynamic of the white folks." According to Willie, "It got to the point where we [as Black students] were like, okay, now, these white folks don't like us . . . so at least we need to get along . . . and that was a conscious decision by teenagers at that time. That's 1974, [when] we made a conscious decision that we were going to get along." To this point, ultimately, Connie concluded, "we were still a neighborhood; we were still one."

Working through these class-based issues was no small feat for Black Waco students. Willie explained that "initially there were" tussles between Black students of different economic classes. He remembered working-class Black students calling him and his Black middle-class peers "Uncle Tom" and proclaiming, "Y'all think y'all know too much; y'all got more than we got." The use of the term "Uncle Tom," a pejorative indicating a Black person's extensive willingness to accommodate white interests while forsaking Black ones to uphold the racial status quo, spoke to the significance of class for working-class Black students.[23] "When they [Black students from low-income families] found out we were just regular folk," Willie continued, and that "our parents taught us to treat everybody right . . . finally they saw that we was all right." Connie explained that although "we separated ourselves [among ourselves], even within our community . . . we were still one cohesive unit. We were still bound by one common thread": racial unity. This shared identity gave Black Waco students assurance that they could depend on one another in foreign settings openly averse to African Americans. Despite these class-based tensions, Black Waco youth grew to see one another through a lens colored in overtly racial terms. This process took some time, but eventually they achieved a measure of Black racial harmony. It required African American students to view their race as their most outwardly salient feature.

These responses served as a way for Black students to reclaim control over their circumstances as the racialized other in a setting where Blackness represented alterity and whiteness ruled supreme.[24] Their words and actions reveal an incredible and mature sense of perception uncharacteristic of many adolescents. The immense responsibility that accompanied being Black in formerly non-Black desegregated schools required forethought and strategizing unnecessary in segregated Black schools. With only themselves to lean on, Black students of all class backgrounds acted in solidarity with one another—because they really were all they had. Such a strategy indicates Black students' efforts to redefine the terms on which they engaged in these new schools—efforts that illustrated their agency clearly.

A staple of many Black Southern communities was a "communal mission," which had undergirded many Black communities for centuries.[25] Black adults as well as Black children like Edwin, Connie, and Willie carried forward this care for one another in thoughtful ways that communicated a strong sense of collective concern for one another's welfare. W. E. B. Du Bois promoted the principle of communal education, observing that "segregation . . . created Negro communal environments in which the sustenance and advancement of the community was contingent on the participation of all members of the group."[26] The sited nature of this conceptualization of community was a critical part of this process, which, as Waco students spoke to, school desegregation compromised, because it removed the schools that educated Black students from Black neighborhoods and, therefore, decreased contact that students had with community elders. These changes manifested in African Americans' loss of control of Black schools, consigning the education of Black children to "bureaucracies outside the community—many of which were not sensitive to the needs of Negro children," pushing Waco's Black students to wrestle more independently with a different care context.[27]

In ways that were less based in students' scruples but were no less important, athletics also offered Black students of varying income levels opportunities to downplay their socioeconomic differences, which fostered racial unity while simultaneously facilitating wider interracial accord across a school. At Lake Air Junior High, Connie noticed that "it was through sport that . . . [we] c[a]me together in a roundabout way. Because our [Black] guys were wanting to play football, and they were good at it, and you wanted to see them excel, so you would rally behind them and wish them well and that helped . . . [us] congeal . . . and learn . . . [from] each other." Sports gave Black students a site through which they could be proud of their Blackness and focus collectively on the task at hand: beating the opposing team. Having this singular mindset gave them a chance to bridge class divides and play a leading role in the larger school community. "If the sports are doing fine," Willie explained, if "your people on your sports teams are getting along, then the high school itself starts to get along, and that's just a natural flow of things." Sociologists studying school desegregation uncovered similar findings, noting that "good schools had higher levels of student participation in extracurricular activities" where students of all races reported participating in "a social program . . . [that] buil[t] student loyalty to the school, provide[d] opportunities for interracial contact, and g[a]ve students opportunities to achieve personal success and establish feelings of personal worth."[28] Despite this ideal circumstance, in Mississippi schools, for instance, "Black students were frequently denied the opportunity to participate in extracurricular activities at the previously all-white schools," something that also occurred in Waco schools.[29] Hence, the racial solidarity that came to define Black Waco students' initiation into desegregated schools served as a crucial starting point for wider school unity.

## "I WON'T BE BACK": TRANSFERRING TO BLACKER SCHOOLS

Some Black Waco students sought out the care they had lost through school desegregation by turning to nominally desegregated but majority-Black schools that more fully humanized Black students. Such an overt act of Black spatial agency highlights Black students' savviness about the broader educational system they were navigating and their refusal to accept inhumane treatment: They applied a capitalistic, consumer-based lens that held white-majority desegregating schools to account and enabled the students to relocate as they saw fit. In many ways, by transferring schools and seeking their education elsewhere to better meet their needs, Black students denied white-dominated schools the power that they tried to wield over them. The irony is that in doing so, they exposed school desegregation's failure to eliminate racial imbalances in schools, a discrepancy that produced school districts like Waco's, where Black students were still concentrated in certain schools while sparsely populating others.

Ever perceptive, several Black Waco students seized on the opportunities this inconsistency presented, designing escape routes to school environments they saw as more conducive to their goals. To access these spaces, they sought both inter- and intra-district transfers, a tremendous undertaking for students in general but particularly for those who were underresourced and oppressed. Nevertheless, many Black Waco students navigated a cumbersome bureaucracy to escape the racial animus that defined their new school lives. Although the specific circumstances that pushed Black students out of white schools sometimes differed, they converged under machinations of antiBlackness that were both gendered and classed. This strategy highlights the students' shrewd problem-solving skills and determination to find educative spaces that would humanize them as Black persons and support them in reaching their goals. This dogged quest for care illuminates what was important to Black Waco students and underscores their savvy resistance and the autonomy they drew on to meet their needs.

With the 1960s ending, public expressions of Black culture grew in popularity across society, and these images were especially accessible to viewers like Edwin James, who tuned in to TV programs like *Soul Train*.[30] At that time, school desegregation was advancing, and more Black students were starting to attend historically non-Black Waco schools. These changes presented new issues for white schools, and many decided to fixate on Black hairstyles. In particular, historically non-Black schools explicitly prohibited the Afro, a popular Black hairstyle, discussed in chapters 3 and 4.

Among the students harassed for their Afros was Edwin, whom Waco High suspended temporarily and threatened to expel permanently. He, however, refused to succumb to the demands that Waco High placed on him and his family and remained determined to maintain this expression of Black culture, which he felt was a fundamental component of his personhood. Because Edwin was part of the class of 1970, he had a unique option for dealing with this issue that younger Black students in Waco lacked: applying for an inter-district transfer to a historically Black school. During his time in high school from 1967 to 1970, both G. W. Carver High School, which closed in 1970, just as the first issue of the Black culture magazine *Essence* was published, and A. J. Moore High School, which closed in 1971, was still in operation. Because A. J. Moore High was in Waco ISD, the same district as Waco High, Edwin assumed transferring there would prove more difficult than seeking an inter-district transfer to G. W. Carver High, which was in La Vega ISD.

Edwin was pointedly committed to keeping his Afro, given its salience to his Blackness. "I'm not cutting my hair," he said. After Waco High threatened his parents with what seemed to have been truancy charges, Edwin facilitated his own inter-district transfer to G. W. Carver High for the 1969–70 school year. He remembered that his grandmother Ms. Laura Mack lived on Preston Street in East Waco, which at the time fell within La Vega ISD. Like many Black children, Edwin was reared in a communal environment marked by robust support networks, through which he maintained a fluid residence status at both his parents' home and his grandmother's home.[31] He recollected, "When I went to Carver, I was on Preston. . . . I used Mama's [Ms. Laura Mack's] address" to go to Carver. This remedy kept his parents out of trouble and allowed Edwin to wear his Afro. Administrators at Waco High, Edwin explained, were displeased that he had, in their eyes, gamed the system, so they warned him that "you can't come back" to Waco High. In response, Edwin doubled down, declaring, "Well, I won't be back." And he didn't go back—an assertion of his agency. He graduated from Carver in 1970 as a member of what he did not know at the time would be the school's final graduating class.

As Edwin predicted, at Carver "there were no issue[s] on hair." As a segregated Black school, G. W. Carver represented a haven for many Black Waco students. The Black staff there cared about Black children and nurtured them in ways that were welcome and familiar to Edwin. In this effort to find the care white Waco schools refused to give Black students, Edwin subverted school desegregation's implementation in Waco. He transferred to and graduated from a Black school that let him proudly wear his Afro. At that school, he found refuge and understanding in an environment that embraced many aspects of Black culture and refused to dwell on cultural expressions that were disconnected from learning and academic achievement.

With the closing of G. W. Carver in 1970, students navigating a hostile racial climate in La Vega or Waco schools had fewer options to which they could turn for escape. Although Debora Wilkerson "had been at Waco High [her] sophomore and junior year," it never crossed her mind that she would graduate from another high school.[32] As she stated, "I just knew that was where I was going to graduate from." When, however, she found out she "was pregnant during the 1970 school year, moving into 1971," she did not disclose it, which allowed her to "continue to go to school into the end of the school year." Her goal was to evade "a requirement that you be removed from that regular school population and . . . required to attend the school that was specifically for pregnant girls." When her child was born in September 1971, she assumed she could "miss a week from school and go ahead and enroll back at Waco High." When she returned "around the first week in October . . . almost immediately . . . a week after my child's birth," Debora was met with hostility. During her meeting with the school counselor, Grace Hamilton, she was told that "because [she] had missed so many days from the start of the school year . . . [she] would not be able to enroll and graduate in time."[33] Debora remembered that "Ms. Hamilton was one of those counselors that . . . Black students wanted to avoid." Hamilton's demeanor and the barrage of questions she asked Debora seeking to uncover how she had successfully concealed her pregnancy conveyed to Debora that "she was angry," and "her sternness . . . let . . . me know that I wouldn't be going back to that school." Despite sharing that she "had gotten married" before "giv[ing] birth to [her] daughter," Debora still received the cold shoulder from Hamilton.

Debora was adamant that "it was important that I graduate," so she made provisions to do just that, despite this major roadblock. "It was just the self-motivation that . . . I wasn't going to stop" trying to find a way to graduate on time. Although she was devasted by the news Hamilton had given her, Debora gave herself little time to wallow in self-pity. She recalled that she immediately got "on the phone and call[ed] . . . another school to find out if what Ms. Hamilton had told me was the truth. . . . I did call Jefferson-Moore, and I did talk to a counselor there. And [they told me] I was able to go to Jefferson-Moore; [I] enroll[ed] and started school that next week." Because Debora was married, the transfer process "did not require that [she] have a legal guardian or my parent there. [She] went in to enroll [her] own self as the adult that [she] was."

Fueled by a relentless drive, Debora said, "I knew that there was another school that housed a majority of Black students compared to where I had been for the past two years, and that the majority of the teachers there were Black." The new Jefferson-Moore High was opening for the 1971–72 school year. Essentially, it assumed A. J. Moore's largely Black student body and a few other non-Black students, making its student body 87 percent Black during the 1972–73 school year.[34] It was in this environment Debora knew she could reach her goal of graduating in 1972. What she had lacked at Waco High in terms of interpersonal and institutional care, she gained at Jefferson-Moore. By returning to what she had known in Black segregated schools, she had her value affirmed as an intelligent, capable student who deserved compassion and assistance instead of judgment and castigation. In the spring of 1972, Debora graduated in Jefferson-Moore High's first graduating class with a husband in Vietnam and a nine-month-old baby girl.

Little changed for Black students the following year in the very same schools. As a member of the class of 1973, Wanda James had to navigate several chaotic schooling climates while migrating between La Vega ISD and Waco ISD. Ultimately, she transferred several times (once involuntarily) during high school, with her voluntary transfer a show of agency reflecting her determination to find a school home that humanized her. From 1969 to 1973, she attended five different high schools, beginning at G. W. Carver High in the wake of its abrupt closure and graduating from Jefferson-Moore in 1973, just as the National Black Feminist Organization was formed. Her route to that point, however, was anything but straight. "I found out I was pregnant at . . . La Vega," she remembered, a place marked by "so much prejudice" because "they [the white stakeholders] didn't want us [Black students] there."[35] This disdain was clear to Wanda, who witnessed "the parents . . . dis-enroll[ing] them [their children] because Blacks was coming. . . . They didn't want us to be mixed with them." This hostile racial climate, explored in chapter 2, made "anybody that could get out of La Vega d[o]" just that. Wanda was one of these students, and she transferred to Waco High in 1971. The transfer process was facilitated by her grandmother's recent move to a new apartment complex; raised in large part by her grandmother Ms. Laura Mack, Wanda recalled that "I used Mama's [her grandmother's] address because we were living in Parkside then, on North Ninth Street."

She was there for only a short time before the school targeted her for expulsion. "Waco High put me out because I was pregnant," Wanda explained. "As soon as I got in Waco High, they found out [about the pregnancy], and I had to transfer to the pregnant school." This news came as a shock to Wanda, who reported that administrators "told me I couldn't go to school there." Local newspapers, however, describe this pregnancy school as a new optional special education initiative, specifically "a voluntary, year-round program for pregnant girls, married and unmarried," that was funded in part by the Model Cities program.[36] Wanda's and Debora's stories bolster each other and help confirm the widespread practice of disappearing openly pregnant girls from schools, which was typical for Black girls and Latinas across the country for decades to come.[37] "I don't know how they found out . . . but I was taken out of class [one] day and told [to] go to the office, [where] I was told that I couldn't go to school there anymore. I was disenrolled," Wanda said. It remains a mystery to Wanda how administrators found out she was expecting, as she "never said anything, because I was too embarrassed, and I never know to this day how they found out." The cold manner in which Wanda's pregnancy was exposed without her permission exemplifies the paucity of care the school showed her, as well as what motivated her to autonomously seek care elsewhere.

After being forced out of Waco High, Wanda completed the Prenatal Continuing Education program and then gave birth to her daughter in early August in time to begin her junior year on time with her classmates. Reflecting on "the way that they did me"—that is, how poorly Waco High had treated her—Wanda said that "I was upset with them." The school's mishandling of her pregnancy gave her the ammunition she needed to decide she did not want to go back. She thus enrolled herself at Jefferson-Moore High in the fall of 1971. The following spring, Wanda married her child's father. She graduated in 1973 with the rest of her class. Although graduation was always her goal, Wanda expressed that it grew in importance to her "because I had a baby." She was adamant that "I wanted to do better, and I kn[e]w I could." So she did.

Her negative experiences at both La Vega High and Waco High pushed her to make the same decision that Debora made. The racial animus both these Black girls faced was unwarranted. While working through difficult and unexpected life circumstances that involved childbearing and marriage, they searched for and found a more humanizing learning environment that did not sabotage or derail their goal of graduating high school.

Unlike the circumstances Debora and other Black students found at Waco High, Black schoolteachers and administrators often extended warm invitations to caretakers and provided a stable environment of support that welcomed Black families to school, motivated African American student success, and created a "segregated school [that] attended to the deeper psychological and sociological needs of students."[38] Starkly absent from most Black Waco students' new schooling arrangement, these elements of Black segregated schools featured a communal vision of care and success that invited families' participation and fostered family advocacy and involvement, which evidence shows was more pronounced in Black segregated schools.[39] This link is corroborated by the robust historical evidence of Black parent-teacher associations, for example.[40] Such an environment fostered shared trust across Black communities like those in Waco and created situations where students' families could rest assured that school staff cared for their children as their own.[41] The "uniformity" that existed between school staff and the children's caretakers, that which school desegregation forced Black Waco children to seek elsewhere, "meant that the students received few conflicting messages about their value in the environment, a consistency which may be speculated to have been a powerful influence on their psychological well-being as they grew to maturity in a segregated society."[42] Negative messages, however, abounded in historically non-Black schools where school desegregation forced Black students to create new care routes to reach their goals.

## MIRRORING THE SCHOOL'S CARE: RECALIBRATING ENGAGEMENT

For many Black Waco students, the extent to which they engaged in their new schools reflected the level of care they felt from these spaces. This recalibration of care and the terms on which Black students autonomously decided how they would achieve that recalibration demonstrated their shrewd perception of the shifting terrain and the different stakes at desegregating schools. Classrooms, clubs, and teams became revealing sites of (un)belonging that indicated their worth in terms of racial and spatial production. Remaking these sites, Black students exposed the disingenuousness of many parts of the broader school desegregation project while working to disprove controlling images about them; this range of responses constitutes Black Waco students' sophisticated understanding of what their Blackness meant to them relative to what it meant to their new school community, and the degree to which the latter demonstrably cared for them.

Segregated Black schools had historically served as a reference point for these expectations. There, school personnel demonstrated repeatedly to Black students that they cared about them on a personal and academic level and prioritized their psychosocial and educational needs as inseparable from their intellectual development. In fact, personal care and academic care were often one and the same—because to care about a child was to care about their academic well-being. "For the students," notes education historian Siddle Walker, "the personal interactions they had with the staff were paramount in their memories of the school. . . . The principal and the teachers cared very much about them as individuals."[43] The staff of segregated Black schools were key figures of Black communities who in many cases shared a broader life with their students and families; these folks often attended the same churches that students and families attended, shopped at the same grocery stores, and sometimes even carpooled with them. They shared a common mission and investment in educating Black children and seeing them reach their highest potential.[44] Feminist scholar and literary critic bell hooks, who attended segregated Kentucky schools in the 1960s, provides this description of the educators in her community: "My teachers made sure they 'knew' us. They knew our parents, our economic status, where we worshipped, what our homes were like, and how we were treated in the family. I went to school at a historical moment where I was being taught by the same teachers who had taught my mother, her sisters, and brothers. My effort and ability to learn was always contextualized within the framework of generational family experience."[45] This dynamic made Black children believe they were important and worth loving. School employees engaged a communal ethic of care, frequently seeing and interacting with Black children to teach, encourage, and humanize them amid the unrelenting racial hostility they faced outside school walls.

When Black students were forced into newly desegregated, predominantly white schools, however, many quickly noticed a diminished ethos of care. When students proved unable to establish caring relationships with adults, they often disengaged from school because they lacked the interpersonal connections that make "students more willing to engage in learning."[46] While it may be tempting to consider this disengagement an instance of Black student failure and to contrast it to the academic success of Black students who were highly engaged in school, I view the former as an important illustration of Black students' agency in responding to the fact that their new school was failing to meet their socioemotional and psychological needs. There were occasional exceptions where school personnel established an interpersonal, caring relationship with a Black student whose caretakers were unable to maintain a high level of school involvement, but this situation often led to students engaging selectively rather than fully in school, usually because of the racism they confronted. Therefore, rather than rank these responses as good, bad, or otherwise, it is important to see each of these responses as a manifestation of Black Waco students' willingness to identify and respond to their psychosocial and emotional needs.

Black Waco students' relationship with the institution of schooling was, of course, complicated, but the role of an adult in the school lives of Black children mattered greatly. Although Black students were able to assert their agency and manifest the care they needed to get through school, they could not rely exclusively on themselves or their peers to navigate these new school settings. They needed adults for that. They needed adult support both in and out of school, because adults have capabilities and power that children lack. Often, this arrangement involved caring relationships with a staff member at school as well as a caretaker at home who was able to establish and maintain an active relationship with the school. By advocating for Black Waco students in ways that tracked with the nature of their engagement, these adults significantly influenced the way the students learned to perceive their desegregated schooling experiences.

Because caring relationships with school personnel were less common in newly desegregated schools, the caretakers of Black children were required to increase their school presence and involvement. There were various consequences of this inconsistency between school staff and Black families regarding a mutual objective of holistic care for Black children that emphasized their academic achievement. One was increased pressure on Black families to stand in the gap between school and home in a way that was not required in Black schools. In practice, this meant that Black families who were able to stand in the gap had to more closely monitor what was going on at their child's school; they had to involve themselves more directly and more often. Establishing and maintaining an active relationship with the school was a significant act of labor that required resources, such as time and transportation, unavailable to all Black families, especially those who were low income and working class. Situations where Black caretakers were well resourced and able to increase their school involvement often correlated with Black children already enjoying a high level of interpersonal care from staff members (though sometimes the relationship was paternalistic); these students were often highly engaged in their school. This point became painfully clear as school desegregation became the new reality in Waco in the 1970s.

### *"Education Meant Nothing. . . . It Was Survival Every Day"*

Connie Oliver's first experience with desegregation was during Waco's period of token desegregation in the late 1960s, when the district placed paltry numbers of Black students in white schools to nominally comply with federal laws.[47] Connie attended West Junior High, a school in north Waco, from which he and his family lived "just six blocks away."[48] The district selected him and six of his friends to desegregate this school, and unbeknownst to him, this was the district's attempt to circumvent the implementation of substantive racial integration in schools. In addition to him, this cast included Anslum Hudlin, Charles Alexander, Raymond Bible, Sammy Cooper, Alvin Cooper, and Timothy Echols. As the self-proclaimed "Magnificent Seven," Connie and his compadres took their new junior high by storm, learning much about "Anglos" and ethnic Mexican students and teachers.

As Connie transitioned from segregated A. J. Moore Junior High to West Junior High, and then on to Waco High, his appreciation for and interest in school generally waned. As he explained, "I lost interest [and went] from, at the all-Black school, [an] A–B honor roll student; when I got to West Junior [High, my] grades started going down. By the time I got to Waco High, I was just barely making it, just keeping my head above water because we were pushed [to excel] in the Black schools. [Teachers would say,] 'Hey, listen! You get out; you go to college; you gon' get your grades up; you [will] go to college! Make something of yourself!'" Connie's gradual decline in school indicated the pivotal role teachers play generally in the lives of students and, more specifically, their power to chart the course of Black students' academic destiny. The spirit of empowerment that had animated his Black teachers in his segregated school taught Connie to expect all teachers to play such roles. He quickly learned, however, that he was mistaken.

> I never got that from any of my teachers at Waco High. It was awful. . . . It was like . . . you do the lesson [but] it's no pushing you to become more than what you are. . . . The difference between the Black school and the white school [was so drastic]. . . . The teachers at Waco High [would say,] "Hey, we got a job to do." And I'm sure some of them had some sense of concern for us, but they couldn't even go [the extra mile] back in '69, '70. . . . And so, I lost a lot of interest in education.

The pointed contrast in the engagement of Connie's various teachers had significant consequences in his broader life. When his father died unexpectedly when Connie was in junior high in 1967, his mother, Anneva Oliver, was left to provide for him and his eight siblings with little support, because they had few family members living in the Waco area. Mrs. Oliver, who had her hands full raising nine children, now had to be the breadwinner as well, working as a domestic laborer for white families. Before his death, Connie's father had strived to make ends meet for his family of eleven by serving as a pastor "at little country churches." With less income, however, Mrs. Oliver now had to sustain the family by joining her earnings with Connie's older siblings' contributions, much like Calvin Jones's family did. Such a situation left Mrs. Oliver little opportunity to be involved in her children's school lives. Connie suspects that this confluence of factors drove him to pursue petty theft; he also had a growing sense of racial rebellion, which was motivated largely by the contemporary Black Power movement.[49] Although school had previously been a place where Connie was once an honor roll student, competed as an athlete, and won school talent shows performing songs by the chart-topping musical group the Temptations, desegregated school offered him no solace and did not serve as the positive outlet he needed. Once he started attending high school, however, school desegregation in Waco ISD had moved to implement more comprehensive student reassignments, heightening the contempt of white supremacist stakeholders. This context likely contributed even more to his disengagement and helps explain why he was engaged in junior high but not in high school.

Connie's story indicates the institutional, not individual, shortcomings of desegregated schools and the tragic yet common sense of unbelonging that Black students experienced in them.[50] Rather than falling in line and investing in a school culture that did not value him, Connie boldly disassociated from a place that refused to give him the care he deserved. This level of perception is commendable, especially for a Black student navigating so much turmoil.

Another member of the Magnificent Seven, Anslum Hudlin struggled at both West Junior High School and Waco High School. Anslum was raised by his grandmother Bessie Hudlin in a home they leased in north Waco. Ms. Hudlin, who worked as a domestic laborer for white Wacoans, did not own a vehicle, so she consistently leased homes either on or very near the public bus route. Like Connie, Anslum transitioned from A. J. Moore Junior High to West Junior High in 1966, attending the latter school during his eighth- and ninth-grade years. He was unable to recall who solicited his grandmother's permission for him to help desegregate that school or if her consent was solicited at all. Although he played sports throughout school, Anslum maintained a fraught relationship with schooling once he started attending racially mixed schools. Only during his senior year was he completely uninvolved, which he attributed to the school's use of corporal punishment and racist threats made by his white basketball coach, Jack Schrader.[51] In large part, his issues stemmed from the constant verbal and physical attacks he and his Black classmates suffered, and unfortunately they were not alone. In fact, Anslum recalled that his classmate Timothy Echols was the only one of the Magnificent Seven who was spared, and that was because his family transported him by car to and from school—allowing him to avoid the optimal times, apparently, to harass Black students. Given their compromised safety, they religiously traveled together in a group and, according to Connie, worked "[in their] first year" to "stick together" to whatever extent possible, much like Edwin and his friends. Believing there to be safety in numbers, the group, as Anslum recounted, readied themselves for battle each day: "After school [his white classmates spent] a lot more energy into making us dis-comfortable [on our way] home. It seemed like we were selected to have to have a street brawl every day. One of us would have to have a street brawl just to prove to them that they've had a battle, they've had a fight with a N[igger]. It was important to those little white kids to have fought an N, for some reason."

The school day failed to offer Black students increased safety. The anxiety and distrust these circumstances fomented in Anslum pushed him to disassociate largely from school. He felt he had no other choice or mental capacity to consider much else. As he recollected, "It was survival. It was survival every day. . . . You couldn't concentrate on nothing if you was constantly dodging something, or making sure nobody's creeping up behind you, or some prank going on." The school seemed to strategically disable Black students' ability to lean on one another in unity, a tactic on which other Black students like Connie Sadler and Willie Williams Jr. relied. Even during his ninth-grade year, when more Black students arrived, Anslum insisted, "It wasn't no more than one or two of us [Black students] at a time in any class." As in other desegregating schools, by precluding Black students from banding together, the school undermined, according to Anslum, "the security of [having] each other [close] during the school day at West Junior."[52]

Anslum's focus on survival prevented him from being able to do much else at school, as surviving required most if not all of his energy; like other Black students, the care and support provided to him at his Black segregated school, however, got him through one of the most difficult periods of his young life.[53] His final two years of junior high disrupted the strong relationship he had built with education in his previous schools. Anslum declared unequivocally that "education meant nothing for two years, for those two years right there," when he attended West Junior High for eighth and ninth grade from 1966 to 1968. Had it not been for his prior segregated education, he doubted whether he would have had the resolve to persist. "I'm thankful for my Barron Springs [Elementary School] education, because that's what carried me through junior high. That carried me," he said. "Never complain[ing] to [his] grandmother," Anslum was unwilling to bother her with his troubles. Her line of work and the lack of transportation available to her would have made it difficult for her to actively advocate for Anslum anyway. And without an adult in the school building to intervene on his behalf, Anslum merely went through the motions of school until he graduated in 1971 from Waco High.

### *"I Was Really Busy"*

Several Black Waco students felt cared for in many respects at their new school, motivating them to get involved in a variety of school activities. Describing themselves as outgoing, these particular students joined a number of clubs and sports teams, excelling academically by utilizing achievement and engagement as acts of resistance against their imposed subordination.[54] Striving to rearticulate the terms on which they would construct a sense of belonging in their new schools, these individuals sought to reclaim their agency by Blackening the racial makeup of highly visible groups and organizations in ways that required white actors to, wittingly or unwittingly, recognize them and the talents they brought to bear. Undergirded by interpersonal care from adults at both home and in school, these Black Waco students were often from middle-class homes with two caretakers and dual incomes, which afforded greater workplace flexibility that was conducive to school advocacy.

One of these hyperinvolved Black students was Richard Jenkins. Richard, a Waco High student, was reared in a Black middle-class neighborhood in East Waco, where his father designed the family's home. His experiences help illustrate the progression of students' racial consciousness as it interacted with their sociopolitical awareness in newly desegregated schools. Various curricular and extracurricular opportunities were sites through which he underscored his sense of self and broadcast his frustrations about racial relations. His account reifies the importance of addressing Black students' needs.

During his track season one year in high school, Richard and his teammates used a relay event as a platform to make a statement that clearly articulated their racial consciousness. Wanting to "do something [specific to the four of them]," they decided "to wear long black socks" as a symbol of their alignment with "the '68 Olympics" protest in Mexico City.[55] During the two-hundred-meter medal ceremony after winning first and third place, respectively, at the Olympics, African Americans Tommie Smith and John Carlos raised their black-gloved fists in a Black Power salute during "The Star-Spangled Banner." This international show of solidarity with human rights struggles has been analyzed by scholars as a pivotal moment in the Black Power movement and as one of the most overtly political moments in sports history.[56] The protest of Waco High athletes took place in 1970, the same year scholar-activist Angela Davis was arrested on federal kidnapping and murder charges. With their long black socks, Richard and his teammates sought to emulate the political message of those Olympic athletes, something specific to Black (male) athletes that showcased their racial awareness and the wide reach of Smith and Carlos's explicit stance against antiBlackness.

Richard's extracurricular activities gave him myriad opportunities to react to racial injustice, including in the school band. One of several Black members in the band, Richard found himself at odds with its white band director,

Richard Perot.[57] During his junior year, Richard struggled to "understand [why] . . . nobody was saying anything about" his band director "ha[ving] us play . . . 'Dixie.'" This song choice felt personal and incendiary to Richard. Examining the song's use in school band contexts, which often included the display of the Confederate flag, historian Derrick White argues that "the song 'Dixie' exemplified America's tortured racial history from the antebellum era through the 1960s, serving as the soundtrack to America's racism."[58] As was the case in other former Confederate states, the use of "Dixie" in Waco schools illustrates how this song in band settings represented a form of what sociologists at the time called "in-school discrimination."[59] Alongside its close cousin "Rebel," "Dixie" became "a white supremacist anthem," and both glorified enslavement.[60] "I'm a Good Ol' Rebel" was the full title of the song that was eventually shortened to "Rebel," and scholars describe it as expressing many white Southerners' angst and anger following the Civil War in which they "cl[u]ng to [their] identity as an unrepentant traitor who twists failed rebellion into victimhood."[61] Debuting in 1859, "Dixie" was originally titled, as White explains, "I Wish I Was in the Dixie's Land," and it quickly became a part of minstrel stage and musical performances nationwide. "During the Civil War, Reconstruction, and the subsequent reconciliation between the white North and the white South under Jim Crow segregation," according to White, "'Dixie' was transformed from a minstrel show ditty, to a white supremacist anthem. The Confederacy appropriated 'Dixie' as its national anthem and battle hymn."[62]

Richard knew this history and the song's firm place in white supremacy and thus felt compelled to challenge it. Richard

> ended up doing . . . a silent protest. Every time he [the band director] . . . called [out] the song ["Dixie"] . . . I would [silence my instrument and] . . . look at him straight in the eye. He'd look over . . . at me. Sometimes, he looked double back at me, and I'd still be looking at him, but it seemed like the harder we would look at each other, the harder he would start with his baton. . . . He was almost sweating . . . pumping his arms.

Richard's Black counterparts in Alabama similarly protested the Confederacy battle cry songs, either by walking out of or refusing to attend games where "Dixie" or "Rebel" were played.[63] This sweaty "firsthand introduction to face-to-face racism" exposed Richard's band director's attitude toward Black students and strengthened Richard's will to push back against white supremacy, even if he only did so silently.

Alongside band, football also demanded much of Richard's time, and in both activities he resisted white subjugation. Recruited by white coaches to join Waco High's football team, Richard was quickly disappointed with his team's performance during his first season in 1968, and he identified poor coaching as a primary reason for their ten-game losing streak. Their 0-and-10 record showed Richard that "we couldn't possibly have been a successful football team because we didn't have the kind of coaches that melded us together. We had the kind of coaches that sowed discord." Deciding that another silent protest was appropriate, Richard "didn't show up for a pep rally" before one of the team's games. After "there was no response the first time," Richard "did it again," missing another pep rally in an attempt to "try . . . to get their [the coaching staff's] attention." He aimed to express that he "wasn't comfortable losing and losing and losing and losing and sitting up at a pep rally where . . . all they [the students] want to do is get out of class," because "they don't care about Tigers . . . winning." Richard did care about whether his team won, so he engaged in absence as an act of resistance to show his coaches how much the game losses mattered to him, losses that he believed the coaching staff could have avoided had they tried harder to help their team address its racial tension.

Richard's turbulent relationship with the football coaching staff came to a head after Wayne Gardner, the head football coach and a white man, made a "very insulting comment" to Richard about his intelligence.[64] Richard recalled that "Coach Gardner had told me I was the smartest colored boy he ever coached," noting that Richard was "even smarter than Mike Tyler," a former Black player on the team who had been captain and played halfback. In addition to football, Mike, who had attended Waco High from 1966 to 1969 as one of the school's first Black students, also participated in numerous activities, including band, track, basketball, choir, and student government.[65] This microaggression enraged Richard, who went home and, as he recollected, "told my dad . . . [who] . . . didn't say another word to me. He just jumped up and grabbed his keys and went out the door." After "he stormed out" to visit the school, where the coaches were still watching film, "Coach Gardner watched his words and his tone after that." Richard had no further issues to report back to his father. This approach to conflict resolution was emblematic of how Richard's mother and father parented; both of them would "just go get things done. . . . They wouldn't say anything about it." Their only instruction to their children after handling a contentious situation was to "make sure you get up to that school and be on time to do what you're supposed to do." Setting himself as an example of this creed, Richard's father, without hesitation, showed up and advocated fiercely for his child, traveling by car in the evening to do so, a course of action facilitated by class privilege not available to all Black children.

In addition to his parents' advocacy, the favor that Richard enjoyed with the adults in the school building was aided, he explained, by his status "as an athlete"; he "didn't have any problems in the classroom." As he remembered, "I was pretty much a teacher's pet . . . [despite] most of the teachers [being] . . . women . . . [who] were all white." Because of his positive relationships with the teachers, he "didn't have any problem with them." This adult support within and outside the classroom positioned Richard to thrive in desegregated schools, to push back against oppression, and to develop into the racially conscious student he became.

Richard's heightened racial consciousness, however, came at a cost. His final two years of high school radicalized him, eventually making him bitter that Waco High was not a meritocracy. He reflected that "I was . . . bitter. . . . That's the main word you could say about me when I was leaving Waco to pursue my future." These feelings grew as Richard realized little by little that he was in many cases equally or "more capable than a lot of my so-called white counterparts, but that it didn't matter. No matter what, somehow, they were going to always slight my efforts." This stark realization cut Richard deep, showing him the extent to which society was engineered to undermine his best efforts and to privilege his less-deserving white peers. Richard's high level of involvement in school showed him this difficult lesson, one he carried with him throughout his life.

Charlotte Adams was a highly involved, high-achieving Black student, and her circumstances helped her cultivate a sense of care that motivated her in school. A 1973 graduate of Waco High School, she, like Richard, had voluntarily helped desegregate the school before the federal government forced Waco ISD to desegregate. Consistent with other Black Waco students, Charlotte recalled her time in segregated schools as positive and excellent, but her parents, Archie and Hattie Mae Adams, felt that better resources and opportunities awaited her at the formerly non-Black schools in the district.

Parental advocacy bolstered Charlotte's school participation. She came from a two-parent, dual-income home, and her parents held the kinds of jobs that allowed them to be active in their daughter's school life.[66] She noted that her dad, who was a caterer with a seventh-grade education, "was a good motivator," and his undereducation made him want better for his own four children.[67] As she explained, "My dad . . . had struggled so much in life [because of] not having a degree and working so hard, and he did not want his children to be like him. . . . Every day it was a conversation. 'What did you learn? What do you need help on? Do we need to go find you a tutor because we can't help you?' Because he . . . couldn't help us at home." Her mother, however, "went all the way" in school, and both parents "volunteered at the school. Whatever they had to do, they [made sure they] were there in the conference[s]. They didn't miss a conference. They were there to support [me]."

Charlotte's parents' visibility facilitated prompt and positive responses from Charlotte's white school administrators. To cite one example, Charlotte recalled how her father met with school administrators after they threatened to decrease the monetary amount of the home economics scholarship she had earned for college. Threatening to divide the scholarship up after Charlotte had been awarded (and rightfully earned) the full amount, the administrators reversed their decision after taking a meeting with Charlotte's father, who pointed out that their use of random metrics was nonsensical and unfair. This scholarship funded her first year of undergraduate study at East Texas State University.

Charlotte's sense of belonging to her new school—which directly affected her level of engagement—was strong and motivated by key school personnel, who expressed care for her in and outside school. Charlotte was actively involved in "several organizations, like Future Teachers of America [and] Future Homemakers of America," and "was involved in volleyball, so I was really busy."[68] The impetus for her being so engaged dated back to her time at G. L. Wiley, the segregated junior high school she attended in the late 1960s. During her final year there, Charlotte explained, a "Black lady counselor," Mrs. Yvonne Mooney, "sat down with me and started talking about clubs and things I should do" in high school. Mrs. Mooney was responsible for bringing to Charlotte and her family information about voluntarily attending Waco High, and Charlotte maintained a relationship with Mrs. Mooney throughout high school. Profound was the legacy of these hardworking, deeply compassionate Black educators.

Once Charlotte arrived at Waco High, the school paired her with a white faculty mentor, Mrs. Ruth Nolte, her home economics teacher.[69] As Charlotte and Nolte grew this connection, Nolte became an in-school resource for Charlotte. Eventually, out of fondness for Charlotte, Nolte invited her mentee to her home to visit with her children, who were roughly the same age as Charlotte. Perhaps drawn to Charlotte's middle-class, albeit Black, world view, Nolte also took Charlotte on outings around Waco, giving her unsolicited etiquette and decorum lessons. This vital mentorship gave Charlotte, who went on to be recognized as Waco High's sole "Who's Who" student in homemaking, a sense of significance that helped her rationalize having invested in her school in such as way.[70] Outside her relationship with Nolte, however, Charlotte kept her interactions with white teachers matter-of-fact by "just go[ing] to class, do[ing] the work . . . turn[ing] in my work, and mov[ing] on. . . . I just . . . did what they said to do. . . . I th[ought] I was just a number to them." Thus, amid her positive experiences, Charlotte remained perceptive and realistic about the realities of racism that animated Waco High and its school desegregation process.

For Russell Livingston, another highly involved Black student in Waco High's class of 1973, extracurricular engagement was such a high priority that he transferred from his advanced courses to regular-level courses to have more time to dedicate to his activities outside academics. As a National Honor Society member during his sophomore year, a Corrigan nominee his junior year, and a Key Club member his senior year—which was the same year he played on the school's basketball team and the student body elected him student government mayor and class president—Russell made his presence known across a variety of school activities.[71] He reported feeling valued by his school community, a sentiment bolstered by his parents, who—like many other Black Waco parents—instructed him to never treat anyone different because of their race. Russell's parents' economic and employment stability placed them squarely in the Black middle class. His mother, Lucille, was a teacher at Dripping Springs Elementary School and his father, Henry, worked at General Tire, a local business near East Waco, where most Black Wacoans were residentially concentrated as a result of housing covenants. Russell owed his socioeconomic security to their careers and also partly to the fact that he was their only child. His two-parent, two-income home helped make him relatable to many white stakeholders in his newly desegregated school; consequently, he accepted invitations to ski trips with white classmates' families and frequented their homes in white west Waco.

Russell's hyperinvolvement failed to leave him completely unscathed by antiBlackness, however. His racial skepticism led him to suspect foul play by the school's administration on multiple occasions. In one instance, Russell explained that when he had been elected both student government mayor and senior class president, "the counselor called me in and said that that was too many 'activity points.' . . . I had never heard about activity points until that happened. So I thought it was something they trumped up, you know, just to try and hold me down." School administrators showed Russell the policies dictating how many activity points students could accumulate and eventually allowed him to choose which of the two positions he wanted to take. That Russell assumed the school would try to sabotage his victory speaks to his awareness of antiBlack racism, which he viewed as something that existed on an individual basis, not a systemic one. A love for public speaking and a desire to give a speech at graduation, an honor reserved for the class president only, influenced Russell's decision to relinquish his post as student government mayor.

Separately, upon reflection, Russell recognized the disinterest—which he suggested was racially motivated—that white Waco High School administrators showed about his future: "When I got ready to go to college, no counselor ever talked to me about . . . going to college. No, not one. And it was just one of those things where in my household, it was like, 'Okay, that's the next step, you get [out] from high school, you go to college. That's the next step in life.'" It was the high academic standards Russell's parent held for him—expectations, he noted, aligned with the education he received at his segregated Black schools—that could be credited for his subsequent matriculation at and graduation from college, not the white school administrators entrusted with such an important task.

### *"They . . . Finally Got Tired . . . and . . . Let It Go"*

Some Black students' school engagement fell somewhere between being deeply involved and disassociating from school. What characterized the involvement of the students who occupied this middle range was their eager yet failed attempts to integrate themselves into the social fabric of their new schools. Although many of these students benefited from the support of an adult in this context, they also met structural obstacles that hindered their ability to feel a full sense of belonging in newly desegregated schools. The struggles of these students showcase their undying will to reclaim and create spaces never meant to hospitably host Black children.

Sarah Johnson's experience with desegregation occurred in 1973 during her eighth-grade year, when she switched from G. L. Wiley to Tennyson Junior High, a historically white school in west Waco. From that point forward, her time in school was marked by antiBlack sexist practices that, despite her best efforts and the support of her parents, precluded her from deeper school engagement. Up to this point, school band had played a meaningful part in Sarah's schooling experiences. But from seventh to eighth grade, she explained, she witnessed a shift in band directors that halted G. L. Wiley's practice of elevating Black music, a demonstration of care for Black culture constitutive of Black schools. Sarah remarked, "At first, [we had] our [Black] culture in band, and we played our kind of music. Once we integrated, we couldn't play that kind of music anymore." Sarah's mother, Mrs. Gladys Johnson, whose sustained support in her daughter's school life provided invaluable perspective on the implementation of school desegregation, expounded by noting that "everything was on the whites' culture. It wasn't on our culture."[72] This exclusionary act pushed Sarah "out of band" and reduced her "interest in band" altogether.

Targeting and punishing Black girls for their racial, gender, and—to some extent—class identities was tragically common. Gladys Johnson underscored that when her daughter was in high school, at Jefferson-Moore High School from 1975 to 1978, the school allowed only "one or two [Black girls to] ma[k]e the drill team" and allowed only "one or two Black cheerleaders. Anything that [required one] to wear short dresses, they [the participants] were just about all white." This pattern persisted despite Jefferson-Moore having a higher Black population than any other high school in Waco ISD. Largely excluded from quintessential school activities like drill team, cheerleading, and baton twirling, Black girls were prohibited from "wear[ing] short dresses" at school events, as Mrs. Johnson observed, because their physical features were associated with the Jezebel, or temptress, controlling image: the antithesis of white femininity, given that it threatened the prevailing social order.[73] Although some Black girls, like Rosalind Russell, were one of few to land a spot on Jefferson-Moore's drill team, they remained in the minority in this organization and in cheerleading—even at majority-Black desegregated schools in Waco through the end of the 1970s.[74] Even at different Waco schools, Black girls like Kay Williams, who graduated from Waco High in the early 1970s, and Beverly Rickford, who graduated from Richfield in the mid-1970s, confronted consistent assumptions about the innate impropriety of their bodies. For Kay, this meant facing unrelenting surveillance in which school counselors regularly measured her and other Black girls' skirts and dresses. For Beverly, this meant white personnel telling her in junior high that her figure was too physically developed for the cheerleading uniform.[75]

This marginalization motivated some Black students like Sarah to form their own organizations, a spatial practice that enhanced their sense of inclusion and through which they engineered the care for which they were searching. According to Mrs. Johnson, Sarah and her friends "form[ed] a pep squad, because they couldn't get into the drill team or be a majorette." "They [the pep squad] s[a]t in the seats," Sarah clarified, "at the game[s]." This attempt by excluded Black girls to reinsert themselves into the fabric of their school, however, was short-lived. Mrs. Johnson explained how the pep squad's elaborate hand cheers and corresponding chants were obscured because they had limited visibility at the games in the stands next to other Jefferson-Moore fans and were only fully visible to the opposing side. Their main competition, "the drill teams and the band" who were "out on the field" or on the court in the center of the sports arena, commanded the audience's focus. Although administrators gave official approval for the pep squad, Mrs. Johnson criticized them for failing to provide sustained support, which, according to her, led to the pep squad "finally g[e]t[ting] tired" and, Sarah interjected, "let[ting] it go." Mrs. Johnson clarified that the pep squad disbanded, explaining how this experience discouraged and disempowered Black girls from trying to create space for themselves more widely. As in many areas of desegregated schooling, in high school sports and related activities, Black girls were reminded of the generally low value schooling structures situated them within, a difficult lesson that pushed many Black girls like Sarah from participating in activities central to many US high school experiences. Mrs. Johnson's involvement in her daughter's school life, facilitated by their family's middle-class standing, inspired Sarah to establish community and create the pep squad, but to no avail. The relatively high number of Black teachers and administrators at Jefferson-Moore High School failed to make a notable difference in Sarah's school engagement, as she proved unable to recall one teacher from Tennyson or Jefferson-Moore who had a significantly positive impact on her.[76] Without an adult figure in the school to whom Sarah could turn for support, she struggled to find a sense of belonging in a place she felt never wanted her there from the start.

Attending racially mixed schools gave some Black students a new, racialized view of economic class dynamics. Like Sarah, Darrick Bledsoe first experienced desegregation in the 1970s in junior high at Tennyson, and he graduated from Jefferson-Moore in 1983 as part of its final graduating class. Growing up in South Terrace public housing, a place his new white classmates called "the projects" but where he felt he had all his immediate needs met, Darrick noted that "it wasn't until middle school [at Tennyson] that I found out I was poor."[77] He refuted this label, declaring, "I'm not poor; my mama can afford my clothes. I got different pairs of pants. I got a different shirt I can wear every day of the week, so I'm not poor." Admitting that "I had no idea what poor was until desegregation and the intermingling," Darrick saw firsthand the wide socioeconomic disparity between himself and his new white classmates, which showed him how class was racialized.

On the sports teams at Jefferson-Moore, Darrick navigated feelings of racial exclusion, an issue with special resonance for a Black boy. As a self-described "tall, lanky fellow" who, as Darrick explained, "could jump out the gym [and] had great hands, [he possessed] a lot of transferable skills from basketball," skills he hoped to employ as a football player during his junior year. However, the head football coach, a white man named Johnny Tusa, soon quashed Darrick's dreams.[78] Tusa, Darrick reported, "tells me, 'No . . . I don't need you.' And I'm like, 'How do you know you don't need me?' I really felt like that was a form of racism because . . . I was one of the fastest guys in school." Although Black football players made up the team's majority during the history of Jefferson-Moore High, Darrick still felt that race in some way explained why Tusa refused to give him an opportunity, and this feeling influenced his relationship to school going forward. Even though Darrick maturely approached Tusa for a conversation, "the door was just literally shut." This denial crushed Darrick, as it would crush any Black male eager to play sports. In a sense, he was another young "black male [who] . . . utilized sports as one means of masculine self-expression within an otherwise limited structure of opportunity."[79]

Adult support for Darrick ebbed and flowed, which led to a similar pattern in his school engagement. His only memory of his mother being able to ardently advocate for him was in elementary school, when they lived in New Orleans before moving to Texas. There, at Nelson Elementary School, Darrick's white teacher and a white administrator pushed to have him placed in special education classes because, as he recalled, they could not reconcile his high-level vocabulary with their stereotypical expectations of the low-achieving Black boy. The overrepresentation of Black children in special education has a long history that school desegregation arguably accelerated.[80] Thus, it was in the mentorship of a Black male teacher at Jefferson-Moore that Darrick found the care that he longed for. Mr. Elverna Williams Jr., his shop teacher, contextualized Darrick's rejection and discouraged him from blaming himself. "Kinda t[aking] to [him] as a surrogate father," Darrick established a connection with Mr. Williams after he, Darrick said, "told me he knew my folks and went to school with them."[81] Darrick said that Williams explained, "Tusa is kind of funny," and he went on to elaborate on some of Tusa's quirks. Serving as Darrick's confidant, Williams quenched Darrick's yearning during his adolescence for a strong male figure in his life, as Darrick returned to his mentor for various forms of advice and guidance that he felt he was unable to access elsewhere, especially in school.

Arguably, Williams's mentorship helped Darrick maintain some investment in school, even if it was not in athletics. Tusa's rejection of him, Darrick explained, "just kinda deflated me, and I think that further led to my anxieties about being in front of folk, talking in front of large groups or performing." The connection Williams and Darrick formed likely inspired Darrick to join the Industrial Arts Club his junior year, when Williams served as its staff sponsor.[82] Additionally, typing class was a place that offered Darrick an opportunity to excel and did not exacerbate his anxiety. There, he made it his personal mission to become one of the five fastest typists in the class. Motivated by a sense of competition, Darrick challenged himself to meet or surpass the typing speed of the white girls, whose names were consistently displayed publicly for typing the most words per minute. Eventually, he succeeded, and this victory gave him confidence in himself and his abilities; he felt that "I can do this." Darrick found a stage on which he could stand out in a new, complicated school context, and key to his small-scale victory was Williams's mentorship: Having someone to whom Darrick could relate, in whom he could confide, and by whom he could be affirmed helped him understand his social milieu and enabled him to more deftly navigate it.

Across a wide range of sites, Black Waco students defined for themselves the terms on which their relationship to their new schools would be based. Central to this deliberation was care, as it shaped Black students' motivation in and reaction to their new educational environment. The deeply contested nature of school desegregation as a political project provoked Black students to craft a distinct practice of Black spatial agency not required of them in segregated schools. Their bravery and self-determination knew few bounds and defined both space and place in multifaceted ways that enabled them to make meaning of their Blackness across various gender and class experiences. Thus, the different engagement practices of Black students reflect the diversity of experience that constituted their foray into school desegregation, which was underpinned and shaped by Blackness, gender, and class. Longing for the Black segregated schools that had made them, Black Waco students left few spaces unmarked by their influence, and the history of this city and its schools will forever bear their imprint. Across school clubs, counselors' offices, and sports teams, Black Waco students remade spaces that white power holders had historically designed to exclude them. Their will to do so speaks to their bravery, which they should not have had to marshal at such an age. Alas, this is a recurring theme in the history of Black struggle.

CONCLUSION

# We Survived It

## SITES OF STRIFE THAT DIDN'T BREAK US

*What he [the Negro] needs more than separate schools is a firm and unshakable belief that twelve million American Negroes have the inborn capacity to accomplish just as much as any nation of twelve million anywhere in the world ever accomplished, and that this is not because they are Negroes but because they are human.*

W. E. B. DU BOIS, "DOES THE NEGRO NEED SEPARATE SCHOOLS?," 1935

*The racist climate of many other Southern communities has stunted the growth of thousands of black children.*

BETSY FANCHER, *VOICES FROM THE SOUTH*, 1970

*The Court's long-overdue finding that Negroes are harmed by racial segregation is, regrettably, unaccompanied by an understanding of the economic, political, and psychological advantages whites gain because of that harm.*

DERRICK BELL, "DISSENTING," 2001

In Katherine Sanford's estimation, "desegregation was good, but it wasn't even." Speaking to how Black communities bore a disproportionate share of the burden required to desegregate schools, Katherine characterized the meaning of Blackness for much of this country's history, because Black people have rarely reaped the full harvest of so-called progress. Following national trends, school desegregation in Waco resulted in the closure of the local Black high schools, G. W. Carver in 1970 and A. J. Moore in 1971. Disappearing the legacy of these schools while leaving intact the historically non-Black schools created a set of circumstances where Waco's high schools, save the newly established Jefferson-Moore, repudiated nearly all expressions of Black culture. Although desegregation was thought to afford Black students the material benefits of a higher-quality education, the intangible benefits were scant in terms of what was lost—namely the compassion and self-determination characteristic of segregated Black schools. North Carolina historians have given us some of the most foundational insights into the importance Black communities have historically placed on Black education in both the segregated and desegregated era. In her poignant rebuke of discourses painting all segregated Black education as deficient, historian Vanessa Siddle Walker documents the care Black Waco students also learned to associate with schooling and thus longed for in historically non-Black schools.[1] Clearly, Black education was something worth fighting for, given the lengths the Black community that historian David Cecelski described went to in boycotting the closing of their school in the wake of school desegregation.[2] Such local histories illuminate how Black emplacement and Black place-making accentuated Black education as a distinctive endeavor that gave schooling deep meaning beyond the white gaze. Once circumstances changed, Black students' time in desegregating schools became punctuated by white supremacy and an acute awareness of the myth of meritocracy.

As the hundreds of scholarly and lay publications on school desegregation attest, these were common—dare I say ordinary—issues that few Southern school districts escaped, issues centered on race in a particular place that interacted with a host of other factors, including, for example, gender, white supremacy, class, and antiBlackness. Ultimately, this project raises and explores questions about how we might more generatively reflect on the implementation of this process, especially as it affected Black students. As a popular topic that has merited significant scholarly attention, it is worth asking what yet another study of this definitive and presumably well-understood chapter in US history stands to still teach us. This book provides a partial response. The ways Black Waco students navigated the implementation of desegregation demonstrates that race, that Blackness, played an outsize part and that race interacted with other social identities, namely gender and class, in deeply spatialized ways that indicated the complex confluence of these factors. Black Waco students teach us that they could never count on a white power structure to respect their humanity or prioritize their dignity. Their stories demonstrate that meaningful efforts to humanize Black children tend to unfold at the behest of Black initiative. They illustrate that even when doing so is well within their right, Black students have rarely if ever assumed victim status. In their recollections of their time in desegregated schools, Black students with different levels of racial consciousness made meaning of their experiences and of their Blackness in profoundly idiosyncratic ways. Finally, their stories reveal that extracurricular spaces provided new opportunities for Black expression and that regular people made history and warrant study.

School desegregation, fundamentally, was about how Black students disrupted status quo spatial arrangements that had long relegated Black bodies to separate and too often inferior spaces. While this implementation process was indeed shaped by Blackness, Blackness was further shaped by gendered and socioeconomic logics that ordered the lives of Waco's Black children. The everyday reality of a Black girl raised in a home with no indoor plumbing by her grandmother who was employed as a domestic laborer differed markedly from that of her Black boy counterpart whose parents were both employed, owned their home, and had college degrees. Both stories, nonetheless, are important. In total, their stories of survival augment a deeply incomplete and flawed written record that never intended to honor them. It is in this spirit that I wrote this book, so they could set the record straight about what they went through and what it meant to them. Doing so matters not only to the historical record but also, and perhaps more important, to their lives and sacrifice.

This book is needed because we don't yet have a historical account of the ways gender and class interacted with Blackness to shape the school desegregation experiences of Black students, particularly ordinary youth who would otherwise escape the annals of history. Top-down legal accounts of school desegregation predominate the literature, important perspectives that nonetheless sideline student experience.[3] While we have a sense of how white women and Black girls have contributed to this historic chapter in US history, our view of gender has yet to seriously consider this analytic outside girlhood or womanhood, leaving major questions unaddressed about Black masculinity or boyhood, notwithstanding how socioeconomic status further complicated these ontologies.[4] Additionally, we don't fully understand what this process entailed for Texas's Black precollegiate students. Texas matters just as every other place does that Black people have historically called home. The historiography of Texas school desegregation, however, will remain incomplete if its primary representations continue to spotlight top-down "omnipresent" renditions, higher education accounts, or those that center on Mexican-origin communities and teachers.[5] And the use of theory as an analytic continues to be a rather contentious matter for both historians and historians of education alike.[6] Departing from convention, this book offers a corrective, using the essential aid of theory as an analytic to argue that race alone is insufficient to fully grapple with school desegregation as an experiential enterprise. Analyses, taking a cue from the one I provide here, must also continue to consider the layered forms of social identity that affected the ways Black students navigated schools and the spatial consequences of their doing so. Last, to examine the implementation of school desegregation, that is, when school desegregation was no longer a voluntary matter but an obligatory one, is to do justice to the ongoing Black freedom struggle in which Black people sought an education in a setting that was largely disinterested in the very objective of Black education. This emphasis expands how we think about the process and enduring consequences of racial mixing in schools.

*Ordinary Sites* and the lessons it offers are much bigger than Waco, Texas, or its Black residents. This book directs the research community to look more closely and carefully at the dynamic social dimensions of taken-for-granted historical chapters we feel we already deeply understand. In particular, it instructs us to ask different questions about human experience, autonomy, and place. Bringing together these constructs stands to enhance the conversation and extant narrative about virtually any topic. The ordinariness of this account, its focus on common people in a common place, makes it relevant for and serviceable to a wide range of communities who have grappled with similar issues—in yet unknown ways that promise to nuance what we think we know about pivotal historical moments.

This narrative about an ordinary place furnishes special insight that extends and complicates the typical school desegregation story. Intending to investigate a place I thought I understood showed me the dubious ways white supremacy may shift in form but not in aim. At the same time, it showed me the creative ways Black peoples fight back to reclaim their humanity and dignity. When I started the research for this book, I assumed I would simply follow Black Waco students back in time through Waco ISD to trace how they went from attending segregated Black schools to desegregated ones; what I uncovered, however, was a far more dynamic set of events. Surprising—to me, at least—was that despite living within Waco city limits, a significant number of Waco's Black students had historically been part of an adjoining school district, La Vega ISD, an arrangement a federal representative from the Office for Civil Rights characterized as indeed odd.[7] To see how this white-dominated school district shut down a Black high school without properly informing its students or their families was not only shocking but grossly disappointing. This important communication detail nuances the historiography of school desegregation. And as much as one might on a conscious level accept the truism that seemingly unremarkable places have their own history, it can be uncanny to grapple with the historical events themselves when they are uncovered, as was the case when I learned that Black Waco students staged a protest—a walkout. This critical episode, however, underscored the sanctity of Black dignity and what regular Black folks were willing to risk in claiming it.

Articulating my rationale to study Waco for this project taught me that there is deep beauty and value in the Black ordinary—that everyday Black life matters and that regular Black people made history. Constructing a narrative that illuminates how seemingly unremarkable Black people made history disproves tacit notions—too often circulating in formal history curricula and classes—that history was something that happened elsewhere, in the big, important places where influential people lived. Conducting this study showed me the flaws in this line of thought and pushed me to dream of a future in which students, K–12 ones especially, engage with a history that represents them, not just in the racial, class, or gender identity of the historical characters they read about but also in the places about which they are asked to learn.

Black students were innovative, self-determining, and set on expressing their humanity and spatial legitimacy in ways that most often centered on race, on their Blackness. I remain convinced they stand as an undertapped resource for insight into the past, and their history, as they tell it, reveals that school desegregation had far from a linear narrative of progress. Given the tenuous nature of school life for many of them, it was important for Black students to maintain a dignified sense of self. Although gender's salience was apparent to me as the researcher intent on exploring it, it is telling that alumni rarely if ever admitted to its significance in their daily lives. Scholars have surmised that the dismissal of gender as an important part of Black baby boomers' identity was related to the racial struggle for justice their generation waged, a fight that pivoted on the metalanguage of race, which has, as historian Evelyn Higginbotham explains, a "totalizing effect in obscuring class and gender."[8]

Sitting at the feet of Black Waco elders taught me that much of the Black history we need resides in their memories, and these memories can only be harnessed if we take the time to conduct oral histories to capture them. This project makes clear that a high level of scrutiny is needed to examine the written record because it is littered with inaccuracies, conjectures, erasures, and distortions that in many cases diametrically oppose the firsthand experiences of African Americans. As one example from this narrative, local newspapers, perhaps at the instruction of Waco ISD spokespersons, described the Prenatal Continuing Education program as a voluntary schooling option for expecting high school mothers. This description countered the testimonies of pregnant Black high schoolers at the time, who were either forced from their home campuses or made to hide their pregnancies to evade temporary banishment. This is just one of the inconsistencies *Ordinary Sites* uncovered, and due diligence to expose and interrogate other instances of the same is critical, because the future of Black history stands in the balance.

The lessons from this book are manifold and resonant with many Black communities across the United States during this era. The story of Waco's Black students who desegregated their schools shows that racism—specifically antiBlackness—was multifaceted and enmeshed in the sited structures that educated students. This narrative also demonstrates how gender and class status interacted with Blackness to distinguish the experiences of Black students in the implementation process of this watershed policy. Retracing their experiences illuminated how spatial contestation was central to school desegregation, which intersected dynamically with the ubiquity of antiBlackness. In this way, both Black geographies and critical race theory clarified the enduring spatial expression of not just racism but antiBlack racism in particular. This oppression, however, failed to totally consume Black life, as Waco's Black students discovered and created ways to reclaim and remake their schooling lives after school desegregation sought to revoke them.

One of the bigger lessons this book grants is that, often, Black students chose life. They chose to live. Contending with the principle of social death in the afterlife of slavery that befell too many African Americans in and after enslavement, Black Waco's children elected to live lives of meaning and purpose.[9] These acts, however, looked very different from common assertions of life. They disassociated. They joined clubs. They leaned on teachers for support. They created alternative organizations. They defied authority. They graduated. They disproved naysayers. They survived.[10] This tenacious spirit lives on in many Black children today, and it behooves educational stakeholders to consider what conditions these students need for their school experience to be less one of resistance and strife and more so one of academic engagement and fortification.

As the 1970s gave rise to the 1980s, racially mixed schools, at least in the South, became the new normal; new yet familiar strategies emerged, however, relative to racial separation inside school walls. One of the most widespread examples was and is schools' use of tracking, which sorted students according to perceived academic ability; this grouping mechanism just so happened to mimic the racial segregation of an earlier era, only inside the same schools.[11] This time, students of different races often found themselves in racially homogeneous classrooms said to be based on academic ability. Akin to white Waco educators deeming a few Black, largely middle-class students "gifted" and inviting them to enroll in advanced courses while purportedly keeping such opportunities from others who failed to meet this proverbial threshold, tracking, as I have shown, has long, ugly roots. Another issue plaguing Black students around the country—one that received significant attention in the lives of Black Waco's students—is hair. Study after study demonstrates how attitudes about Black hair led to the creation of cultural pathologies that made way for the disproportionate discipline of Black children. These responses to one of the most recognizable markers that distinguishes Black hair—and Black people—from that of other races is representative of the wider discriminatory discipline trends in too many of today's schools. Some researchers have been able to link the rise in these disparities between Black and white students in particular back to the era of school desegregation, when they say this unique discipline gap began to emerge.[12] Since 1988, when school desegregation, according to expert Gary Orfield, reached its peak, Black students have found themselves in increasingly more racially homogeneous school settings.[13] Under the guise of reform, familiar efforts are driving this retrenchment. Today, neoliberal interests seeking to deregulate public schooling draw on capitalist, corporate accountability structures that undermine the academic achievement of Black students and many of their racially and ethnically marginalized counterparts.[14] Strikingly, this issue is most evident outside the South.

Cumulatively, these issues raise pressing questions about how Black children are treated inside the schools they attend and what their treatment says about how Black children of the past were often treated in segregated Black schools. Overwhelmingly, Black students today face a schooling reality that notably differentiates their experiences from those of Black students who attended segregated Black schools for their entire education. The compassionate environments that promoted academic excellence and marked segregated

Black schools of the past are now, in many cases, missing the Black educators that once animated them. This is one of the many vestiges of school desegregation with which we as a country continue to grapple. Since the dissolution of Black schools, few researchers have been able to show that Black students in schools today articulate the prominent sense of belonging or affirmation that was characteristic of Black students educated in segregated Black schools. This disparity begs the pressing question of how Black students' holistic well-being was prioritized in the school desegregation process.

These persistent matters indicate that rearranging differently racialized bodies in and between schools is insufficient for remedying the racial injustice that proliferates both within and outside school walls. One of the grave missteps, I argue, in taking a primarily legal approach to desegregating schools was that issues of power were left in the balance. Without economic, political, or social power, change, even on a policy or legal level, means little. As just one example, the battle that Waco's first Black school board trustees waged reveals as much.[15] Thus, future endeavors to meaningfully improve the educational plight of Black children might do well to consider how not only bodies but also power can be redistributed in a way that bolsters racial justice and looks to eradicate antiBlackness.

We cannot, therefore, assume the past is no longer with us, that it is no longer informing our present and future. To do so would constitute ahistoricism. Back in 1935, W. E. B. Du Bois told us that to ask whether Black children needed separate schools was an unproductive way to frame the issue. He implored us to remember that what they needed, in whatever racial context and in whichever place, was to be humanized and to be taught that Black people are capable, are intelligent, and matter.[16] The educational story of Black Waco's children relays much the same message. For all the resisting they did, it is imperative to remember that they should not have had to. Thus, this book stands not only as a reminder of their strength and will to live but also as a critique of the circumstances in which school desegregation placed them. This emplacement necessitated that they fight back in a variety of ways that hinged largely on their social position as differently gendered and classed Black students in the spatially contested terrain of historically non-Black schools. Their account of this history should compel us to continue the fight to create the schools they always deserved to attend.

# APPENDIX: ORAL HISTORY INTERVIEWS

All interviews were conducted by the author, unless otherwise noted, between 2018 and 2023 in either Waco, Texas, or Champaign, Illinois, via phone or video call. Recordings are in the author's possession.

* *Indicates multiple interviews*
^ *Indicates pseudonym (which required anonymizing identifying details in the text)*

Adams, Charlotte
Baldwin, Marshall, interview by Sean Sutcliffe, transcript housed at Baylor University Institute for Oral History, Waco, Texas
Bass, Michael
Bledsoe, Darrick
Brown, Willie
Haliburton, Carol
Hudlin, Anslum
James, Edwin Earl
*James, Pamela
*James, Wanda
^Jenkins, Richard
^Johnson, Gladys
^Johnson, Sarah
Jones, Calvin
Livingston, Russell
Mosley, Jacqueline Elaine
Oliver, Connie
^Rickford, Beverly
Russell, Rosalind

Sadler, Constance
^Sanford, Katherine
*Wilkerson, Debora
Williams, Kay Cheryl
Williams, Willie, Jr.

# NOTES

## ABBREVIATIONS

**LVISD Trustees** La Vega Independent School District Board of Trustees, Board of Trustees Records, La Vega Independent School District, Bellmead, Texas
**WISD Trustees** Waco Independent School District Board of Trustees, Board of Trustees Records, Waco Independent School District, Waco, Texas

## INTRODUCTION

1. In 1875, Alexander James Moore and his wife Mary Moore started teaching groups of students from their home, and in 1881 they opened their first school building.

2. Renee Tweedle, "Appeal Readied for School Board," *Waco Times-Tribune*, September 3, 1970, 34.

3. Renee Tweedle, "Pressure on Board for Name Decision," *Waco Times-Tribune*, November 4, 1970, 25.

4. "Students Will Appeal Name of School Today," *Waco News-Tribune*, December 17, 1970, 43; "Students Will Present Appeal to Board Here," *Waco Times-Tribune*, December 16, 1970, 39.

5. Tweedle, "Pressure on Board," 25.

6. "Students Will Present Appeal," 39.

7. Tweedle, "Appeal Readied," 34.

8. Minutes, October 13, 1970, "Naming New High Schools" section under Superintendent's Reports and Recommendations, WISD Trustees.

9. Tweedle, "Pressure on Board," 25.

10. Curtis Lee Wilburn, interview by James M. SoRelle and Bettie Beard, August 15, 1985, 151, 153, transcript, Institute for Oral History, Baylor University, Waco, Texas, https://digitalcollections-baylor.quartexcollections.com/documents/detail/1718819.

11. "Students Will Present Appeal," 39.

12. "No Name Change for Jefferson-Moore," *Waco Citizen*, December 24, 1970, 5.

13. Renee Tweedle, "Final Goodbyes at Two Schools," *Waco Times-Herald*, June 3, 1971, 6.

14. Derrick Bell, "Racial Realism," *Connecticut Law Review* 24, no. 2 (1992): 363–79.

15. Charise L. Cheney, *Blacks Against Brown: The Intra-Racial Struggle over Segregated Schools in Topeka, Kansas* (Chapel Hill: University of North Carolina Press, 2024).

16. *The Lion*, yearbook, 1969, 44, A. J. Moore High School, Waco, Texas.

17. Alessandro Portelli, *The Death of Luigi Trastulli: Form and Meaning in Oral History* (Albany: State University of New York Press, 1991).

18. Jordan P. Brasher, Derek H. Alderman, and Joshua Inwood, "Applying Critical Race and Memory Studies to University Place Naming Controversies: Toward a Responsible Landscape Policy," *Papers in Applied Geography* 3, no. 3–4 (2017): 292–307; Karen Till, "Wounded Cities: Memory-Work and a Place-Based Ethics of Care," *Political Geography* 31, no. 1 (2012): 3–14.

19. On the limitations of the written archive for Black history, see Saidiya Hartman, *Wayward Lives, Beautiful Experiments: Intimate Histories of Riotous Black Girls, Troublesome Women, and Queer Radicals* (New York: W. W. Norton, 2020); and Marisa J. Fuentes, *Dispossessed Lives: Enslaved Women, Violence, and the Archive* (Philadelphia: University of Pennsylvania Press, 2016).

20. Vanessa Siddle Walker, *Their Highest Potential: An African American School Community in the Segregated South* (Chapel Hill: University of North Carolina Press, 1996); Michael Fultz, "African American Teachers in the South, 1890–1940: Powerlessness and the Ironies of Expectations and Protest," *History of Education Quarterly* 35, no. 4 (1995): 401–22; Michael Fultz, "The Displacement of Black Educators Post-*Brown*: An Overview and Analysis," *History of Education Quarterly* 44, no. 1 (2004): 11–45.

21. Rachel Devlin, *A Girl Stands at the Door: The Generation of Young Women Who Desegregated America's Schools* (New York: Basic Books, 2018); Karen Anderson, *Little Rock: Race and Resistance at Central High School* (Princeton, NJ: Princeton University Press, 2010).

22. Richard Kluger, *Simple Justice: The History of Brown v. Board of Education and Black America's Struggle for Equality* (New York: Vintage Books, 1976); Mark V. Tushnet, *The NAACP's Legal Strategy Against Segregated Education, 1925–1950* (Chapel Hill: University of North Carolina Press, 1987); James T. Patterson, *Brown v. Board of Education: A Civil Rights Milestone and Its Troubled Legacy* (New York: Oxford University Press, 2001); J. Harvie Wilkinson III, *From Brown to Bakke: The Supreme Court and School Integration; 1954–1978* (New York: Oxford University Press, 1979).

23. Leslie T. Fenwick, *Jim Crow's Pink Slip: The Untold Story of Black Principal and Teacher Leadership* (Cambridge, MA: Harvard Education, 2022); David. S. Cecelski, *Along Freedom Road: Hyde County, North Carolina, and the Fate of Black Schools in the South* (Chapel Hill: University of North Carolina Press, 1994); Anna Victoria Wilson and William E. Segall, *Oh, Do I Remember! Experiences of Teachers During the Desegregation of Austin's Schools, 1964–1971* (Albany: State University of New York Press, 2001).

24. For Texas higher education examples, see Merline Pitre, *Born to Serve: A History of Texas Southern University* (Norman: University of Oklahoma Press, 2018); Dwonna Naomi Goldstone, *Integrating the 40 Acres: The Fifty-Year Struggle for Racial Equality at the University of Texas* (Athens: University of Georgia Press, 2006); and Amilcar Shabazz, *Advancing Democracy: African Americans and the Struggle for Access and Equity in Higher Education in Texas* (Chapel Hill: University of North Carolina Press, 2004). For elite private schools, see Michelle Purdy, *Transforming the Elite: Black Students and the Desegregation of Private Schools* (Chapel Hill: University of North Carolina Press, 2018).

25. Gary Orfield and Chungmei Lee, *Historic Reversals, Accelerating Resegregation, and the Need for New Integration Strategies* (Los Angeles: Civil Rights Project / Proyecto Derechos Civiles, 2007). See also Gary Orfield, *The Reconstruction of Southern Education: The Schools and the 1964 Civil Rights Act* (New York: John Wiley and Sons, 1969).

26. Charles C. Bolton, *The Hardest Deal of All: The Battle over School Integration in Mississippi, 1870–1980* (Oxford: University Press of Mississippi, 2005); Scott Baker, *Paradoxes of Desegregation: African American Struggles for Educational Equity in Charleston, South Carolina, 1926–1972* (Columbia: University of South Carolina Press, 2006); Purdy, *Transforming the Elite*; Vincent D. Willis, *Audacious Agitation: The Uncompromising Commitment of Black Youth to Equal Education after Brown* (Athens: University of Georgia Press, 2021); Davison M. Douglas, *Reading, Writing, and Race: The Desegregation of the Charlotte Schools* (Chapel Hill: University of North Carolina Press, 1995).

27. Douglas, *Reading, Writing, and Race*; Tracy E. K'Meyer, *From Brown to Meredith: The Long Struggle for School Desegregation in Louisville* (Chapel Hill: University of North Carolina Press, 2013); Ansley Erickson, *Making the Unequal Metropolis: School Desegregation and Its Limits* (Chicago: University of Chicago Press, 2016); Purdy, *Transforming the Elite*; Dionne Danns, *Something Better for Our Children: Black Organizing in Chicago Public Schools, 1963–1971* (New York: Routledge, 2003); Dionne Danns, *Desegregating Chicago's Public Schools: Policy Implementation, Politics, and Protest, 1965–1985* (New York: Palgrave Macmillan, 2014); Dionne Danns, *Crossing Segregated Boundaries: Remembering Chicago School Desegregation* (New Brunswick, NJ: Rutgers University Press, 2020); Jack Dougherty, *More Than One Struggle: The Evolution of Black School Reform in Milwaukee* (Chapel Hill: University of North Carolina Press, 2004); Davison M. Douglas, *Jim Crow Moves North: The Battle over Northern School Segregation, 1865–1954* (New York: Cambridge University Press, 2005); Guadalupe San Miguel, *Brown, Not White: School Integration and the Chicano Movement in Houston* (College Station: Texas A&M University Press, 2005); William Henry Kellar, *Make Haste Slowly: Moderates, Conservatives, and School Desegregation in Houston* (College Station: Texas A&M University Press, 1999); David G. García, *Strategies of Segregation: Race, Residence, and the Struggle for Educational Equality* (Berkeley: University of California Press, 2018).

28. Virginia, albeit significant, is one of the best examples. See Brian J. Daugherity, *Keep on Keeping On: The NAACP and the Implementation of Brown v. Board of Education in Virginia* (Charlottesville: University of Virginia Press, 2016); Jill Ogline Titus, *Brown's Battleground: Students, Segregationists, and the Struggle for Justice in Prince Edward County, Virginia* (Chapel Hill: University of North Carolina Press, 2011); Christopher Bonastia, *Southern Stalemate: Five Years Without Public Education in Prince Edward County, Virginia* (Chicago: University of Chicago Press, 2012); Robert A. Pratt, *The Color of Their Skin: Education and Race in Richmond, Virginia, 1954–89* (Charlottesville: University Press of Virginia, 1992); Matthew D. Lassiter and Andrew B. Lewis, eds., *The Moderates' Dilemma: Massive Resistance to School Desegregation in Virginia* (Charlottesville: University of Virginia Press, 1998); and Jeffrey L. Littlejohn and Charles H. Ford, *Elusive Equality: Desegregation and Resegregation in Norfolk's Public Schools* (Charlottesville: University of Virginia Press, 2012).

29. Cecelski, *Along Freedom Road*.

30. Wilson and Segall, *Oh, Do I Remember!*; Kellar, *Make Haste Slowly*; San Miguel, *Brown, Not White*; Glenn M. Linden, *Desegregating Schools in Dallas: Four Decades in the Federal Courts* (Dallas, TX: Three Forks, 1995); Robyn Duff Ladino, *Desegregating Texas*

*Schools: Eisenhower, Shivers, and the Crisis at Mansfield High* (Austin: University of Texas Press, 1996); Shabazz, *Advancing Democracy*; Goldstone, *Integrating the 40 Acres*; Pitre, *Born to Serve*.

31. See, e.g., Brett Gadsden, *Between North and South: Delaware, Desegregation, and the Myth of American Sectionalism* (Philadelphia: University of Pennsylvania Press, 2012).

32. Deirdre M. Dougherty, "Urban Redevelopment, School Closure, and the Abstract Space of Black Schooling in Prince George's County, Maryland, 1968–1972," *Journal of Urban History* 46, no. 5 (2020): 1117–41; Darius Scott, "Oral History and Emplacement in 'Nowhere at All': The Role of Personal and Family Narratives in Rural Black Community-Building," *Social and Cultural Geography* 20, no. 8 (2019): 1094–113; Walter C. Stern, "'We Got to Fight for What We Want': Black School Rebellions in Louisiana, 1965–1974," *Teachers College Record* 125, no. 3 (2023): 319–49.

33. García, *Strategies of Segregation*; James B. Barrera, *"We Want Better Education!": The 1960s Chicano Student Movement, School Walkouts, and the Quest for Educational Reform in South Texas* (College Station: Texas A&M University Press, 2023); Jesús Jesse Esparza, *Raza Schools: The Fight for Latino Educational Autonomy in a West Texas Borderlands Town* (Norman: University of Oklahoma Press, 2023).

34. ArCasia D. James-Gallaway, "Under a Black Light: Implications of Mexican American School Segregation Challenges for African Americans in Texas," *Teachers College Record* 124, no. 12 (2022): 220–51.

35. Derrick Bell, "Serving Two Masters: Integration Ideals and Client Interests in School Desegregation Litigation," *Yale Law Journal* 85, no. 4 (1976): 470–516. See also Derrick Bell, *Ethical Ambition: Living a Life of Meaning and Worth* (New York: Bloomsbury, 2003); and Derrick Bell, *Silent Covenants: Brown v. Board of Education and the Unfulfilled Hopes for Racial Reform* (New York: Oxford University Press, 2004).

36. Gloria Ladson-Billings and William F. Tate, "Toward a Critical Race Theory of Education," *Teachers College Record* 97, no. 1 (1995): 47–68; Adrienne D. Dixson and Celia K. Rousseau, eds., *Critical Race Theory in Education: All God's Children Got a Song* (New York: Routledge, 2006).

37. Bell, "Racial Realism."

38. Mari Matsuda, "Looking to the Bottom: Critical Legal Studies and Reparations," *Harvard Civil Rights–Civil Liberties Law Review* 22, no. 2 (1987): 323–99.

39. Richard Delgado, "Storytelling for Oppositionists and Others: A Plea for Narrative," *Michigan Law Review* 87, no. 8 (1989): 2411–41; Derrick Bell, "The Power of Narrative," *Legal Studies Forum* 23, no. 3 (1999): 315–48; Derrick Bell, *Faces at the Bottom of the Well: The Permanence of Racism* (New York: Basic Books, 1992).

40. Cheryl I. Harris, "Whiteness as Property," *Harvard Law Review* 106, no. 8 (1993): 1707–91.

41. Katherine McKittrick and Clyde Woods, eds., *Black Geographies and the Politics of Place* (Cambridge, MA: South End, 2007); Katherine McKittrick, *Demonic Grounds: Black Women and the Cartographies of Struggle* (Minneapolis: University of Minnesota Press, 2006); Ruth Wilson Gilmore, *Golden Gulag: Prisons, Surplus, Crisis, and Opposition in Globalizing California* (Berkeley: University of California Press, 2007); Clyde Woods, *Development Arrested: The Blues and Plantation Power in the Mississippi Delta* (London: Verso, 2000).

42. Frank B. Wilderson, *Afropessimism* (New York: W. W. Norton, 2020); Jared Sexton, "Afro-Pessimism: The Unclear Word," *Rhizomes*, no. 29 (2016), www.rhizomes.net/issue29/sexton.html.

43. Katherine McKittrick, "On Plantations, Prisons, and a Black Sense of Place," *Social and Cultural Geography* 12, no. 8 (2011): 950.

44. McKittrick, "On Plantations," 949.

45. James-Gallaway, "Under a Black Light," 222.

46. See Scott Nakagawa, "Blackness Is the Fulcrum," *Race Files*, May 4, 2012, www.racefiles.com/2012/05/04/blackness-is-the-fulcrum; and Alicia Garza's remarks in Keeanga-Yamahtta Taylor, ed., *How We Get Free: Black Feminism and the Combahee River Collective* (Chicago: Haymarket Books, 2017), 163–64.

47. Kimberlé Crenshaw, "Mapping the Margins: Intersectionality, Identity Politics, and Violence Against Women of Color," *Stanford Law Review* 43, no. 6 (1991): 1241–99; Kimberlé Crenshaw, "Demarginalizing the Intersection of Race and Sex: A Black Feminist Critique of Antidiscrimination Doctrine, Feminist Theory and Antiracist Politics," *University of Chicago Legal Forum*, 1989, no. 8 (1989): 139–67.

48. Matthew D. Lassiter and Joseph Crespino, eds., *The Myth of Southern Exceptionalism* (New York: Oxford University Press, 2009); Hartman, *Wayward Lives, Beautiful Experiments*; Danns, *Desegregating Chicago's Public Schools*; Danns, *Something Better*; Jack Dougherty, *More Than One Struggle*; Gregory S. Jacobs, *Getting Around Brown: Desegregation, Development, and the Columbus Public Schools* (Columbus: Ohio State University Press, 1998).

49. James D. Anderson, "A Tale of Two *Browns*: Constitutional Equality and Unequal Education," *Yearbook of the National Society for the Study of Education* 105, no. 2 (2006): 14–35.

50. Ronald P. Formisano, *Boston Against Busing: Race, Class, and Ethnicity in the 1960s and 1970s* (Chapel Hill: University of North Carolina Press, 1991).

51. Neil Foley, *Quest for Equality: The Failed Promise of Black-Brown Solidarity* (Cambridge, MA: Harvard University Press, 2010), 118–19.

52. Toni Morrison, *Playing in the Dark: Whiteness and the Literary Imagination* (Cambridge, MA: Harvard University Press, 1992); Bell, *Faces at the Bottom*; James-Gallaway, "Under a Black Light."

53. Wilma King, *Stolen Childhood: Slave Youth in Nineteenth-Century America* (Bloomington: Indiana University Press, 1995).

54. Cecelski, *Along Freedom Road.*

## CHAPTER 1

1. Rachel Devlin, *A Girl Stands at the Door: The Generation of Young Women Who Desegregated America's Schools* (New York: Basic Books, 2018).

2. Debora Wilkerson, in discussion with the author, February 2018. All references in this chapter to Debora Wilkerson's oral history interview are from this discussion.

3. Patricia Bernstein, *The First Waco Horror: The Lynching of Jesse Washington and the Rise of the NAACP* (College Station: Texas A&M University Press, 2006); William Carrigan, *The Making of a Lynching Culture: Violence and Vigilantism in Central Texas, 1836–1916* (Urbana: University of Illinois Press, 2006); James M. SoRelle, "The 'Waco Horror': The

Lynching of Jesse Washington," *Southwestern Historical Quarterly* 86, no. 4 (1983): 517–36; Alwyn Barr, *Black Texans: A History of African Americans in Texas, 1528–1995* (Norman: University of Oklahoma Press, 1996), 136–37.

4. "The Waco Horror," supplement, *Crisis*, July 1, 1916, 1–8.

5. Terry Anne Scott, *Lynching and Leisure: Race and the Transformation of Mob Violence in Texas* (Fayetteville: University of Arkansas Press, 2022).

6. H. L. Jaworski, "The Waco Tornado Disaster," *American Journal of Surgery* 87, no. 3 (1954): 484–86.

7. Bernstein, *First Waco Horror*; Rasul Mowatt, "The King of the Damned: Reading Lynching as Leisure," *Policy Futures in Education* 7, no. 2 (2009): 185–99; Scott, *Lynching and Leisure*.

8. SoRelle, "'Waco Horror,'" 527.

9. SoRelle, "'Waco Horror,'" 530–31.

10. ArCasia D. James-Gallaway, "What Got Them Through: Community Cultural Wealth, Black Students, and Texas School Desegregation," *Race Ethnicity and Education* 25, no. 2 (2022): 173–91.

11. Katherine McKittrick, "On Plantations, Prisons, and a Black Sense of Place," *Social and Cultural Geography* 12, no. 8 (2011): 947–63; Kevin Quashie, *Black Aliveness, or a Poetics of Being* (Durham, NC: Duke University Press, 2021).

12. See, e.g., Melba Beals, *Warriors Don't Cry: Searing Memoir of Battle to Integrate Little Rock* (New York: Simon and Schuster, 1995); Michelle Purdy, *Transforming the Elite: Black Students and the Desegregation of Private Schools* (Chapel Hill: University of North Carolina Press, 2018); Tracy E. K'Meyer, *From Brown to Meredith: The Long Struggle for School Desegregation in Louisville* (Chapel Hill: University of North Carolina Press, 2013); and Charles C. Bolton, *The Hardest Deal of All: The Battle over School Integration in Mississippi, 1870–1980* (Oxford: University Press of Mississippi, 2005).

13. I analyze these constructions in chapter 3.

14. SoRelle, "'Waco Horror,'" 520.

15. McKittrick, "On Plantations," 948.

16. I discuss these ideas more thoroughly in chapter 3.

17. Annette Gordon-Reed, *On Juneteenth* (New York: Liveright, 2021).

18. Randolph Campbell, *An Empire for Slavery: The Peculiar Institution in Texas, 1821–1865* (Baton Rouge: Louisiana State University Press, 1991); Walter L. Buenger, "Texas and the South," *Southwestern Historical Quarterly* 103, no. 3 (2000): 308–24; Gregg Cantrell, "Racial Violence and Reconstruction Politics in Texas, 1867–1868," *Southwestern Historical Quarterly* 93, no. 3 (1990): 333–55; Tyina L. Steptoe, *Houston Bound: Culture and Color in a Jim Crow City* (Berkeley: University of California Press, 2015); Neil Foley, *The White Scourge: Mexicans, Blacks, and Poor Whites in Texas Cotton Culture* (Berkeley: University of California Press, 1998).

19. Walter L. Buenger, "Texas Identity: Alternatives to the Terrible Triplets," in *This Corner of Canaan: Essays on Texas in Honor of Randolph B. Campbell*, ed. Richard B. McCaslin, Donald E. Chipman, and Andrew J. Torget (Denton: University of North Texas Press, 2013), 9.

20. William Poage, *McLennan County, Before 1980* (Waco, TX: Texian, 1981); Dayton Kelley, ed., *The Handbook of Waco and McLennan County, Texas* (Waco, TX: Texian, 1972);

Sharon Bracken, *Historic McLennan County: An Illustrated History* (San Antonio, TX: Historical Publishing Network, 2010), 20, 29.

21. Equal Justice Initiative, *Lynching in America: Confronting the Legacy of Racial Terror* (Montgomery, AL: Equal Justice Initiative, 2015), 10, https://eji.org/sites/default/files/lynching-in-america-third-edition-summary.pdf. Waco and Bellmead are part of the Waco metropolitan statistical area, which corresponds with McLennan County; for details, see US Department of Agriculture, "1974 Rural-Urban Continuum Codes," Economic Research Service, Microsoft Excel document, updated August 2003, www.ers.usda.gov/data-products/rural-urban-continuum-codes.

22. Thomas Russell, "'Keep Negroes Out of Most Classes Where There Are a Large Number of Girls': The Unseen Power of the Ku Klux Klan and Standardized Testing at the University of Texas, 1899–1999," *South Texas Law Review* 52, no. 1 (2010): 1–35.

23. This quotation is from a transcript of a meeting between the La Vega ISD school board and Don Vernon, an attorney from the federal Office for Civil Rights. See minutes, March 12, 1968, LVISD Trustees.

24. Wei-ling Gong, "A History of Integration of the Waco Public Schools, 1954 to the Present" (master's thesis, Baylor University, 1987); Samuel W. Newman, *History of the Waco Public School System* (Waco, TX: Waco Independent School District, 1976).

25. Adam Bledsoe, "The Primacy of Anti-Blackness," *Area* 52, no. 3 (2020): 472–79.

26. Richard Rothstein, *The Color of Law: A Forgotten History of How Our Government Segregated America* (New York: Liveright, 2017); Ansley Erickson, *Making the Unequal Metropolis: School Desegregation and Its Limits* (Chicago: University of Chicago Press, 2016); Matthew D. Lassiter, "Schools and Housing in Metropolitan History: An Introduction," *Journal of Urban History* 38, no. 2 (2012): 195–204; Gary Orfield, "School Segregation and Residential Segregation," in *School Desegregation: Past, Present and Future*, ed. Walter Stephan and Joe Feagin (New York: Plenum, 1980), 227–47; Michael Meier and Joe Feagin, *A Comparative Analysis of Black and Mexican American Residential Segregation in Southwestern Cities*, report no. ED 076267 (Washington, DC: US Department of Health, Education, and Welfare, Office of Education, 1972), 15, 19.

27. Virginia Lee Spurlin, "The Conners of Waco: Black Professionals in Twentieth Century Texas" (PhD diss., Texas Tech University, 1991), vi.

28. I capitalize *East Waco*, following the preference of the city's local publications, to recognize this part of the city's distinct Black character and cultural significance.

29. Erickson, *Making the Unequal Metropolis*.

30. LaDale C. Winling and Todd M. Michney, "The Roots of Redlining: Academic, Governmental, and Professional Networks in the Making of the New Deal Lending Regime," *Journal of American History* 108, no. 1 (2021): 42.

31. See the finalized area description at "Waco, TX" (1934), Mapping Inequality, accessed October 9, 2024, https://dsl.richmond.edu/panorama/redlining/map/TX/Waco/areas#loc=15/31.5666/-97.1177.

32. Anna Livia Brand, "Claiborne Love Song: Black Place-Making Toward a Vast Imaginary of Freedom," *Urban Geography*, April 2023, 2, 13.

33. Darius Scott, "Oral History and Emplacement in 'Nowhere at All': The Role of Personal and Family Narratives in Rural Black Community-Building," *Social and Cultural Geography* 20, no. 8 (2019): 1108.

34. Brand, "Claiborne Love Song," 17, 13.

35. Marcus Anthony Hunter, Mary Pattillo, Zandria F. Robinson, and Keeanga-Yamahtta Taylor, "Black Placemaking: Celebration, Play, and Poetry," *Theory, Culture and Society* 33, no. 7–8 (2016): 32.

36. US Department of Commerce, Social and Economic Statistics Administration, and US Bureau of the Census, *Waco, Tex. Standard Metropolitan Statistical Area: 1970 Census of Population and Housing*, Census Tracts (Washington, DC: US Department of Commerce, 1972), www2.census.gov/library/publications/decennial/1970/phc-1/39204513p22ch10.pdf, table P-1 (tracts 0016, 0017, and 0018). Additionally, the median income in 1970 of Waco ISD households was $7,857. See Michael Blackmon, *Preparation for Parenthood: Evaluation Plan and Program Evaluation* (Bethesda, MD: National Institutes of Health and Waco Independent School District, 1973), 12.

37. US Bureau of the Census, *Income in 1970 of Families and Persons in the United States*, Current Population Reports, series P60-80 (Washington, DC: US Government Printing Office, 1971), 14, www2.census.gov/library/publications/1971/demographics/p60-80.pdf.

38. "Maxey Homes Open House Set," *Waco Tribune-Herald*, June 7, 1959, 29; Official Records: Report of Deeds, *Waco News-Tribune*, January 12, 1948, 8, November 5, 1946, 12; "X-Real Estate: 116-Colored Properties," *Waco Tribune-Herald*, February 3, 1952, 25; "Busy Day for City Council," *Waco Tribune-Herald*, September 24, 1964, 1.

39. US Department of Commerce et al., *Waco, Tex.*, tables P-1, P-2 (tracts 0014, 0015, and 0016).

40. "Parkside Village Apartments to Start Taking Applications," *Waco Tribune-Herald*, January 3, 1971, 13. For a discussion of urban renewal's impact on Texas broadly and in Waco specifically, see Robert B. Fairbanks, "Federal Urban Renewal in Three Small Texas Cities: A Mixed Legacy," *Journal of Planning History* 19, no. 3 (2020): 187–203.

41. James Baldwin, "Urban Renewal . . . Means Negro Removal," interview by Kenneth Clark, 1963, posted June 3, 2015, by Vince Graham, YouTube, 1 min., 14 sec., www.youtube.com/watch?v=T8Abhj17kYU.

42. Allie Roberts, "Urban Renewal: Baylor University Project," *Waco History*, accessed July 1, 2024, https://wacohistory.org/items/show/229; Geoff Hunt, "Urban Renewal, 1966: The Year Waco's Alico Building Meets Midcentury Modern," *Texas Collection* (blog), Baylor University, July 17, 2015, https://blogs.baylor.edu/texascollection/category/urban-renewal.

43. Robert Darden, "Vivienne Malone-Mayes: First African-American Professor at Baylor Receives Recognition," *Wacoan*, accessed June 27, 2024, www.wacoan.com/vivienne-malone-mayes.

44. See, e.g., St. Clair Drake, "The Social and Economic Status of the Negro in the United States," *Daedalus* 94, no. 4 (1965): 771–814.

45. US Department of Commerce and US Bureau of the Census, *Census of Population: 1950*, vol. 1, *Number of Inhabitants* (Washington, DC: US Government Printing Office, 1952), chap. 43, "Texas," www.census.gov/library/publications/1952/dec/population-vol-01.html. See also Douglas S. Massey and Nancy A. Denton, *American Apartheid: Segregation and the Making of the Underclass* (Cambridge, MA: Harvard University Press, 1993); and Rothstein, *Color of Law*.

46. "116 Colored Properties," *Waco News-Tribune*, April 28, 1955, 31; "GI Homes (for Colored Only) FOR SALE: No Down Payment," *Waco Tribune-Herald*, February 26, 1950, 27; "More Housing Is Seen Here," *Waco Tribune-Herald*, March 5, 1950, 25.

47. Glenn Altschuler and Stuart Blumin, *The GI Bill: The New Deal for Veterans* (New York: Oxford University Press, 2009).

48. This base was renamed Fort Cavazos in 2022.

49. See, e.g., deed for Carver Park addition, January 21, 1948, vol. 604, p. 342; and deed for River Oaks addition, September 26 and 27, 1956, vol. 792, p. 550, both in Deed Records, McLennan County Clerk's Office, Waco, Texas.

50. Plat of the Hirsch Heights addition, March 19, 1950, annex 3 to the City of Waco, Deed Records, McLennan County Clerk's Office, Waco, Texas.

51. "Area Neighborhoods to Celebrate Legacy Neighborhoods," *Waco Tribune-Herald*, June 4, 2017, 8B.

52. "GI Homes," 27; Louis Lee Woods II, "Almost 'No Negro Veteran . . . Could Get a Loan': African Americans, the GI Bill, and the NAACP Campaign Against Residential Segregation, 1917–1960," *Journal of African American History* 98, no. 3 (2013): 392–417.

53. US Department of Commerce et al., *Waco, Tex.*, tables P-1, P-2 (tracts 0012 and 0013).

54. Connie Oliver, in discussion with the author, May 2019. All references in this chapter to Connie Oliver's oral history interview are from this discussion.

55. Plat of the Hirsch Heights addition, March 19, 1950, annex 3 to the City of Waco, Deed Records, McLennan County Clerk's Office, Waco, Texas.

56. Deed for Sycamore addition, February 15, 1950, vol. 647, p. 354, Deed Records, McLennan County Clerk's Office, Waco, Texas.

57. Anslum Hudlin, in discussion with the author, August 7, 2023. All references in this chapter to Anslum Hudlin's oral history interview are from this discussion.

58. For more on white flight, see Kevin M. Kruse, *White Flight: Atlanta and the Making of Modern Conservatism* (Princeton, NJ: Princeton University Press, 2005). For a historical view of the racial wealth gap, see Ellora Derenoncourt, Chi Hyun Kim, Moritz Kuhn, and Moritz Schularick, "Wealth of Two Nations: The US Racial Wealth Gap, 1860–2020," *Quarterly Journal of Economics* 139, no. 2 (2024): 693–750.

59. George Lipsitz, *How Racism Takes Place* (Philadelphia: Temple University Press, 2011).

60. "Members of Housing Authority Want Complaints Before Board," *Waco Tribune-Herald*, October 9, 1975, 5.

61. US Department of Commerce et al., *Waco, Tex.*, tables P-1, P-3 (tracts 0026, 0027, and 0028).

62. Stacey Floyd-Thomas, Juan M. Floyd-Thomas, Carol B. Duncan, Stephen G. Ray Jr., and Nancy Lynne Westfield, *Black Church Studies: An Introduction* (Nashville, TN: Abingdon, 2007); Henry Louis Gates Jr., *The Black Church: This Is Our Story, This Is Our Song* (New York: Penguin, 2022).

63. ArCasia D. James-Gallaway, "Waco's First Black School Board Trustees: Navigating Institutional White Supremacy in 1970s Texas," *History of Education Quarterly* 63, no. 1 (2023): 59–83.

64. Gates, *Black Church*; Barbara Dianne Savage, *Your Spirits Walk Beside Us: The Politics of Black Religion* (Cambridge, MA: Harvard University Press, 2012).

65. For more on Smith and the Farmers' Home Improvement Society, see Merline Pitre, "Robert Lloyd Smith: A Black Lawmaker in the Shadow of Booker T. Washington," *Phylon* 46, no. 3 (1985): 262–68; and Andrea R. Roberts, "The Farmers' Improvement Society and the Women's Barnyard Auxiliary of Texas: African American Community Building in the Progressive Era," *Journal of Planning History* 16, no. 3 (2017): 222–45.

66. "History: G. L. Wiley Opportunity Center," Waco Independent School District, accessed March 6, 2026, https://woc.wacoisd.org/about-us/about-woc/history. Initially, the building that became Wiley was white segregated East Waco Junior High School, but in 1958 when Waco ISD decided to make it a segregated Black school—four years after the Supreme Court outlawed school segregation—the Black community changed its name. This school plant signified an upgrade in resources and facilities for Black Waco students.

67. "Phil Teeling New Head of School Board," *Waco News-Tribune*, April 17, 1952, 6; James H. Hines Jr. death certificate, Texas Department of Health, Bureau of Vital Statistics, April 26, 1944, application number 19698, Ancestry.com.

68. Newman, *History*, 112.

69. "School Holds Unveiling of Oil Painting," *Waco Tribune-Herald*, September 2, 1951, 20. Savage (*Your Spirits Walk*) writes about the inherently political nature of many Black churches and their leaders.

70. Although the 1970 Census did not disaggregate occupational information by race, racial observations can be gleaned from its presentation of neighborhood tracts, which in many cases were racially exclusive given the strength of residential segregation. See the following supporting literature: Stanley Lieberson, *A Piece of the Pie: Blacks and White Immigrants Since 1880* (Berkeley: University of California Press, 1980); Stewart E. Tolnay, "Trends in the Relative Occupational Status of African Americans and European Immigrants in Northern Cities, 1880–1970," *Social Science Research* 32, no. 4 (2003): 603–32; and Robert M. Adelman and Stewart E. Tolnay, "Occupational Status of Immigrants and African Americans at the Beginning and End of the Great Migration," *Sociological Perspectives* 46, no. 2 (2003): 179–206.

71. US Department of Commerce et al., *Waco, Tex.*, table P-3 (tracts 0014, 0015, 0016, 0026, 0027, and 0028).

72. For a discussion of these trends, see Jacqueline Jones, *Labor of Love, Labor of Sorrow: Black Women, Work, and the Family, from Slavery to the Present* (New York: Basic Books, 1985); and Victoria W. Wolcott, *Remaking Respectability: African American Women in Interwar Detroit* (Chapel Hill: University of North Carolina Press, 2013).

73. ArCasia D. James-Gallaway and Adah Ward Randolph, "Critical Race Theory and Education History: Constructing a Race-Centered History of School Desegregation," in *Handbook of Critical Race Theory in Education*, ed. Marvin Lynn and Adrienne D. Dixson (New York: Routledge, 2021), 330–42.

74. Newman, *History*, 15.

75. James D. Anderson, *The Education of Blacks in the South, 1860–1935* (Chapel Hill: University of North Carolina Press, 1988).

76. Newman, *History*, 31. "Trustee Meeting: Selection of Teachers for the Coming Scholastic Years," *Waco Daily Examiner*, July 30, 1882, 1. "Public Schools: Opening of the Fall Term in Waco," *Waco Daily Examiner*, October 2, 1883, 4. "School Board Meeting," *Waco Daily Day Globe*, August 2, 1893, 3.

77. Anderson, *Education of Blacks*.

78. Anderson, *Education of Blacks*.

79. Newman, *History*, 111.

80. Woodbert Andruss Porter, "A Survey of the La Vega Public School System" (PhD diss., University of Texas, 1940), 4; Bracken, *Historic McLennan County*, 17. A 1955 newspaper

article notes that "La Vega Independent School district was formed on July 14, 1927 when citizens of the old Pecan Grove Common School District voted to become an independent district. . . . In July 1941, Waco annexed a portion of the La Vega district. Portions of Lakeview and Malley districts were annexed to La Vega in 1946, 1947, and 1948." See Reba Campbell, "Desegregation Issue in La Vega: At Least Two Major Questions Face District," *Waco Times-Herald*, August 3, 1955, 6.

81. Porter, "Survey," 28–29. Old Zion served grades 1–7 and Olive Heights grades 1–9.

82. La Vega Public Schools, *The La Vega Public Schools . . . Their Beginning and Growth* (Bellmead, TX: La Vega Public School District, n.d.), 26. Although the brochure is undated, contextual details suggest it was likely published in the early to mid-1950s, circa 1953.

83. "Waco Boys Attend 4-H Meet at Prairie View," *Waco Tribune-Herald*, June 5, 1949, 22; "Olive Heights School Children Exhibit Their Canning," *Waco Sunday Tribune-Herald*, December 15, 1946, 24.

84. "Negroes Exhibit 1500 Containers of Canned Foods: Extension Workers Tour of County Reveals Excellent Progress Being Made in McLennan," *Waco Tribune-Herald*, July 14, 1935, 12.

85. "School Named in Honor of Former Waco Leader," *Waco Tribune-Herald*, August 26, 1951, 26; "Rev. Griffin Is Given Call," *Waco Tribune-Herald*, July 15, 1951, 25.

86. "Olive Heights School Plans Due," *Waco Tribune-Herald*, February 25, 1951, 29.

87. La Vega Public Schools, *La Vega Public Schools*, 26; "Cornerstone Ceremonies Held for Jenkins Schools," *Waco Tribune-Herald*, September 2, 1951, 20.

88. "Cornerstone Ceremonies Held," 20; "Jenkins School Opening Rites Are Conducted," *Waco Tribune-Herald*, May 4, 1952, 37; "News of the Negro Community," *Waco Tribune-Herald*, March 23, 1952, 27.

89. US Department of Commerce and US Bureau of the Census, *Census of Population: 1950*, chap. 43, "Texas."

90. Minutes, November 23, December 3, 1954, LVISD Trustees.

91. In 1955, 70 of the total 861 Black La Vega ISD students lived in Bellmead. See Campbell, "Desegregation Issue," 6.

92. Minutes, November 23, 1954, LVISD Trustees.

93. Campbell, "Desegregation Issue," 6.

94. Gong, "History of Integration," 14–15.

95. Gong, "History of Integration," 22. Article 2900a of the 1958 Supplement to *Vernon's Texas Statutes* of 1948, 1950, 1952, and 1956 stipulates, "No board of trustees nor any other school authority shall have the right to abolish the dual public school system nor to abolish arrangements for transfer out of the district for students of any minority race, unless by a prior vote of the qualified electors residing in such district the dual school system therein is abolished." See 55th Texas Legislature, *Vernon's Texas Statutes 1958 Supplement: Including General and Permanent Laws of the 55th Legislature, Regular Session and First and Second Called Session* (Kansas City, MO: Vernon Law, 1958), 275.

96. For example, there was an unofficial agreement between Black community activists and newspaper reporters "to downplay news coverage of public protests in return for quiet, behind-the-scenes pressure for integration." See Carl Hoover, "Dr Pepper Museum Exhibit Highlights Countertop Civil Rights Struggle," *Waco Tribune-Herald*, December 4, 2021, https://wacotrib.com/news/local/history/dr-pepper-museum-exhibit-highlights-countertop-civil-rights-struggle/article_6e83882c-547b-11ec-b465-7b0bfddaa219.html.

97. K'Meyer, *From Brown to Meredith.*

98. The all-white board approved the adult education request on a trial basis. See minutes, June 14, 1954, LVISD Trustees (the district was not located solely in Bellmead at this point). For the banquet request, see minutes, March 3, 1955; and Yancy to P. W. Shelton (La Vega ISD superintendent), March 2, 1955, both in LVISD Trustees. Regarding Yancy's request for a scholarship fundraiser, according to the board, the proposed event failed to "conform . . . to school policy [because the event] was not directly sponsored by the school and was to raise money for outside interests," so his motion was denied. See minutes, October 6, 1955, LVISD Trustees.

99. William Henry Chafe, Raymond Gavins, and Robert Korstad, eds., *Remembering Jim Crow: African Americans Tell About Life in the Segregated South* (New York: New Press, 2011).

100. His request was approved. Minutes, March 3, 1955, LVISD Trustees; Yancy to Shelton, March 2, 1955.

101. McLennan County Colored Teachers' Association to Shelton and La Vega ISD school board, February 22, 1954, LVISD Trustees.

102. Minutes, November 21, 1955, LVISD Trustees.

103. Minutes, December 1, 1955, LVISD Trustees. Although the minutes note that the petition would be "inserted in these minutes," said petition does not appear.

104. "Texas Supreme Court Knocks Out School Segregation Law," *Southern School News*, November 1955, 6; Anna Victoria Wilson and William E. Segall, *Oh, Do I Remember! Experiences of Teachers During the Desegregation of Austin's Schools, 1964–1971* (Albany: State University of New York Press, 2001), 146n32, 147n35.

105. Neil R. McMillen, *The Citizens' Council: Organized Resistance to the Second Reconstruction, 1954–64* (Urbana: University of Illinois Press, 1994), 11. See also Stephanie R. Rolph, *Resisting Equality: The Citizens' Council, 1954–1989* (Baton Rouge: Louisiana State University Press, 2018).

106. "Texas Supreme Court," 6.

107. Minutes, December 20, 1955, LVISD Trustees.

108. Minutes, March 19, 1956, LVISD Trustees.

109. Minutes, April 9, 1956, LVISD Trustees.

110. Meredith Haas, "History Behind the Name: G. W. Carver Middle School Gets a New Look While Reflecting on the Past," KCEN, February 15, 2024, www.kcentv.com/article/news/local/black-history/history-behind-the-name-gw-carver-middle-school-gets-a-new-look-while-reflecting-on-the-past-kcen-kags/500-11b51af7-8d38-4abc-b00f-ffbb347d8dab.

111. Charles C. Bolton, "Mississippi's School Equalization Program, 1945–1954: A Last Gasp to Try to Maintain a Segregated Educational System," *Journal of Southern History* 66, no. 4 (2000): 784.

112. Bolton, "Mississippi's School Equalization Program."

113. Regular requests from Black citizens asking to use the school appear in La Vega ISD school board minutes from 1956 to 1970, the year the school closed.

114. "Carver High P-TA to Give Music Fete," *Waco Tribune-Herald*, May 5, 1957, 29.

115. "Rev. W. L. Shaw Heads District 3 in East Waco," *Waco News-Tribune*, September 30, 1962, 33. The board permitted the group to use the school a total of five times. Minutes, June 4, 1963, August 23, 1956, LVISD Trustees.

116. Evans's request was denied. Minutes, June 4, 1963, LVISD Trustees.

117. For more on Evans's residential efforts for Black Wacoans, see "Ceremonies Open Work on All-Negro Home Area," *Waco News-Tribune*, February 27, 1956, 13; and "Cultural Landmarks and Celebrations," Baylor University (website), accessed January 1, 2026, https://waco.web.baylor.edu/waco-guides/waco-culture-guide/african-americans-waco/cultural-landmarks-celebrations.

118. Robyn Duff Ladino, *Desegregating Texas Schools: Eisenhower, Shivers, and the Crisis at Mansfield High* (Austin: University of Texas Press, 1996).

119. Wilson and Segall, *Oh, I Do Remember!*, 49–50; Ladino, *Desegregating Texas Schools*.

120. For a critical history of the Texas Rangers, see Monica Muñoz Martinez, *The Injustice Never Leaves You: Anti-Mexican Violence in Texas* (Cambridge, MA: Harvard University Press, 2018).

121. Tina M. Kibbe, "School Desegregation in Port Arthur: The Battle Between the Community, the Board, and the Justice Department," *East Texas Historical Journal* 44, no. 2 (2006): 4. Also see Article 2900a in 55th Texas Legislature, *Vernon's Texas Statutes*, 275.

122. Gong, "History of Integration," 14–15, 22–23.

123. James Hershman, "Public School Bonds and Virginia's Massive Resistance," *Journal of Negro Education* 52, no. 4 (1983): 398–409.

124. Davison M. Douglas, *Reading, Writing, and Race: The Desegregation of the Charlotte Schools* (Chapel Hill: University of North Carolina Press, 1995).

125. Michael Hurd, *Thursday Night Lights: The Story of Black High School Football in Texas* (Austin: University of Texas Press, 2017), 94–99.

126. Hurd, *Thursday Night Lights*.

127. Shardae LaRae, "'It Was a Family School': Before the Middle School, G. W. Carver HS Served as an Area School for Black students," KXXV, March 7, 2024, www.kxxv.com/news/black-history-month/it-was-a-family-school-before-the-middle-school-g-w-carver-hs-served-as-an-area-school-for-black-students.

128. Willie Brown, in discussion with the author, November 2018. All references in this chapter to Willie Brown's oral history interview are from this discussion.

129. Gong, "History of Integration," 24.

130. Newman, *History*, 79.

131. Gong, "History of Integration," 28.

132. Newman, *History*, 79.

133. Gong, "History of Integration," 27.

134. Gong, "History of Integration," 26–27.

135. Jane Williamson, "Downing Explains Problems: Shifting Population One Major Cause," *Waco News-Tribune*, September 22, 1964, 1, 12. Baylor University's urban renewal project, discussed in the introduction, caused this shift.

136. Minutes, June 4, 1963, LVISD Trustees.

137. In the La Vega ISD school board's records, a resolution appears after the minutes for this June 4 meeting and before the next set of board meeting minutes for August. Later, it is dated June 25, 1963.

138. Robert A. Pratt, *The Color of Their Skin: Education and Race in Richmond, Virginia, 1954–89* (Charlottesville: University Press of Virginia, 1992), 25; J. Harvie Wilkinson III, *From Brown to Bakke: The Supreme Court and School Integration: 1954–1978* (New York: Oxford University Press, 1979), 45, 109; Richard Kluger, *Simple Justice: The History of*

*Brown v. Board of Education and Black America's Struggle for Equality* (New York: Vintage Books, 1976).

139. Article 2900a in 55th Texas Legislature, *Vernon's Texas Statutes*, 275.

140. "In La Vega Controversy: Black Leaders Report Outside Agitators Here," *Waco News-Tribune*, September 16, 1970, 1.

141. "School Enrollment Up Slightly Here," *Waco News-Tribune*, September 4, 1964, 1, 4.

142. "Waco Area Enrollment Gains Higher," *Waco News-Tribune*, September 4, 1964, 1.

143. Stephen J. Caldas and Carl L. Bankston III, *Forced to Fail: The Paradox of School Desegregation* (Westport, CT: Praeger, 2005), 29.

144. Caldas and Bankston, *Forced to Fail*, 29–30; Wilkinson, *From Brown to Bakke*; Jill Ogline Titus, *Brown's Battleground: Students, Segregationists, and the Struggle for Justice in Prince Edward County, Virginia* (Chapel Hill: University of North Carolina Press, 2011); Christopher Bonastia, *Southern Stalemate: Five Years Without Public Education in Prince Edward County, Virginia* (Chicago: University of Chicago Press, 2012). The 1964 Civil Rights Act ushered in the freedom-of-choice era. This act saw "in 1965 federal education officials set minimum civil rights standards for choice, including (1) a clear chance for every family to make choices each year, (2) a guarantee that these choices be honored, (3) a guarantee of free transportation to receiving schools, (4) a prohibition on transfers that would increase segregation, and (5) a requirement of fair treatment of new students in receiving schools." See Gary Orfield and Erica Frankenberg, *Why Choice Can Deepen Inequality and How to Make Schools Fair* (Berkeley: University of California Press, 2013), 10.

145. Bolton, *Hardest Deal of All*, xiv–xv.

146. Bolton, *Hardest Deal of All*, 194.

147. Cranfill to Edgar, May 5, 1965, LVISD Trustees.

148. Wilkinson, *From Brown to Bakke*; Titus, *Brown's Battleground*; Bonastia, *Southern Stalemate*.

149. "In La Vega Controversy," 1.

150. Zoning descriptions and maps included in Cranfill's letter to Edgar maintain a similar racial distribution of students in the district's seven schools. For example, students living in the Dripping Springs or Jenkins zones are to attend Carver for high school. Dripping Springs opened in 1963 and was one of the two Black elementary schools in La Vega ISD; Jenkins was the other, and it was built in 1951. Students living on the other side of the secondary boundary line, where the district's white elementary schools were, are to attend La Vega High School. Thus, schools' racial composition was unchanged per the "new" plan.

151. Minutes, March 18, 1968, LVISD Trustees. Two attorneys in the US Department of Health, Education, and Welfare's Office for Civil Rights—Don Vernon, who worked in the Washington, DC, headquarters, and Douglas Clay, who worked in the Dallas regional office—visited La Vega ISD on March 12, 1968, to inform the board it was in violation of operating dual schooling systems. The meeting was transcribed verbatim in twenty-three single-spaced pages.

152. Minutes, March 18, 1968, LVISD Trustees.

153. Cranfill to Edgar, May 5, 1965, LVISD Trustees.

154. Marshall Baldwin, interview by Sean Sutcliffe, June 24, 2016, 40, Oral History Memoir interview 1, transcript, Baylor University Institute for Oral History, Waco, Texas.

155. "At Tri-State Festival: Carver High Wins Top Band Honors," *Waco News-Tribune*, May 8, 1967, 1.

156. "At Tri-State Festival," 1.

157. "At Tri-State Festival," 5.

158. "Carver Band Gets Praise from Enid," *Waco News-Tribune*, May 18, 1967, 21.

159. "Carver High Continues Fund Drive," *Waco News-Tribune*, June 16, 1967, 12; "Carver Band Still Selling Barbecue," *Waco News-Tribune*, June 22, 1967, 9; Roger Cantrell, "5 P.M. Departure: Carver Band, Needing Funds, Delays Leaving," *Waco News-Tribune*, June 28, 1967, 7.

160. Cantrell, "5 P.M. Departure," 7; Roger Cantrell, "Expo Date Off: Band Wows Canadians," *Waco News-Tribune*, July 3, 1967, 1. Lee ensured that the trip served also as a vacation of sorts for his hardworking band by stopping in Washington, DC, New York City, and Niagara Falls.

161. Cantrell, "5 P.M. Departure," 7.

162. Wanda James, in discussion with the author, April 2019. All references in this chapter to Wanda James's oral history interview are from this discussion.

163. Hurd, *Thursday Night Lights*.

164. Louise Later, "Bacon, Eggs and Red Carpet for Carver Band: There'll Never Be Another Homecoming Just Like It," *Waco News-Tribune*, July 10, 1967, 1.

165. "Carver Band Still Selling Barbecue," 9; "Raising Funds for Trip: Carver Band Holds Concert Here Tonight," *Waco News-Tribune*, June 15, 1967, 1, 3.

## CHAPTER 2

1. Charles C. Bolton, *The Hardest Deal of All: The Battle over School Integration in Mississippi, 1870–1980* (Oxford: University Press of Mississippi, 2005), 169–73.

2. J. Harvie Wilkinson III, *From Brown to Bakke: The Supreme Court and School Integration: 1954–1978* (New York: Oxford University Press, 1979), 120.

3. Wilkinson, *From Brown to Bakke*, 118.

4. Wilkinson, *From Brown to Bakke*, 118.

5. The *Swann* case is discussed in more detail later in this chapter.

6. Peter Irons, *Jim Crow's Children: The Broken Promise of the Brown Decision* (New York: Viking, 2002), 199.

7. Irons, *Jim Crow's Children*, 204.

8. Richard Kluger, *Simple Justice: The History of Brown v. Board of Education and Black America's Struggle for Equality* (New York: Vintage Books, 1976), 766; Wilkinson, *From Brown to Bakke*, 116–17.

9. Stephen J. Caldas and Carl L. Bankston III, *Forced to Fail: The Paradox of School Desegregation* (Westport, CT: Praeger, 2005), 32.

10. Irons, *Jim Crow's Children*, 204–5.

11. This is also indicated in minutes, May 27, 1969, LVISD Trustees. Specifically, grades 1–2 would go to La Vega Elementary School; grade 3 would go to East La Vega Elementary School; grades 4–5 would go to Dripping Springs Elementary School; grades 6–7 would go to La Vega Intermediate School; grades 8–9 would go to Carver High School (which was to be renamed); and grades 10–12 would go to La Vega High School. This plan is corroborated by a newspaper article published on May 30 of the same year. See Ernie Makovy, "300 Bellmead Citizens Protest Integration Plan," *Waco News-Herald*, May 30, 1969.

12. The closing of Black segregated schools was all too common in efforts to achieve school desegregation. See, e.g., David S. Cecelski, *Along Freedom Road: Hyde County, North Carolina, and the Fate of Black Schools in the South* (Chapel Hill: University of North Carolina Press, 1994).

13. "School Elections," *Waco Citizen*, April 10, 1969. This article discusses the election of LaDell Thomas. "Rev. Thomas to Run Again at La Vega," *Waco News-Tribune*, February 24, 1971; minutes, May 28, 1970, LVISD Trustees. Although Thomas and another Black man, Samuel Forney, were elected to the board at the same time and were its first Black members, just a few months into his term Forney resigned from this and his other civic posts due to declining health, and he died just a few years later in 1974. Forney had been a science teacher at A. J. Moore High since the 1950s. See "La Vega School Board Integrated," *Waco Citizen*, April 17, 1969, 1; "Four File for La Vega School Board Positions," *Waco News-Tribune*, December 16, 1970, 10; "Council Defers Curb, Gutter Action," *Waco News-Tribune*, March 3, 1971, 11; and *The Lion*, yearbook, 1956, A. J. Moore High School, Waco, Texas.

14. *The Treasure Chest*, yearbook, 1970, 39, La Vega High School, Bellmead, Texas.

15. Minutes, May 28, 1970, LVISD Trustees.

16. Minutes, July 28, 31, 1970, LVISD Trustees.

17. Minutes, August 13, 1970, LVISD Trustees. At this meeting, trustees decided to present the plan as a "narrative description."

18. Minutes, August 18, 1970, LVISD Trustees.

19. Linda C. Tillman, "(Un)intended Consequences? The Impact of the *Brown v. Board of Education* Decision on the Employment Status of Black Educators," *Education and Urban Society* 36, no. 3 (2004): 280–303; Michael Fultz, "The Displacement of Black Educators Post-*Brown*: An Overview and Analysis," *History of Education Quarterly* 44, no. 1 (2004): 11–45; Leslie T. Fenwick, *Jim Crow's Pink Slip: The Untold Story of Black Principal and Teacher Leadership* (Cambridge, MA: Harvard Education, 2022).

20. Bolton, *Hardest Deal of All*, 214.

21. Bolton, *Hardest Deal of All*, 163.

22. Associated Press, "Negro Pupils Walk Out in Protest," *Del Rio (TX) News Herald*, September 15, 1970, 6.

23. Terri Jo Ryan, "Residents Remember Waco's Segregated Past: Segregation Focus of Waco History Project Program," Waco History Project, accessed January 1, 2026, wacohistoryproject.org/Moments/segregated.htm.

24. Makovy, "300 Bellmead Citizens Protest."

25. "La Vega Reviews Complaints," *Waco News-Tribune*, September 16, 1970, 1A.

26. "La Vega Reviews Complaints," 1A.

27. The first quote is from "La Vega Reviews Complaints," 1A. The final two quotes are from Ira Royals, "La Vega Board Votes to Accept Unit Plan," *Waco News-Tribune*, September 18, 1970, 1A.

28. "La Vega Reviews Complaints," 1A. Once schools desegregated, the trustees of majority-white school boards regularly employed similar antics to curb Black power. See, e.g., ArCasia D. James-Gallaway, "Waco's First Black School Board Trustees: Navigating Institutional White Supremacy in 1970s Texas," *History of Education Quarterly* 63, no. 1 (2023): 59–83.

29. Royals, "La Vega Board Votes."

30. Marshall Baldwin, interview by Sean Sutcliffe, June 24, 2016, 33, Oral History Memoir interview 1, transcript, Baylor University Institute for Oral History, Waco, Texas.

31. Shardae LaRae, "'It Was a Family School': Before the Middle School, G. W. Carver HS Served as an Area School for Black Students," KXXV, March 7, 2024, www.kxxv.com/news/black-history-month/it-was-a-family-school-before-the-middle-school-g-w-carver-hs-served-as-an-area-school-for-black-students.

32. Baldwin, interview, 33.

33. Beverly Rickford, in discussion with the author, January 2019. All references in this chapter to Beverly Rickford's oral history interview are from this discussion. Contact issues prevented me from obtaining permission to use Beverly's de-identified interviews before book production began; thus, I created a pseudonym to protect her privacy.

34. Michael Bass, in discussion with the author, June 2019. All references in this chapter to Michael Bass's oral history interview are from this discussion.

35. See, e.g., Gael Graham, *Young Activists: American High School Students in the Age of Protest* (DeKalb: Northern Illinois University Press, 2006); Vincent D. Willis, *Audacious Agitation: The Uncompromising Commitment of Black Youth to Equal Education After Brown* (Athens: University of Georgia Press, 2021); Jon N. Hale, *The Freedom Schools: Student Activists in the Mississippi Civil Rights Movement* (New York: Columbia University Press, 2016); Jon N. Hale, *A New Kind of Youth: Historically Black High Schools and Southern Student Activism, 1920–1975* (Chapel Hill: University of North Carolina Press, 2022); Jeanne Theoharis, "'W-A-L-K-O-U-T!': High School Students and the Development of Black Power in L.A," in *Neighborhood Rebels: Black Power at the Local Level* (New York: Palgrave Macmillan, 2010), 107–29; and Walter C. Stern, "'We Got to Fight for What We Want': Black School Rebellions in Louisiana, 1965–1974," *Teachers College Record* 125, no. 3 (2023): 319–49.

36. Anna Livia Brand, "Claiborne Love Song: Black Place-Making Toward a Vast Imaginary of Freedom," *Urban Geography*, April 2023, 1–21.

37. Thomas Bynum, *NAACP Youth and the Fight for Black Freedom, 1936–1965* (Knoxville: University of Tennessee Press, 2013).

38. Rev. M. L. Cooper Jr., "Local NAACP Picket 7–11 Store: Negro's Viewpoint," *Waco News Citizen*, June 5, 1962, 1.

39. Tess Bundy, "'Revolutions Happen Through Young People!': The Black Student Movement in the Boston Public Schools, 1968–1971," *Journal of Urban History* 43, no. 2 (2017): 273–93; Leonard Nathaniel Moore, "The School Desegregation Crisis of Cleveland, Ohio, 1963–1964: The Catalyst for Black Political Power in a Northern City," *Journal of Urban History* 28, no. 2 (2002): 135–57; Jeanne Theoharis, "'We Saved the City': Black Struggles for Educational Equality in Boston, 1960–1976," *Radical History Review* 81, no. 1 (2001): 61–93.

40. Alexander Hyres, "'The Whole Mess Is American History': Protest, Pedagogy, and Black Studies at a Desegregated High School in the South, 1967–1974," *Journal of African American History* 107, no. 1 (2022): 55–78.

41. Ibram X. Kendi, *The Black Campus Movement: Black Students and the Racial Reconstitution of Higher Education, 1965–1972* (New York: Palgrave Macmillan, 2012).

42. Baldwin, interview, 38. Secondary literature supports this point about antiBlack racial violence. See Patricia Bernstein, *The First Waco Horror: The Lynching of Jesse Washington and the Rise of the NAACP* (College Station: Texas A&M University Press, 2006); William Carrigan, *The Making of a Lynching Culture: Violence and Vigilantism in Central Texas,*

*1836–1916* (Urbana: University of Illinois Press, 2006); and Walter L. Buenger, "Texas and the South," *Southwestern Historical Quarterly* 103, no. 3 (2000): 308–24.

43. Dara Walker, "Learning to Struggle, Learning to Govern: How Black Youth Marshaled Education to Navigate Urban Transformations in the Motor City, 1967–1972," *Journal of Urban History* 51, no. 2 (2025): 441.

44. Waco's median income was roughly double that of Bellmead. See US Department of Commerce, Social and Economic Statistics Administration, and US Bureau of the Census, *Waco, Tex. Standard Metropolitan Statistical Area: 1970 Census of Population and Housing*, Census Tracts (Washington, DC: US Department of Commerce, 1972), www2.census.gov/library/publications/decennial/1970/phc-1/39204513p22ch10.pdf, table P-1.

45. The first quote is from Derrick Bell, "The Dialects of School Desegregation," *Alabama Law Review* 32, no. 2 (1980): 293. The second quote is from Lani Guinier, "From Racial Liberalism to Racial Literacy: *Brown v. Board of Education* and the Interest-Divergence Dilemma," *Journal of American History* 91, no. 1 (2004): 101.

46. Barbara J. Love, "*Brown* Plus 50 Counter-Storytelling: A Critical Race Theory Analysis of the 'Majoritarian Achievement Gap' Story," *Equity and Excellence in Education* 37, no. 3 (2004): 228–29.

47. Aja Y. Martinez, "A Plea for Critical Race Theory Counterstory: Stock Story Versus Counterstory Dialogues Concerning Alejandra's 'Fit' in the Academy," *Composition Studies* 42, no. 2 (2014): 38. See also Richard Delgado, "Storytelling for Oppositionists and Others: A Plea for Narrative," *Michigan Law Review* 87, no. 8 (1989): 2411–41; and Derrick Bell, *Faces at the Bottom of the Well: The Permanence of Racism* (New York: Basic Books, 1992).

48. Willis, *Audacious Agitation*, 70.

49. Ryan, "Residents Remember."

50. Vincent P. Franklin, *The Young Crusaders: The Untold Story of the Children and Teenagers Who Galvanized the Civil Rights Movement* (New York: Beacon, 2021), 194.

51. "La Vega Boycott Continues: Black Students Demand Changes," *Waco News-Tribune*, September 15, 1970, 10A.

52. This issue is enduring. See, e.g., Chaddrick D. James-Gallaway, ArCasia D. James-Gallaway, and Autumn A. Griffin, "'It's in [Their] Roots': A Critical Race Discourse Analysis of Media Accounts Depicting Black Hair Discrimination in K–12 School," *Urban Review* 56, no. 1 (2024): 35–58.

53. Dismissing the major issues that Black students articulated in educational protests was common. See, e.g., Francena Turner, "Black Women and Student Activism at Fayetteville State, 1960–1972" (PhD diss., University of Illinois, 2020); and Francena Turner, "'Girls Don't Strike Without Provocation': African American Women, the General Strike, and the Good Samaritan Hospital School of Nursing, Charlotte, North Carolina, 1956–1959," *Nursing History Review* 32, no. 1 (2024): 142–64.

54. Baldwin, interview, 35–36.

55. Associated Press, "Negro Pupils Walk Out," 6.

56. Tondra L. Loder-Jackson, *Schoolhouse Activists: African American Educators and the Long Birmingham Civil Rights Movement* (Albany: State University of New York Press, 2015).

57. United Press International, "Violence Feared at Tense Texas School," *Monitor* (McAllen, TX), September 21, 1970, 3.

58. ArCasia D. James-Gallaway and Chaddrick D. James-Gallaway, "A Historical Analysis of Education Leadership During Texas School Desegregation: Viewing Racial Literacy on

a Gradient," *Journal of Educational Foundations* 36, no. 1 (2023): 49–72, https://files.eric.ed.gov/fulltext/EJ1438770.pdf.

59. Baldwin, interview, 38.

60. Tera Eva Agyepong, *The Criminalization of Black Children: Race, Gender, and Delinquency in Chicago's Juvenile Justice System, 1899–1945* (Chapel Hill: University of North Carolina Press, 2018).

61. Derrick Bell, *Silent Covenants: Brown v. Board of Education and the Unfulfilled Hopes for Racial Reform* (New York: Oxford University Press, 2004).

62. Cheryl I. Harris, "Whiteness as Property," *Harvard Law Review* 106, no. 8 (1993): 1707–91.

63. Adam Bledsoe, Latoya E. Eaves, and Brian Williams, "Black Geographies in and of the United States South," *Southeastern Geographer* 57, no. 1 (2017): 6–11.

64. Tracy Lachica Buenavista, Stephanie Cariaga, Edward R. Curammeng, et al., "A Praxis of Critical Race Love: Toward the Abolition of Cisheteropatriarchy and Toxic Masculinity in Educational Justice Formations," *Educational Studies* 57, no. 3 (2021): 238–49.

65. Rachel Devlin, *A Girl Stands at the Door: The Generation of Young Women Who Desegregated America's Schools* (New York: Basic Books, 2018).

66. La Vega ISD school board minutes indicate that on November 17, 1970, Ivy Branch was suspended at the behest of the school's white principal, Donald Richardson. See minutes, November 17, 1970, LVISD Trustees; and Willie Brown, in discussion with the author, November 2018. All references in this chapter to Willie Brown's oral history interview are from this discussion.

67. ArCasia D. James-Gallaway, "Tacit Curriculum of Black Intellectual Ineptitude: Black Girls' Perspectives on Texas School Desegregation Implementation in the 1970s," *History of Education Review* 51, no. 1 (2022): 81–95.

68. Belinda Robnett, *How Long? How Long? African American Women in the Struggle for Civil Rights* (New York: Oxford University Press, 2000), 5.

69. Ryan, "Residents Remember."

70. "La Vega Boycott Continues," 10A.

71. Ryan, "Residents Remember." Another news article substantiates the claim that La Vega ISD reappointed Clarence Chase as the district's athletic director. See "Football, Baseball, and Integration Coincide," *Waco Citizen*, August 27, 1970, 8.

72. Franklin, *Young Crusaders*, 14, 75.

73. Elizabeth A. Roumell and ArCasia D. James-Gallaway, "Social Movements, Community Education, and the Fight for Racial Justice: Black Women and Social Transformation," *New Directions for Adult and Continuing Education* 2021, no. 170 (2021): 21–31; Bettye Collier-Thomas and Vincent P. Franklin, eds., *Sisters in the Struggle: African American Women in the Civil Rights–Black Power Movement* (New York: New York University Press, 2001); Barbara Ransby, *Ella Baker and the Black Freedom Movement: A Radical Democratic Vision* (Chapel Hill: University of North Carolina Press, 2003); Chana Kai Lee, *For Freedom's Sake: The Life of Fannie Lou Hamer* (Urbana-Champaign: University of Illinois Press, 2000).

74. James-Gallaway, "Waco's First"; Virginia Lee Spurlin, "The Conners of Waco: Black Professionals in Twentieth Century Texas" (PhD diss., Texas Tech University, 1991).

75. Robnett, *How Long?*

76. Carl Hoover, "Dr Pepper Museum Exhibit Highlights Countertop Civil Rights Struggle," *Waco Tribune-Herald*, December 4, 2021, https://wacotrib.com/news/local/history/dr

-pepper-museum-exhibit-highlights-countertop-civil-rights-struggle/article_6e83882c-547b-11ec-b465-7b0bfddaa219.html.

77. "La Vega Boycott Continues," 10A.

78. "La Vega Boycott Continues," 1.

79. "La Vega Boycott Continues," 1.

80. "La Vega Boycott Continues," 1.

81. Vincent P. Franklin, *Black Self-Determination: A Cultural History of African American Resistance* (Chicago: Lawrence Hill, 1992).

82. "King Urges La Vega Students to Return," *Waco News-Tribune*, September 20, 1970, 13; "Group Urges Show of Unity at La Vega," *Waco News-Tribune*, September 21, 1970, 13.

83. Royals, "La Vega Board Votes," 1A; Thom Matthews, "La Vega School Nears 50 Percent Absenteeism," *Waco Tribune-Herald*, September 18, 1970, 1A.

84. John Black, "Unity Among Whites Urged in La Vega School Issues," *Waco News-Tribune*, December 4, 1970, 2.

85. Black, "Unity Among Whites Urged," 2.

86. Tracy E. K'Meyer, *From Brown to Meredith: The Long Struggle for School Desegregation in Louisville* (Chapel Hill: University of North Carolina Press, 2013), 40, 42; Bolton, *Hardest Deal of All*, 155, 160.

87. Vivian Gunn Morris and Curtis L. Morris, *The Price They Paid: Desegregation in an African American Community* (New York: Teachers College Press, 2002); Russell Skiba and Ashley White, "Ever Since Little Rock: The History of Disciplinary Disparities in America's Schools," in *Disproportionality and Social Justice in Education*, ed. Nicholas Gage, Luke J. Rapa, Denise K. Whitford, and Antonis Katsiyanis (Cham, Switzerland: Springer International, 2022), 3–33.

88. Vanessa Siddle Walker, *Their Highest Potential: An African American School Community in the Segregated South* (Chapel Hill: University of North Carolina Press, 1996); ArCasia D. James-Gallaway and Tiffany Harris, "We Been Relevant: Culturally Relevant Pedagogy and Black Women Teachers in Segregated Schools," *Educational Studies* 57, no. 2 (2021): 124–41.

89. Walker, "Learning to Struggle," 441.

90. James-Gallaway, "Tacit Curriculum."

91. *Treasure Chest*, 1972, 44–54.

92. Maryam M. Jernigan and Jessica Henderson Daniel, "Racial Trauma in the Lives of Black Children and Adolescents: Challenges and Clinical Implications," *Journal of Child and Adolescent Trauma* 4, no. 2 (2011): 123–41.

93. Constance Sadler, in discussion with the author, May 2019. All references in this chapter to Constance "Connie" Sadler's oral history interview are from this discussion.

94. Baldwin, interview, 44.

95. Patricia Hill Collins, *Black Sexual Politics: African Americans, Gender, and the New Racism* (New York: Routledge, 2004), 194. See also chapter 4 of this book.

96. Bundy, "'Revolutions Happen Through Young People!,'" 283.

97. Mary Ellen Hanson, *Go! Fight! Win! Cheerleading in American Culture* (Bowling Green, OH: Bowling Green State University Popular Press, 1995), 34.

98. Skylar Ray, "Marvin C. Griffin," *Waco History*, accessed January 1, 2026, https://wacohistory.org/items/show/204; Marvin C. Griffin, interview by Thomas L. Charlton,

June 23, 1972, audio recording, Baylor University Institute for Oral History, Waco, Texas, https://digitalcollections-baylor.quartexcollections.com/Documents/Detail/oral-memoirs-of-marvin-c.-griffin-series-1-audio/1602109?item=1602110.

99. Baldwin, interview, 42.

100. On May 31, the La Vega ISD board meeting minutes note, "All members present expressed the desire that letters of thanks and appreciation be sent to all governmental bodies whose policemen gave assistance to the district during the last three days of the school year ending May 28, 1971." Additional letters were dated June 3, 1971. See minutes, May 31, 1971, LVISD Trustees.

101. Wei-ling Gong, "A History of Integration of the Waco Public Schools, 1954 to the Present" (master's thesis, Baylor University, 1987), 33–41.

102. Spurlin, "Conners of Waco."

103. Spurlin, "Conners of Waco," 151–56.

104. Tillman, "(Un)intended Consequences?"; Fultz, "Displacement of Black Educators"; Fenwick, *Jim Crow's Pink Slip.*

105. James-Gallaway, "Waco's First," 80–81.

106. Richard L. Schott and Isabel Marcus, *School Desegregation in Texas: The Implementation of United States v. Texas*, Policy Research Report 51 (Austin: Lyndon B. Johnson School of Public Affairs, University of Texas, 1982).

107. Schott and Marcus, *School Desegregation in Texas*, 58.

108. Frank R. Kemerer, *William Wayne Justice: A Judicial Biography* (Austin: University of Texas Press, 1991).

109. Schott and Marcus, *School Desegregation in Texas*, 4.

110. Renee Tweedle, "Waco School System Seen as Splintering," *Waco News-Tribune*, December 9, 1970, 1B; Renee Tweedle, "Immediate Faculty Integration Asked," *Waco Times-Herald*, November 20, 1970, 1, 7.

111. "Eighty-white/twenty Black" refers to the racial ratio set for Waco ISD, wherein 80 percent of the study body at all schools would be not Black and 20 percent would be Black. At this time, Mexican American students were considered white.

112. Bolton, *Hardest Deal of All*, 169–73; Wilkinson, *From Brown to Bakke*, 120, 118.

113. "High School Boundaries: Public Meetings May 10-11-12," *Waco Citizen*, May 6, 1971; and W. C. Roper Jr., DDS, to Citizens Advisory Committee, May 12, 1971; and R. L. Zeigler, MD, to Citizens Advisory Committee, May 11, 1971, both in box 1, folder 2, Raymond E. Biles Collection, Texas Collection, Baylor University, Waco, Texas.

114. "High School Boundaries"; Roper to Citizens Advisory Committee, May 12, 1971; Zeigler to Citizens Advisory Committee, May 11, 1971.

115. Minutes, July 15, 1971, WISD Trustees. Claiming the school board had "missed the entire point of view" in failing to recognize that for many Mexican Americans, "damage has already been done" to prevent them from staying in school, Muniz urged the school board to address the wishes of local Mexican American residents, who were "asking for equal education," a plea that squared with that of Black Waco residents.

116. Minutes, April 20, 1971, LVISD Trustees.

117. Minutes, July 20, 1971, LVISD Trustees.

118. Minutes, July 20, 1971, LVISD Trustees.

119. Minutes, July 22, 1971, LVISD Trustees.

120. Hinsley to Henry Cranfill, August 16, 1971, LVISD Trustees.

121. See John Black, "NAACP Discusses Plans for Equality at La Vega," *Waco Tribune-Herald*, December 5, 1970, 1; and "La Vega Files Suit on NAACP," *Waco News-Tribune*, December 22, 1970, 1.

122. Hinsley to Cranfill, August 16, 1971.

123. Terri Jo Ryan, "Racial Segregation Created G. W. Carver," Waco History Project, January 16, 2006, http://wacohistoryproject.org/Places/CarverHigh.htm.

124. "Seminar on Civil Rights Voted Here," *Waco News-Tribune*, January 22, 1971, 7B; Sean Sutcliffe, "La Vega ISD Shrinks, Waco ISD Grows: School Integration, July 1971," *Local History Stories* (blog), Waco-McLennan County Library, July 23, 2021, https://libguides.wacolibrary.org/localhistory/stories/La-Vega-ISD-shrinks-Waco-ISD-grows-school-integration-July-1971.

125. In a map of new boundary changes, General Tire appears within Waco ISD lines. See "La Vega-Waco: School Boundaries Changed," *Waco Citizen*, July 29, 1971; and Ryan, "Racial Segregation."

126. Black, "Unity Among Whites Urged," 2.

127. Samuel W. Newman, *History of the Waco Public School System* (Waco, TX: Waco Independent School District, 1976), 80.

128. Newman, *History*, 80.

129. Debora Wilkerson, in discussion with the author, February 2018 and September 2023. All references in this chapter to Debora Wilkerson's oral history interview are from these discussions.

130. Newman, *History*, 80.

131. James-Gallaway, "Waco's First," 70.

132. Minutes, August 19, 1971, WISD Trustees.

133. "Model City Funds: $7.2 Million for City-Wide Use," *Waco Citizen*, August 19, 1971, 1.

134. "Model City Funds," 1.

135. Ansley Erickson, *Making the Unequal Metropolis: School Desegregation and Its Limits* (Chicago: University of Chicago Press, 2016), chap. 5; Walter Stern, *Race and Education in New Orleans: Creating the Segregated City, 1764–1960* (Baton Rouge: Louisiana State University Press, 2018), chap. 4; Andrew R. Highsmith, *Demolition Means Progress: Flint, Michigan, and the Fate of the American Metropolis* (Chicago: University of Chicago Press, 2019), chap. 9.

136. Minutes, July 15, 1971, WISD Trustees.

## CHAPTER 3

1. Willie Brown, in discussion with the author, November 2018. All references in this chapter to Willie Brown's oral history interview are from this discussion. Rather than censor the antiBlack epithet "Nigga" or any of its derivatives, I feature the language as reported to me in interviews or as I uncovered it in historical records. I make this choice to accurately and precisely represent the history I am seeking to portray, which is animated by the heavy, negative baggage the terms summon.

2. Adam Bledsoe, "The Primacy of Anti-Blackness," *Area* 52, no. 3 (2020): 472–79; Adam Bledsoe, LaToya Eaves, Brian Williams, and Willie Jamaal Wright, "Enacting Black

Geographies," in "Black Geographies," special virtual issue 2, *Southeastern Geographer*, 2018, 1–18, https://muse.jhu.edu/issue/38075.

3. Charles C. Bolton, *The Hardest Deal of All: The Battle over School Integration in Mississippi, 1870–1980* (Oxford: University Press of Mississippi, 2005), 160.

4. The white student body at Richfield was generally more affluent, as the residential values in the local neighborhoods show, which resulted in generally more positive interactions with Black students. See chapter 1 for a longer discussion on this phenomenon.

5. Dixie Shipp, "School Status Here Uncertain," *Waco Times-Herald*, January 28, 1970, 6.

6. Shipp, "School Status Here Uncertain," 6. See chapter 2 of this book for more details on this sudden rise in Richfield's Black student population.

7. Patricia Bernstein, *The First Waco Horror: The Lynching of Jesse Washington and the Rise of the NAACP* (College Station: Texas A&M University Press, 2006); James M. SoRelle, "The 'Waco Horror': The Lynching of Jesse Washington," *Southwestern Historical Quarterly* 86, no. 4 (1983): 517–36; Herbert Shapiro, *White Violence and Black Response: From Reconstruction to Montgomery* (Amherst: University of Massachusetts Press, 1988).

8. Claude M. Steele and Joshua Aronson, "Stereotype Threat and the Intellectual Test Performance of African Americans," *Journal of Personality and Social Psychology* 69, no. 5 (1995): 797–811.

9. Patricia Hill Collins, *Black Feminist Thought: Knowledge, Consciousness, and the Politics of Empowerment*, 2nd ed. (New York: Routledge, 2002).

10. Saidiya Hartman describes the "afterlife of slavery" as "a measure of man and a ranking of life and worth that has yet to be undone . . . a racial calculus and a political arithmetic that were entrenched centuries ago." See Saidiya Hartman, *Lose Your Mother: A Journey Along the Atlantic Slave Route* (New York: Farrar, Straus and Giroux, 2007), 6.

11. George M. Fredrickson, *The Black Image in the White Mind: The Debate on Afro-American Character and Destiny, 1817–1914* (New York: Harper and Row, 1971); Michelle M. Wright, *Physics of Blackness: Beyond the Middle Passage Epistemology* (Minneapolis: University of Minnesota Press, 2015).

12. Patricia Hill Collins, *Black Sexual Politics: African Americans, Gender and the New Racism* (New York: Routledge, 2004); bell hooks, *We Real Cool: Black Men and Masculinity* (New York: Routledge, 2004); Fredrickson, *Black Image*; Tracey Owens Patton and Julie Snyder-Yuly, "Any Four Black Men Will Do: Rape, Race, and the Ultimate Scapegoat," *Journal of Black Studies* 37, no. 6 (2007): 859–95; Bettina L. Love, "'I See Trayvon Martin': What Teachers Can Learn from the Tragic Death of a Young Black Male," *Urban Review* 46, no. 2 (2014): 292–306.

13. "Best Dressed: Bill (Willie) Brown and Marcella Sexton," in *The Treasure Chest*, yearbook, 1971, 93, La Vega High School, Bellmead, Texas. Willie, who is misnamed in this yearbook as Bill, followed directions from the yearbook photographer to sit behind the white classmate named Best-Dressed Girl.

14. Donald Bogle, *Toms, Coons, Mulattoes, Mammies, and Bucks: An Interpretive History of Blacks in American Films* (New York: Viking, 1973); Stefanie Laufs, *Fighting a Movie with Lightning: "The Birth of a Nation" and the Black Community* (Hamburg, Germany: Anchor Academic, 2013); Sylvia E. White and Tania Fuentez, "Analysis of Black Images in Comic Strips, 1915–1995," *Newspaper Research Journal* 18, no. 1–2 (1997): 72–85.

15. Angela Y. Davis, "Rape, Racism and the Capitalist Setting," *Black Scholar* 12, no. 6 (1981): 40.

16. Paula J. Giddings, *Ida: A Sword Among Lions; Ida B. Wells and the Campaign Against Lynching* (New York: Amistad, 2008). See also Collins, *Black Sexual Politics*; hooks, *We Real Cool*; Fredrickson, *Black Image*; Patton and Snyder-Yuly, "Any Four Black Men"; and Bogle, *Toms, Coons, Mulattoes, Mammies.*

17. Bolton, *Hardest Deal of All*, 207.

18. See *Treasure Chest*, 1971, 90–100; and *The Daisy Chain*, yearbook, 1969–73, Waco High School, Waco, Texas.

19. Thomas S. Martin, "Inequality in Desegregation: Black School Closings," *University of Chicago Law Review* 39, no. 3 (1972): 658–72; David. S. Cecelski, *Along Freedom Road: Hyde County, North Carolina, and the Fate of Black Schools in the South* (Chapel Hill: University of North Carolina Press, 1994).

20. Refer to chapter 1 for a discussion of the economic differences between these areas of the city, as Willie's analysis is supported by economic data.

21. Cedric Robinson, *Black Marxism: The Making of the Black Radical Tradition* (1983; repr., Chapel Hill: University of North Carolina Press, 2000); Jodi Melamed, "Racial Capitalism," *Critical Ethnic Studies* 1, no. 1 (2015): 76–85.

22. Charles S. Bullock III, "Interracial Contact and Student Prejudice: The Impact of Southern School Desegregation," *Youth and Society* 7, no. 3 (1976): 279.

23. Russell Livingston, in discussion with the author, December 2018. All references in this chapter to Russell Livingston's oral history interview are from this discussion.

24. Karen Anderson, *Little Rock: Race and Resistance at Central High School* (Princeton, NJ: Princeton University Press, 2010), 106.

25. Darrick Bledsoe, in discussion with the author, October 2018. All references in this chapter to Darrick Bledsoe's oral history interview are from this discussion.

26. Thomas Russell, "'Keep Negroes Out of Most Classes Where There Are a Large Number of Girls': The Unseen Power of the Ku Klux Klan and Standardized Testing at the University of Texas, 1899–1999," *South Texas Law Review* 52, no. 1 (2010): 1–2.

27. Bernstein, *First Waco Horror*; SoRelle, "'Waco Horror.'"

28. ArCasia D. James-Gallaway, "Under a Black Light: Implications of Mexican American School Segregation Challenges for African Americans in Texas," *Teachers College Record* 124, no. 12 (2022): 220–51; Laura Gómez, *Manifest Destinies: The Making of the Mexican American Race* (New York: New York University Press, 2018); Guadalupe San Miguel, *Brown, Not White: School Integration and the Chicano Movement in Houston* (College Station: Texas A&M University Press, 2005); Rubén Donato, *The Other Struggle for Equal Schools: Mexican Americans During the Civil Rights Era* (Albany: State University of New York Press, 1997).

29. Bogle, *Toms, Coons, Mulattoes, Mammies.*

30. ArCasia D. James-Gallaway, "Alive and Well: Enduring Stereotypes in School Desegregation," *American Educational History Journal* 46, no. 1–2 (2019): 51.

31. Calvin Jones, in discussion with the author, May 2019; Connie Oliver, in discussion with the author, May 2019. All references in this chapter to Calvin Jones's and Connie Oliver's oral history interviews are from these respective discussions.

32. Anderson, *Little Rock*, 122.

33. Anderson, *Little Rock*; Tracy E. K'Meyer, *From Brown to Meredith: The Long Struggle for School Desegregation in Louisville* (Chapel Hill: University of North Carolina Press, 2013).

34. Martha Hodes, *White Women, Black Men: Illicit Sex in the Nineteenth-Century South* (New Haven, CT: Yale University Press, 2014).

35. Amy Stuart Wells, Jennifer Jellison Holme, Anita Tijerina Revilla, and Awo Korantemaa Atanda, *Both Sides Now: The Story of School Desegregation's Graduates* (Berkeley: University of California Press; 2008), 197.

36. D. W. Griffith, dir., *The Birth of a Nation* (Hollywood, CA: David W. Griffith Corporation, 1915); Anderson, *Little Rock*; James-Gallaway, "Alive and Well."

37. Richard Jenkins, in discussion with the author, October 2023. All references in this chapter to Richard Jenkins's oral history interview are from this discussion. Contact issues prevented me from obtaining permission to use Richard's de-identified interviews before book production began; thus, I created a pseudonym to protect his privacy.

38. Roberta G. Simmons, Leslie Brown, Diane Mitsch Bush, and Dale A. Blyth, "Self-Esteem and Achievement of Black and White Adolescents," *Social Problems* 26, no. 1 (1978): 86–96; Florence R. Rosenberg and Roberta G. Simmons, "Sex Differences in the Self-Concept in Adolescence," *Sex Roles* 1, no. 2 (1975): 147–59.

39. Maria Josefina Saldaña-Portillo, "Consuming Malcolm X: Prophecy and Performative Masculinity," *Novel* 30, no. 3 (1997): 295.

40. Derrick Bell, "Racial Realism," *Connecticut Law Review* 24, no. 2 (1992): 363–79.

41. Russell Livingston is pictured wearing a suit his junior year for Waco High School's student government photo. See *Daisy Chain*, 1972, 55.

42. Robert Wuthnow, *Rough Country: How Texas Became America's Most Powerful Bible-Belt State* (Princeton, NJ: Princeton University Press, 2014), 5.

43. For more on the racism embedded within Waco's residential covenants, see chapter 1.

44. Russell Livingston is pictured with a group of white students holding a mega-size check for Young Life in the 1973 Waco High School yearbook. *Daisy Chain*, 1973, n.p.

45. See also Ray C. Rist, "School Integration and Minority Student Tokenism," *Integrated Education* 14, no. 1 (1976): 18–20.

46. Malcolm X, *The Autobiography of Malcolm X*, with Alex Haley (New York: Grove, 1964), 37.

47. See, e.g., Darrell Steffensmeier, Jeffery Ulmer, and John Kramer, "The Interaction of Race, Gender, and Age in Criminal Sentencing: The Punishment Cost of Being Young, Black, and Male," *Criminology* 36, no. 4 (1998): 763–98; and Cassia Spohn, "Race, Crime, and Punishment in the Twentieth and Twenty-First Centuries," *Crime and Justice* 44, no. 1 (2015): 49–97.

48. Linda Grant, "Uneasy Alliances: Black Males, Teachers, and Peers in Desegregated Classrooms," 30, paper prepared for the Annual Meeting of the American Educational Research Association, Chicago, IL, April 1, 1985, https://files.eric.ed.gov/fulltext/ED262115.pdf.

49. Malcolm X, *Autobiography of Malcolm X*, 28.

50. Malcolm X, *Autobiography of Malcolm X*, 31.

51. See, e.g., *Daisy Chain*, 1973, 46, 93.

52. During his senior year alone, Russell was documented in the yearbook to have belonged to five different student organizations. See *Daisy Chain*, 1973, 15 (theater department), 93 (senior honors), 96 (pep rally skit), 104 (Key Club), 117 (Junior Classical League), 118 (Journalism Club).

53. See chapter 4 for a fuller account of each Black girl's experiences.

54. K'Meyer, *From Brown to Meredith*, 39.

55. Calvin's working-class upbringing was evident in his reflection about "having it made" as one of the youngest of six children in his family because his "older [siblings] . . . bought [him and the other younger siblings] clothes."

56. Adrienne D. Dixson and Celia K. Rousseau, "And We Are Still Not Saved: Critical Race Theory in Education Ten Years Later," *Race Ethnicity and Education* 8, no. 1 (2005): 15.

57. Grant, "Uneasy Alliances," 4.

58. K'Meyer, *From Brown to Meredith*, 44.

59. *Spirit*, yearbook, 1976, 27 (Citizen of the Year), 54–55 (Best All-Around), University High School, Waco, Texas.

60. *Spirit*, 1976, 151.

61. Carol Haliburton, in discussion with the author, May 2019. All references in this chapter to Carol Haliburton's oral history interview are from this discussion. *Spirit*, 1976, 109; *Spirit*, 1974, 151. The year 1976 was Carol's and Calvin's senior year; 1974 was their sophomore year. For more on the struggle around Black students being accepted in white schools, see Melba Beals, *Warriors Don't Cry: Searing Memoir of Battle to Integrate Little Rock* (New York: Simon and Schuster, 1995); Michelle Purdy, *Transforming the Elite: Black Students and the Desegregation of Private Schools* (Chapel Hill: University of North Carolina Press, 2018); Anderson, *Little Rock*; and K'Meyer, *From Brown to Meredith*.

62. Malcolm X, *Autobiography of Malcolm X*.

63. A core tenet of Black geographies is Black spatial agency. See Pat Noxolo, "Geographies of Race and Ethnicity 1: Black Geographies," *Progress in Human Geography* 46, no. 5 (2022): 1232–240; and Adam Bledsoe and Willie Jamaal Wright, "The Anti-Blackness of Global Capital," *Environment and Planning D: Society and Space* 37, no. 1 (2019): 8–26.

64. Ashley Atkins, "Black Lives Matter or All Lives Matter? Color-Blindness and Epistemic Injustice," *Social Epistemology* 33, no. 1 (2019): 1–22.

65. Jacqueline Elaine Mosley's picture appears in *Daisy Chain*, 1972, 44, 72 (homecoming court), 109, 116 (Junior Classical League), 127 (choir). Elaine went by her middle name.

66. Grant, "Uneasy Alliances," 30.

67. Bettye Collier-Thomas and Vincent P. Franklin, eds., *Sisters in the Struggle: African American Women in the Civil Rights–Black Power Movement* (New York: New York University Press, 2001); Bernice McNair Barnett, "Invisible Southern Black Women Leaders in the Civil Rights Movement: The Triple Constraints of Gender, Race, and Class," *Gender and Society* 7, no. 2 (1993): 162–82; ArCasia D. James-Gallaway, "Waco's First Black School Board Trustees: Navigating Institutional White Supremacy in 1970s Texas," *History of Education Quarterly* 63, no. 1 (2023): 220–51.

68. James-Gallaway, "Waco's First."

69. W. E. B. Du Bois, "Strivings of the Negro People," *Atlantic*, August 1897, 194–98.

70. Scott Baker, *Paradoxes of Desegregation: African American Struggles for Educational Equity in Charleston, South Carolina, 1926–1972* (Columbia: University of South Carolina Press, 2006), 164.

71. Purdy, *Transforming the Elite*, 136.

72. Deborah Gray White, *Ar'n't I a Woman? Female Slaves in the Plantation South* (New York: W. W. Norton, 1999), chap. 1; Kimberly Wallace-Sanders, *Mammy: A Century of Race, Gender, and Southern Memory* (Ann Arbor: University of Michigan Press, 2008); K. Sue Jewell, *From Mammy to Miss America and Beyond: Cultural Images and the Shaping of US Social Policy* (London: Routledge, 2012).

73. Ruth Nolte is named as a teacher in the school's annual yearbook. See *Daisy Chain*, 1971, 22.

74. Mary Pattillo-McCoy, *Black Picket Fences: Privilege and Peril Among the Black Middle Class* (Chicago: University of Chicago Press, 1999); Melvin Oliver and Thomas Shapiro, *Black Wealth / White Wealth: A New Perspective on Racial Inequality* (New York: Routledge, 1995).

75. ArCasia D. James-Gallaway and Adah Ward Randolph, "Critical Race Theory and Education History: Constructing a Race-Centered History of School Desegregation," in *Handbook of Critical Race Theory in Education*, ed. Marvin Lynn and Adrienne D. Dixson (New York: Routledge, 2021), 337–38.

76. Charlotte Adams, in discussion with the author, December 2018. All references in this chapter to Charlotte Adams's oral history interview are from this discussion.

77. Joe R. Feagin, *The White Racial Frame: Centuries of Racial Framing and Counter-Framing* (New York: Routledge, 2010).

78. Pamela James, in discussion with the author, August 2018. All references in this chapter to Pamela James's oral history interview are from this discussion.

79. Charlotte Adams's résumé indicates that she went on to earn multiple advanced degrees and enjoyed a long and accomplished career as an educator in Texas.

80. William A. Sundstrom, "The Geography of Wage Discrimination in the Pre–Civil Rights South," *Journal of Economic History* 67, no. 2 (2007): 410–44; Stanley Lieberson, *A Piece of the Pie: Blacks and White Immigrants Since 1880* (Berkeley: University of California Press, 1980); William A. Darity and Patrick L. Mason, "Evidence on Discrimination in Employment: Codes of Color, Codes of Gender," *Journal of Economic Perspectives* 12, no. 2 (1998): 63–90; Celeste K. Carruthers and Marianne H. Wanamaker, "Separate and Unequal in the Labor Market: Human Capital and the Jim Crow Wage Gap," *Journal of Labor Economics* 35, no. 3 (2017): 655–96.

81. Katherine Sanford, in discussion with the author, May 2019. All references in this chapter to Katherine Sanford's oral history interview are from this discussion. Contact issues prevented me from obtaining permission to use Katherine's de-identified interviews before book production began; thus, I created a pseudonym to protect her privacy.

82. White, *Ar'n't I a Woman?*, 27–61; Regina Austin, "Sapphire Bound!," *Wisconsin Law Review* 3 (1989): 539–78; Carolyn M. West, "Mammy, Sapphire, and Jezebel: Historical Images of Black Women and Their Implications for Psychotherapy," *Psychotherapy* 32, no. 3 (1995): 458–66; Joan Marie Johnson, "'Ye Gave Them a Stone': African American Women's Clubs, the Frederick Douglass Home, and the Black Mammy Monument," *Journal of Women's History* 17, no. 1 (2005): 62–86; Wallace-Sanders, *Mammy*.

83. Angela Jill Cooley, "'Eating with Negroes': Food and Racial Taboo in the Twentieth-Century South," *Southern Quarterly* 52, no. 2 (2015): 72.

84. West, "Mammy, Sapphire, and Jezebel," 459–61, 462–63; White, *Ar'n't I a Woman?*, 27–61; James-Gallaway, "Alive and Well." See also Rachel Feinstein, *When Rape Was Legal: The Untold History of Sexual Violence During Slavery* (New York: Routledge, 2018).

85. Bolton, *Hardest Deal of All*, 160.

86. The quotation is taken from Lindsey Elizabeth Jones, "'The Most Unprotected of All Human Beings': Black Girls, State Violence, and the Limits of Protection in Jim Crow Virginia," *Souls* 20, no. 1 (2018): 16. See also Kellie Carter Jackson, *We Refuse: A Forceful History of Black Resistance* (New York: Seal, 2024).

87. K'Meyer, *From Brown to Meredith*, 37.

88. Ruth Frankenberg, *White Women, Race Matters: The Social Construction of Whiteness* (Minneapolis: University of Minnesota Press, 1993); Sarita Srivastava, "'You're Calling Me a Racist?' The Moral and Emotional Regulation of Antiracism and Feminism," *Signs* 31, no. 1 (2005): 29–62; Nancy MacLean, "White Women and Klan Violence in the 1920s: Agency, Complicity and the Politics of Women's History," *Gender and History* 3, no. 3 (1991): 285–303.

89. Waco ISD school board minutes from October 1974 highlight the board's decision to demolish West Junior High given its age and deterioration. It is curious that some of Waco ISD's first Black students to desegregate were forced into one of the oldest buildings in the district. See minutes, October 1974, WISD Trustees.

90. Rachel Devlin, *A Girl Stands at the Door: The Generation of Young Women Who Desegregated America's Schools* (New York: Basic Books, 2018).

91. Anslum Hudlin, in discussion with the author, August 2023. All references in this chapter to Anslum Hudlin's oral history interview are from this discussion.

92. Dara Walker, "Learning to Struggle, Learning to Govern: How Black Youth Marshaled Education to Navigate Urban Transformations in the Motor City, 1967–1972," *Journal of Urban History* 51, no. 2 (2025): 441.

93. Mona Domosh, "Genealogies of Race, Gender, and Place," *Annals of the American Association of Geographers* 107, no. 3 (2017): 766. See also Cheryl I. Harris, "Whiteness as Property," *Harvard Law Review* 106, no. 8 (1993): 1707–91; and James Loewen, *Sundown Towns: A Hidden Dimension of American Racism* (New York: New Press, 2005).

94. Purdy, *Transforming the Elite*, 118–19.

95. Edwin Earl James, in discussion with the author, July 2023. All references in this chapter to Edwin Earl James's oral history interview are from this discussion. Edwin, Wanda, and Pamela are siblings who grew up in different households.

96. "La Vega Boycott Continues: Black Students Demand Changes," *Waco News-Tribune*, September 15, 1970, 10A.

97. See chapter 5 for more details on this strategy.

98. W. E. B. Du Bois, *The Souls of Black Folk* (1903; Mineola, NY: Dover, 1994), 1; Hartman, *Lose Your Mother*; Christina Sharpe, *In the Wake: On Blackness and Being* (Durham, NC: Duke University Press, 2016).

99. Katherine McKittrick "On Plantations, Prisons, and a Black Sense of Place," *Social and Cultural Geography* 12, no. 8 (2011): 954. See also Domosh, "Genealogies of Race," 765–78.

100. Emilie V. Siddle Walker, "Interpersonal Caring in the 'Good' Segregated Schooling of African-American Children: Evidence from the Case of Caswell County Training School," *Urban Review* 25, no. 1 (1993): 63–77; Van Dempsey and George Noblit, "The Demise of Caring in an African-American Community: One Consequence of School Desegregation," *Urban Review* 25, no. 1 (1993): 47–61. See chapter 5 of this book for a fuller discussion of this theme.

101. Wanda James, in discussion with the author, April 2019. All references in this chapter to Wanda James's oral history interview are from this discussion.

102. "La Vega Boycott Continues," 10A.

103. Recent scholarship has explored the prevalence of the Black criminal stereotype. See Kelly Welch, "Black Criminal Stereotypes and Racial Profiling," *Journal of Contemporary Criminal Justice* 23, no. 3 (2007): 276–88; and Mark W. Bennett and Victoria C. Plaut,

"Looking Criminal and the Presumption of Dangerousness: Afrocentric Facial Features, Skin Tone, and Criminal Justice," *UC Davis Law Review* 51, no. 3 (2017): 745.

104. "La Vega Boycott Continues," 10A.

105. W. E. B. Du Bois, *The Philadelphia Negro: A Social Study* (New York: Benjamin Blom, 1899); Du Bois, *Souls of Black Folk.*

106. Du Bois, *Souls of Black Folk*, 1.

107. Russell Skiba and Ashley White, "Ever Since Little Rock: The History of Disciplinary Disparities in America's Schools," in *Disproportionality and Social Justice in Education*, ed. Nicholas Gage, Luke J. Rapa, Denise K. Whitford, and Antonis Katsiyanis (Cham, Switzerland: Springer International, 2022), 3–33.

108. Michael Bass, in discussion with the author, June 2019. All references in this chapter to Michael Bass's oral history interview are from this discussion. Sarah Johnson and Gladys Johnson, in discussion with the author, November 2018. All references in this chapter to Sarah Johnson's and Gladys Johnson's oral history interviews are from this discussion. Of note is that I conducted Sarah's interview with her mother, Gladys Johnson, because this was Sarah's stipulation for being interviewed. Sarah was the only narrator who requested that I use pseudonyms for her and her mother. I have honored her request in accordance with the Black feminist claim that Black women reserve the right to define themselves. See the following article for a more thorough discussion: ArCasia D. James-Gallaway, "Tacit Curriculum of Black Intellectual Ineptitude: Black Girls' Perspectives on Texas School Desegregation Implementation in the 1970s," *History of Education Review* 51, no. 1 (2022): 81–95. Although Sarah and her mother were the only narrators who requested pseudonyms, I use pseudonyms for three others: Beverly Rickford, Katherine Sanford, and Richard Jenkins, given contact issues that prevented me from obtaining their permission to use their de-identified interviews before book production began.

109. bell hooks, *Teaching to Transgress: Education as the Practice of Freedom* (New York: Routledge, 1994), 3.

110. At a reunion of Black alumni of Waco ISD in September 2023, former students reflected openly on this point.

111. Bolton, *Hardest Deal of All*, 206.

112. Kimberlé Crenshaw, Priscilla Ocen, and Jyoti Nanda, *Black Girls Matter: Pushed Out, Overpoliced and Underprotected* (New York: Center for Intersectionality and Social Policy Studies at Columbia University and African American Policy Forum, 2015), www.aapf.org/blackgirlsmatter; Tera Eva Agyepong, *The Criminalization of Black Children: Race, Gender, and Delinquency in Chicago's Juvenile Justice System, 1899–1945* (Chapel Hill: University of North Carolina Press, 2018); Monique Morris, *Pushout: The Criminalization of Black Girls in Schools* (New York: New Press, 2016).

113. A review of Waco ISD school board minutes from 1974–76, the years Carol Haliburton was in high school, supports this assessment.

114. See Discipline Committee report, February 1973, WISD Trustees.

115. Cheryl Nelson Butler, "Blackness as Delinquency," *Washington University Law Review* 90, no. 5 (2012): 1335–97.

116. For example, at the Waco ISD school board meeting on December 20, 1973, the Black Federation requested that Dane Scott be reinstated after being suspended, offering to "put their full support behind the student and help him as much as possible to continue his

education." The board voted in favor of the motion and Dane was reinstated. See minutes, December 20, 1973, WISD Trustees.

117. James-Gallaway, "Waco's First"; minutes, 1976–78, WISD Trustees.

118. Carter Jackson, *We Refuse.*

119. W. E. B. Du Bois, "Does the Negro Need Separate Schools?," *Journal of Negro Education* 4, no. 3 (1935): 328–35.

## CHAPTER 4

1. Cheryl Kay Williams, in discussion with the author, October 2023. All references in this chapter to Kay Williams's oral history interview are from this discussion. Kay went by her middle name. She is pictured in her yearbook as a homecoming nominee and in her senior class photo. See *The Daisy Chain*, yearbook, 1970, 39, 80, Waco High School, Waco, Texas.

2. *Daisy Chain*, 1972, 103.

3. Constance Sadler, in discussion with the author, May 2018. All references in this chapter to Constance "Connie" Sadler's oral history interview are from this discussion.

4. Connie Sadler appears in yearbook photos with her Afro. See *Aries*, yearbook, 1976, 24, 25, Richfield High School, Waco, Texas; and *Aries*, 1974, 166. See note 1 of this chapter for Kay Williams's photos.

5. The Miss America and the Miss Black America pageants were both held in Atlantic City, New Jersey. See Georgia Paige Welch, "'Up Against the Wall Miss America': Women's Liberation and Miss Black America in Atlantic City, 1968," *Feminist Formations* 27, no. 2 (2015): 70–97; and Maxine Leeds Craig, *Ain't I a Beauty Queen? Black Women, Beauty, and the Politics of Race* (New York: Oxford University Press, 2002).

6. Noliwe M. Rooks, *Hair Raising: Beauty, Culture, and African American Women* (New Brunswick, NJ: Rutgers University Press, 1996); Ayana D. Byrd and Lori L. Tharps, *Hair Story: Untangling the Roots of Black Hair in America* (New York: Macmillan, 2014); quotation from Paulette M. Caldwell, "A Hair Piece: Perspectives on the Intersection of Race and Gender," *Duke Law Journal* 1991, no. 2 (1991): 384.

7. On Madame C. J. Walker as one example, see Paula J. Giddings, *When and Where I Enter: The Impact of Black Women on Race and Sex in America* (New York: Bantam Books, 1984), 187–89.

8. LaKisha Simmons, *Crescent City Girls: The Lives of Young Black Women in Segregated New Orleans* (Chapel Hill: University of North Carolina Press, 2015); Corinne Field, *The Struggle for Equal Adulthood: Gender, Race, Age, and the Fight for Citizenship in Antebellum America* (Chapel Hill: University of North Carolina Press, 2014); Corinne Field, Tammy-Charelle Owens, Marcia Chatelain, LaKisha Simmons, Abosede George, and Rhian Keyse, "The History of Black Girlhood: Recent Innovations and Future Directions," *Journal of the History of Childhood and Youth* 9, no. 3 (2016): 383–401; Marcia Chatelain, *South Side Girls: Growing Up in the Great Migration* (Durham, NC: Duke University Press, 2015); Rachel Devlin, *A Girl Stands at the Door: The Generation of Young Women Who Desegregated America's Schools* (New York: Basic Books, 2018).

9. Kevin Quashie, "To Be (a) One: Notes on Coupling and Black Female Audacity," *differences* 29, no. 2 (2018): 68–95; Simmons, *Crescent City Girls.*

10. Aimee Meredith Cox, *Shapeshifters: Black Girls and the Choreography of Citizenship* (Durham, NC: Duke University Press, 2015), 29.

11. Cox, *Shapeshifters*, 29.

12. Tondra L. Loder-Jackson, *Schoolhouse Activists: African American Educators and the Long Birmingham Civil Rights Movement* (Albany: State University of New York Press, 2015).

13. ArCasia D. James-Gallaway, "What Got Them Through: Community Cultural Wealth, Black Students, and Texas School Desegregation," *Race Ethnicity and Education* 25, no. 2 (2022): 173–91; Michelle Purdy, *Transforming the Elite: Black Students and the Desegregation of Private Schools* (Chapel Hill: University of North Carolina Press, 2018), 138.

14. Pamela James, in discussion with the author, August 2018 and July 2023. All references in this chapter to Pamela James's oral history interview are from these discussions.

15. Minutes, April 16 and June 18, 1970, WISD Trustees. According to scholars writing about the history of kindergarten programs in Austin, Texas, "The development of the state law [to make kindergarten universal] was prompted by the success of the federal Head Start program." Curtis Brewer, John W. Gasko, and Derek Miller, "Have We Been Here Before? Lessons Learned from a Microhistory of the Policy Development of Universal Kindergarten," *Educational Policy* 25, no. 1 (2011): 27.

16. James-Gallaway, "What Got Them Through."

17. Margaret L. Hunter, *Race, Gender, and the Politics of Skin Tone* (New York: Routledge, 2013); Toni Morrison, *The Bluest Eye* (New York: Pocket Books, 1970).

18. Mary Beth Rogers, "The School Years of Barbara Jordan," *Journal of Blacks in Higher Education* 23 (1999): 116.

19. See chapter 1 for a detailed analysis of these home value and homeownership trends.

20. Sharon M. Collins, "The Making of the Black Middle Class," *Social Problems* 30, no. 4 (1983): 369; Thomas J. Durant and Joyce S. Louden, "The Black Middle Class in America: Historical and Contemporary Perspectives," *Phylon* 47, no. 4 (1986): 257; Mary Pattillo, *Black Picket Fences: Privilege and Peril Among the Black Middle Class* (Chicago: University of Chicago Press, 2013).

21. Gretchen Sorin, *Driving While Black: African American Travel and the Road to Civil Rights* (New York: Liveright, 2020).

22. Michelle L. Stevenson, Tammy L. Henderson, and Eboni Baugh, "Vital Defenses: Social Support Appraisals of Black Grandmothers Parenting Grandchildren," *Journal of Family Issues* 28, no. 2 (2007): 182–211; Jillian Jimenez, "The History of Grandmothers in the African-American Community," *Social Service Review* 76, no. 4 (2002): 523–51.

23. Wanda James, in discussion with the author, April 2019 and October 2023. All references in this chapter to Wanda James's oral history interview are from these discussions.

24. Patricia Hill Collins, *Black Feminist Thought: Knowledge, Consciousness, and the Politics of Empowerment*, 2nd ed. (New York: Routledge, 2002), chap. 4.

25. Debora Wilkerson, in discussion with the author, February 2018 and September 2023. All references in this chapter to Debora Wilkerson's oral history interview are from these discussions.

26. *Daisy Chain*, 1970, 80–81 (Future Homemakers of America club), 101 (Personality Development Club).

27. *Daisy Chain*, 1970, 137 (wearing pants to school), 93 (Nike Club).

28. Jennifer Mittelstadt, "Educating 'Our Girls' and 'Welfare Mothers': Discussions of Education Policy for Pregnant and Parenting Adolescents in Federal Hearings, 1975–1995,"

*Journal of Family History* 22, no. 3 (1997): 326–53; Wanda Pillow, "Teen Pregnancy and Education: Politics of Knowledge, Research, and Practice," *Educational Policy* 20, no. 1 (2006): 59–84.

29. Jerome Dees, "Access or Interest: Why *Brown* Has Benefitted African-American Women More Than Title IX," *University of Missouri Kansas City Law Review* 76, no. 1 (2008): 629–34.

30. Jacqueline Elaine Mosley, in discussion with the author, September 2023. All references in this chapter to Elaine Mosley's oral history interview are from this discussion. Elaine went by her middle name.

31. Image of Debora Wilkerson and Elaine Mosley at G. L. Wiley Junior High's prom in spring 1969, Elaine Mosley private collection.

32. The first quote is from Thomas Collins, "Reconstructing a High School Society After Court-Ordered Desegregation," *Anthropology of Education Quarterly* 9, no. 4 (1978): 249–50. The second quote is from A. Guy Larkins and Sally E. Oldham, "Patterns of Racial Separation in a Desegregated High School," *Theory and Research in Social Education* 4, no. 2 (1976): 31. For further discussion, see Charles T. Clotfelter, "Interracial Contact in High School Extracurricular Activities," *Urban Review* 34, no. 1 (2002): 25–46.

33. Laura Grindstaff and Emily West, "Cheerleading and the Gendered Politics of Sport," *Social Problems* 53, no. 4 (2006): 500–501. For further discussion, see Mary Ellen Hanson, *Go! Fight! Win! Cheerleading in American Culture* (Bowling Green, OH: Bowling Green State University Popular Press, 1995).

34. Daniel U. Levine and Ronald Brink, eds., *Perspectives and Suggestions for Teaching in Desegregated Schools*, ERIC 033895 (Kansas City: Kansas City School District and School of Education, Missouri University, 1969), 3.

35. Robert E. Anderson Jr., ed., *The South and Her Children: School Desegregation, 1970–1971* (Atlanta: Southern Regional Council, 1971), http://files.eric.ed.gov/fulltext/ED049327.pdf.

36. Linda M. Perkins, *To Advance the Race: Black Women's Higher Education from the Antebellum Era to the 1960s* (Urbana: University of Illinois Press, 2024), 200–205.

37. Hanson, *Go! Fight! Win!*, 33–34.

38. Hanson, *Go! Fight! Win!*, 34.

39. Beverly Rickford, in discussion with the author, January 2019. All references in this chapter to Beverly Rickford's oral history interview are from this discussion.

40. Caldwell, "Hair Piece," 383.

41. Carol E. Henderson, "AKA: Sarah Baartman, the Hottentot Venus, and Black Women's Identity," *Women's Studies* 43, no. 7 (2014): 946–59; Katherine McKittrick, "Science Quarrels Sculpture: The Politics of Reading Sarah Baartman," in "Sculpture," special issue, *Mosaic* 42, no. 2 (2010): 113–30.

42. Patricia Hill Collins, *Black Sexual Politics: African Americans, Gender and the New Racism* (New York: Routledge, 2004), 193.

43. Rogers, "School Years," 117.

44. Saidiya Hartman, "Seduction and the Ruses of Power," *Callaloo* 19, no. 2 (1996): 537.

45. Wilma King, *Stolen Childhood: Slave Youth in Nineteenth-Century America* (Bloomington: Indiana University Press, 1995); Kimberlé Crenshaw, "Demarginalizing the Intersection of Race and Sex: A Black Feminist Critique of Antidiscrimination Doctrine, Feminist

Theory and Antiracist Politics," *University of Chicago Legal Forum*, 1989, no. 8 (1989), 139, 145; Giddings, *When and Where.*

46. Patricia Hill Collins, *Black Sexual Politics*, 194.

47. While it is likely that exceptions did exist, this study found little to no evidence of such within the context of newly desegregated schools in Waco.

48. Carol Haliburton, in discussion with the author, May 2019. All references in this chapter to Carol Haliburton's oral history interview are from this discussion.

49. Sarah Johnson, in discussion with the author, November 2018. All references in this chapter to Sarah Johnson's oral history interview are from this discussion.

50. Katherine McKittrick, "'Who Do You Talk To, When a Body's in Trouble?': M. Nourbese Philip's (Un)silencing of Black Bodies in the Diaspora," *Social and Cultural Geography* 1, no. 2 (2000): 223–36.

51. Some of the only scholarship on this topic focuses on Black higher education dance teams. J'aime Griffith, "Historically Black College and University Dance Lines: Redefining and Identifying Elements to Determine Aesthetic Value" (master's thesis, University of Oklahoma, 2022); Chelsea Mary Elise Johnson, "'Just Because I Dance Like a Ho I'm Not a Ho': Cheerleading at the Intersection of Race, Class, and Gender," *Sociology of Sport Journal* 32, no. 4 (2015): 377–94.

52. Walda Kennedy is pictured as a student at Waco High School in two issues of the school's yearbook. See *Daisy Chain*, 1967, 53 (sophomore year), 98 (Future Secretaries Club); and *Daisy Chain*, 1968, 120 (junior year).

53. Patricia Hill Collins, *Black Sexual Politics*, 193–98.

54. Cox, *Shapeshifters*, 29.

55. Patricia G. Davis, "The Other Southern Belles: Civil War Reenactment, African American Women, and the Performance of Idealized Femininity," *Text and Performance Quarterly* 32, no. 4 (2012): 308–31; Crenshaw, "Demarginalizing the Intersection"; Giddings, *When and Where*; Hortense Spillers, "Mama's Baby, Papa's Maybe: An American Grammar Book," *Diacritics* 17, no. 2 (1987): 65–81.

56. Davis, "Other Southern Belles," 311.

57. Davis, "Other Southern Belles," 311.

58. Margaret Smith Crocco and Catty L. Waite, "Education and Marginality: Race and Gender in Higher Education, 1940–1955," *History of Education Quarterly* 47, no. 1 (2007): 73.

59. Crocco and Waite, "Education and Marginality," 73; direct quote from Stephanie J. Shaw, *What a Woman Ought to Be and to Do: Black Professional Women Workers During the Jim Crow Era* (Chicago: University of Chicago Press, 1996), 2.

60. Crocco and Waite, "Education and Marginality," 73.

61. Anslum Hudlin, in discussion with the author, August 2023. All references in this chapter to Anslum Hudlin's oral history interview are from this discussion.

62. Richard and Katherine were pictured throughout their yearbook. See *Daisy Chain*, 1971.

63. Levine and Brink, *Perspectives and Suggestions*, 4.

64. Richard Jenkins, in discussion with the author, October 2023. All references in this chapter to Richard Jenkins's oral history interview are from this discussion.

65. Tracy E. K'Meyer, *From Brown to Meredith: The Long Struggle for School Desegregation in Louisville* (Chapel Hill: University of North Carolina Press, 2013), 37–38.

66. Ann Patterson, "Waco's Junior Miss Pageant to Be Held Saturday Night," *Waco Citizen*, November 19, 1970, 1.

67. Scott Baker, *Paradoxes of Desegregation: African American Struggles for Educational Equity in Charleston, South Carolina, 1926–1972* (Columbia: University of South Carolina Press, 2006), 164.

68. Rogers, "School Years," 117.

69. Richard Jenkins is pictured throughout his yearbook. See *Daisy Chain*, 1971.

70. Kurt Conklin, "'We Can't Let Chicago Outdo Us, Can We?': Sex Education and Desegregation in New York City's Public Schools," *History of Education Quarterly* 53, no. 4 (2013): 335–68.

71. Jonathan Zimmerman, *Whose America? Culture Wars in the Public Schools*, 2nd ed. (Chicago: University of Chicago Press, 2022), 173.

72. Kathi Bolt, "Red Cross Class Stresses Care for Expectant Mother," *Waco Times-Herald*, February 8, 1971, 9A. This article described what to expect during pregnancy, previewing the progression of a typical pregnancy and the warning signs of complications. "Birth Control Increases Even as Legal Abortions Increase," *Waco Citizen*, November 20, 1975, 3. This article sounded moral alarms about the rises in both these health resources. "Junior League Hears: Teen Pregnancies at Epidemic Stage," *Waco Times-Herald*, October 14, 1976, 16. This article referred to pregnant teens as "moral outcasts." "Teen Births Risky," *Waco Tribune-Herald*, April 19, 1978, 15. This article summarized and explained how to purchase a pamphlet entitled *Teenage Pregnancy: Everybody's Problem*, created by the US Department of Health, Education, and Welfare.

73. Elsa Barkley Brown, "'What Has Happened Here': The Politics of Difference in Women's History and Feminist Politics," *Feminist Studies* 18, no. 2 (1992): 306. See also Darlene Clark Hine, "Rape and the Inner Lives of Black Women in the Middle West," *Signs* 14, no. 4 (1989): 912–20.

74. "Birth Control Increases," 3.

75. Brown, "'What Has Happened Here,'" 306. See also Darlene Clark Hine, "Rape and the Inner Lives of Black Women in the Middle West," *Signs: Journal of Women in Culture and Society* 14, no. 4 (1989): 912–20.

76. Evelyn Brooks Higginbotham, "African-American Women's History and the Metalanguage of Race," *Signs* 17, no. 2 (1992): 271.

77. Pillow, "Teen Pregnancy and Education," 72.

78. On the murky relationship between school desegregation and birth rates, see Sze Yan Liu, Crystal D. Linkletter, Eric B. Loucks, M. Maria Glymour, and Stephen L. Buka, "Decreased Births Among Black Female Adolescents Following School Desegregation," *Social Science and Medicine* 74, no. 7 (2012): 982–88; and Robert Bifulco, Leonard M. Lopoo, and Sun Jung Oh, "School Desegregation and Teenage Fertility," *Educational Evaluation and Policy Analysis* 37, no. 4 (2015): 591–611.

79. Jill Ogline Titus, "Living on the Frontlines: Black Teenagers on the Move to Freedom," *Journal of the History of Childhood and Youth* 2, no. 3 (2009): 440.

80. Stephanie J. Ventura and Mary Anne Freedman, "Teenage Childbearing in the United States, 1960–1997," *American Journal of Preventive Medicine* 19, no. 1 (2000): 22.

81. Pillow, "Teen Pregnancy and Education," 59–84, 71.

82. Chatelain, *South Side Girls*, 4.

83. Dorothy Roberts, *Killing the Black Body: Race, Reproduction, and the Meaning of Liberty* (New York: Vintage, 1997).

84. Rickie Solinger, *Wake Up Little Susie: Single Pregnancy and Race Before Roe v. Wade* (New York: Routledge, 1992); Loretta J. Ross, "African-American Women and Abortion: 1800–1970," in *Theorizing Black Feminisms: The Visionary Pragmatism of Black Women*, ed. Stanley M. James and Abena P. A. Busia (New York: Routledge, 1993), 155–74.

85. Quashie, "To Be (a) One."

86. Kevin Quashie, "The Trouble with Publicness: Toward a Theory of Black Quiet," *African American Review* 43, no. 2–3 (2009): 334.

87. Quashie, "To Be (a) One."

88. Katherine Sanford is pictured in her yearbook. See *Daisy Chain*, 1971.

89. Katherine Sanford, in discussion with the author, May 2019. All references in this chapter to Katherine Sanford's oral history interview are from this discussion.

90. Simmons, *Crescent City Girls*.

91. Evelyn Brooks Higginbotham, *Righteous Discontent: The Women's Movement in the Black Baptist Church, 1880–1920* (Cambridge, MA: Harvard University Press, 1994), 187. See also Kevin Gaines, *Uplifting the Race: Black Leadership, Politics, and Culture in the Twentieth Century* (Chapel Hill: University of North Carolina Press, 1996).

92. Gloria T. Hull, Patricia Bell Scott, and Barbara Smith, eds., *All the Women Are White, All the Blacks Are Men, but Some of Us Are Brave: Black Women's Studies* (Old Westbury, NY: Feminist, 1982); Angela Y. Davis, *Women, Race and Class* (New York: Vintage, 1983).

93. Founded in the 1920s, the *Waco Messenger* was published by members of the local Black elite, namely R. L. Rhone, through the 1980s. The *Waco Messenger* archive, Texas Collection, Carroll Library, Baylor University, Waco, Texas.

94. Cox, *Shapeshifters*, 7.

95. Stephen Jay Gould, *The Mismeasure of Man* (New York: W. W. Norton, 1981).

96. Charles C. Bolton, *The Hardest Deal of All: The Battle over School Integration in Mississippi, 1870–1980* (Oxford: University Press of Mississippi, 2005), 159.

97. Rosalee A. Clawson, "Poor People, Black Faces: The Portrayal of Poverty in Economics Textbooks," *Journal of Black Studies* 32, no. 3 (2002): 352–61; Rosalee A. Clawson and Elizabeth R. Kegler, "The Race Coding of Poverty in American Government College Textbooks," *Howard Journal of Communication* 11, no. 3 (2000): 179–88.

98. Devlin, *Girl Stands*, 104.

99. Pamela James's various school activities are depicted in the school yearbook. See *Daisy Chain*, 1972, 36 (homecoming court), 40 (choir), 103 (cheerleading).

100. ArCasia D. James-Gallaway, "Tacit Curriculum of Black Intellectual Ineptitude: Black Girls' Perspectives on Texas School Desegregation Implementation in the 1970s," *History of Education Review* 51, no. 1 (2022): 81–95.

101. Cox, *Shapeshifters*, 28.

102. Grace Hamilton is pictured in the 1970 yearbook. See *Daisy Chain*, 1970, 13.

103. See chapter 5 for more details.

104. Wei-ling Gong, "A History of Integration of the Waco Public Schools, 1954 to the Present" (master's thesis, Baylor University, 1987), 82. A review of Richfield High's yearbook, *Aries*, throughout the 1960s and 1970s continues to show a majority-white student body as well.

105. Levine and Brink, *Perspectives and Suggestions*, 2; Larkins and Oldham, "Patterns of Racial Separation," 33.

106. Beverly Rickford is pictured in the Richfield High School 1975 yearbook. See *Aries*, 1970.

107. Jean Wyatt, "Patricia Hill Collins's *Black Sexual Politics* and the Genealogy of the Strong Black Woman," *Studies in Gender and Sexuality* 9, no. 1 (2008): 52–67; Patricia Hill Collins, "Reply to Commentaries: *Black Sexual Politics* Revisited," *Studies in Gender and Sexuality* 9, no. 1 (2008): 82–85.

108. Kathleen M. Blee, *Women of the Klan: Racism and Gender in the 1920s* (Berkeley: University of California Press, 1991); Kristina DuRocher, *Raising Racists: The Socialization of White Children in the Jim Crow South* (Lexington: University Press of Kentucky, 2011).

109. Elizabeth Gillespie McRae, *Mothers of Massive Resistance: White Women and the Politics of White Supremacy* (Oxford: Oxford University Press, 2018); Karen Anderson, *Little Rock: Race and Resistance at Central High School* (Princeton, NJ: Princeton University Press, 2010).

110. See, e.g., Thavolia Glymph, *Out of the House of Bondage: The Transformation of the Plantation Household* (New York: Cambridge University Press, 2008); and Stephanie E. Jones-Rogers, *They Were Her Property: White Women as Slave Owners in the American South* (New Haven, CT: Yale University Press, 2019).

111. Patricia Hill Collins, *Black Sexual Politics*; Patricia Hill Collins, *Black Feminist Thought*, chap. 4.

112. See chapter 5 for a fuller discussion of Debora's encounters with her counselor, Grace Hamilton.

113. Cox, *Shapeshifters*, 29.

114. Sherri Fudge, "Pregnant School Girls Across U.S. Don't Have to Interrupt Education," *Waco Times-Herald*, June 22, 1972, 35.

115. Monica J. Stamm, "A Skeleton in the Closet: Single-Sex Schools for Pregnant Girls," *Columbia Law Review* 98, no. 5 (1998): 1203.

116. Regina Austin, "Sapphire Bound!," *Wisconsin Law Review* 3 (1989): 539–78; Patricia J. Williams, *The Rooster's Egg* (Cambridge, MA: Harvard University Press, 1995); Patricia Hill Collins, *Black Feminist Thought*. On services for pregnant students, see Cynthia Barnett, "An Assessment of Educational Services for Pregnant Students and Teenage Mothers" (PhD diss., Columbia University, 1988).

117. Fudge, "Pregnant School Girls," 35; Stamm, "Skeleton in the Closet," 1203; Pillow, "Teen Pregnancy and Education," 71.

118. Stamm, "Skeleton in the Closet," 1229.

119. Cox, *Shapeshifters*, 29–30.

120. Patricia Hill Collins, "Black Feminist Thought in the Matrix of Domination," in *Social Theory: The Multicultural and Classic Readings*, ed. Charles Lemert (San Francisco: Westview, 1993), 615–26.

## CHAPTER 5

1. Carol Haliburton lived with her parents in "No Man's Land," an underserved, unincorporated area where the cities of Waco and Bellmead connect; during her early

childhood, they lacked indoor plumbing and running water, having to use an outhouse into the 1960s. This area just south of Waco was historically home to concentrations of Black and Mexican American populations. Although her mother was able to transport her to and from school and the doctor, and her father visited University High School when administrators called with discipline concerns, it was only in extreme circumstances that they were able to be present in her school life. Carol's father's visit to University High is detailed in chapter 3.

2. Carol Haliburton, in discussion with the author, May 2019. All references in this chapter to Carol Haliburton's oral history interview are from this discussion.

3. Gary Lavergne, *Before Brown: Heman Marion Sweatt, Thurgood Marshall, and the Long Road to Justice* (Austin: University of Texas Press, 2010), 280.

4. Scott Baker, *Paradoxes of Desegregation: African American Struggles for Educational Equity in Charleston, South Carolina, 1926–1972* (Columbia: University of South Carolina Press, 2006), 164.

5. This event is discussed in chapter 3.

6. Russell Skiba and Ashley White, "Ever Since Little Rock: The History of Disciplinary Disparities in America's Schools," in *Disproportionality and Social Justice in Education*, ed. Nicholas Gage, Luke J. Rapa, Denise K. Whitford, and Antonis Katsiyanis (Cham, Switzerland: Springer International, 2022).

7. ArCasia D. James-Gallaway, "Waco's First Black School Board Trustees: Navigating Institutional White Supremacy in 1970s Texas," *History of Education Quarterly* 63, no. 1 (2023): 59–83.

8. Jay McCullough appears in the Waco ISD Board of Trustees minutes and in the yearbook during Carol's time at University High School. See minutes, March 21, 1974, WISD Trustees; and *Spirit*, yearbook, 1975, 75, University High School, Waco, Texas.

9. Monique Morris, *Pushout: The Criminalization of Black Girls in Schools* (New York: New Press, 2016).

10. Van Dempsey and George Noblit, "The Demise of Caring in an African-American Community: One Consequence of School Desegregation," *Urban Review* 25, no. 1 (1993): 47–61; Van Dempsey and George W. Noblit, "Cultural Ignorance and School Desegregation: Reconstructing a Silenced Narrative," *Educational Policy* 7, no. 3 (1993): 318–39.

11. Emilie V. Siddle Walker, "Interpersonal Caring in the 'Good' Segregated Schooling of African-American Children: Evidence from the Case of Caswell County Training School," *Urban Review* 25, no. 1 (1993): 65.

12. La Vega ISD closed G. W. Carver High School in 1970. Waco ISD closed A. J. Moore High School in 1971. These adjoining school districts shut down these segregated Black schools to comply with desegregation mandates because they were under court orders to meet the requirements of the 1968 *Green v. County School Board of New Kent County* decision, which outlawed the token desegregation both districts were practicing. See chapters 1 and 2 for further discussion.

13. Derrick Bell, "Racial Realism," *Connecticut Law Review* 24, no. 2 (1992): 363–79.

14. Quotation is from Alexander Hyres, "'The Whole Mess Is American History': Protest, Pedagogy, and Black Studies at a Desegregated High School in the South, 1967–1974," *Journal of African American History* 107, no. 1 (2022): 65. The Boston example is from Tess Bundy, "'Revolutions Happen Through Young People!': The Black Student Movement in the Boston Public Schools, 1968–1971," *Journal of Urban History* 43, no. 2 (2017): 273–93.

15. For a racialized discussion of Waco's economic context, see chapter 1. Additionally, multiple narrators such as Carol Haliburton and Darrick Bledsoe underscored that they were unaware they were impoverished until they attended desegregated schools.

16. Edwin James's family rented their home rather than owned it, and his caretakers were wage laborers. Edwin Earl James, in discussion with the author, July 2023. All references in this chapter to Edwin Earl James's oral history interview are from this discussion.

17. Melba Beals, *Warriors Don't Cry: Searing Memoir of Battle to Integrate Little Rock* (New York: Simon and Schuster, 1995), 119.

18. William J. Baxley, George L. Beck Jr., Ed Carnes, and Myron H. Thompson, "In Pursuit of Justice: The Investigation, Historic Trial and Conviction of the First Klansman for the Sixteenth Street Baptist Church Bombing," *Alabama Law Review* 71, no. 3 (2020): 605.

19. John Dittmer, *Local People: The Struggle for Civil Rights in Mississippi* (Urbana: University of Illinois Press, 1994).

20. Joy Ann Williamson, *Black Power on Campus: The University of Illinois, 1965–75* (Urbana: University of Illinois Press, 2003).

21. Connie's father served in the military, and her mother, who worked intermittently when her father was alive and consistently upon his passing when Connie was a teenager, worked as a domestic laborer in west Waco. It is likely that Connie's father's military service benefits helped the family maintain their home, a valuable asset, and the security that housing stability provided. Willie's parents were both educators, who worked as teachers and administrators in La Vega and Waco schools. Constance "Connie" Sadler, in discussion with the author, May 2019. All references in this chapter to Connie Sadler's oral history interview are from this discussion. Willie Williams Jr., in discussion with the author, April 2019. All references in this chapter to Willie Williams Jr.'s oral history interview are from this discussion.

22. These single-family homes, which middle-class Black families started to purchase in the 1950s and 1960s, tended to be in three distinct East Waco neighborhoods: Sharondale, where Willie Williams Jr. lived; Hollywood; and Carver Park, where Connie Sadler's family resided.

23. Cheryl Thompson, *Uncle: Race, Nostalgia, and the Politics of Loyalty* (Toronto, ON: Coach House Books, 2021).

24. Sylvia Wynter, "Alterity," in *Dictionary of Multicultural Education*, ed. Carl Grant and Gloria Ladson-Billings (New York: Oryx, 1997), 13–14.

25. Kabria Baumgartner, *In Pursuit of Knowledge: Black Women and Educational Activism in Antebellum America* (New York: New York University Press, 2022), 14.

26. Derrick P. Alridge, "Conceptualizing a Du Boisian Philosophy of Education: Toward a Model for African-American Education," *Educational Theory* 49, no. 3 (1999): 372.

27. Alridge, "Conceptualizing a Du Boisian Philosophy," 373.

28. Robert L. Crain, "Making Desegregation Work: Extracurricular Activities," *Urban Review* 13, no. 2 (1981): 124.

29. Charles C. Bolton, *The Hardest Deal of All: The Battle over School Integration in Mississippi, 1870–1980* (Oxford: University Press of Mississippi, 2005), 161.

30. During his interview, Edwin noted that *Soul Train*, an hour-long show that aired on weekdays and was created and hosted by Don Cornelius from 1970 to 1993, significantly influenced his desire to grow his hair out into an Afro and adopt a contemporary, quintessential Black aesthetic. See Christopher P. Lehman, *A Critical History of Soul Train on Television* (Jefferson, NC: McFarland, 2008).

31. Carol B. Stack, *All Our Kin: Strategies for Survival in a Black Community* (New York: Harper and Row, 1974).

32. Debora Wilkerson, in discussion with the author, February 2018. All references in this chapter to Debora Wilkerson's oral history interview are from this discussion.

33. I have confirmed the name of the school counselor. *The Daisy Chain*, yearbook, 1970, 13, Waco High School, Waco, Texas.

34. Arvizu v. Waco Independent School District, 373 F. Supp. 1264 (W.D. Tex. 1973), https://law.justia.com/cases/federal/district-courts/FSupp/373/1264/2097664.

35. Wanda James, in discussion with the author, April 2019. All references in this chapter to Wanda James's oral history interview are from this discussion.

36. "Waco Working Out a Program for Girls Who Become Pregnant," *Waco Times-Herald*, August 12, 1970, 18. Known as "Preparation for Parenthood," Waco ISD's Prenatal Continuing Education program was funded by the larger, federal Model Cities program in which Waco participated. See Renee Tweedle, "Pregnancy Doesn't Have to Mean End of School," *Waco Times-Herald*, October 21, 1971, 3; and Michael E. Blackmon, *Preparation for Parenthood: Prenatal Continuing Education Evaluation* (Waco, TX: Waco Independent School District and National Institutes of Health, 1973), https://files.eric.ed.gov/fulltext/ED091632.pdf.

37. Wanda Pillow, "Teen Pregnancy and Education: Politics of Knowledge, Research, and Practice," *Educational Policy* 20, no. 1 (2006): 59–84.

38. Russell W. Irvine and Jacqueline Jordan Irvine, "The Impact of the Desegregation Process on the Education of Black Students: Key Variables," *Journal of Negro Education* 52, no. 4 (1983): 410–22.

39. Irvine and Irvine, "Impact"; Cheryl Fields-Smith, "African American Parents Before and after *Brown*," *Journal of Curriculum and Supervision* 20, no. 2 (2005): 129–35; Patricia A. Edwards, "Before and After School Desegregation: African-American Parents' Involvement in Schools," *Educational Policy* 7, no. 3 (1993): 340–69; Vanessa Siddle Walker, *Their Highest Potential: An African American School Community in the Segregated South* (Chapel Hill: University of North Carolina Press, 1996).

40. Christine Woyshner, *The National PTA, Race, and Civic Engagement, 1897–1970* (Columbus: Ohio State University Press, 2009).

41. See *The Lion*, yearbook, 1881–1971, A. J. Moore High School, Waco, Texas.

42. Siddle Walker, "Interpersonal Caring," 75.

43. Siddle Walker, "Interpersonal Caring," 72.

44. James-Gallaway, "What Got Them Through."

45. bell hooks, *Teaching to Transgress: Education as the Practice of Freedom* (New York: Routledge, 1994), 3.

46. Siddle Walker, "Interpersonal Caring," 67.

47. Wei-ling Gong, "A History of Integration of the Waco Public Schools, 1954 to the Present" (master's thesis, Baylor University, 1987). Anslum Hudlin, in discussion with the author, August 2023. All references in this chapter to Anslum Hudlin's oral history interview are from this discussion.

48. Connie Oliver, in discussion with the author, May 2019. All references in this chapter to Connie Oliver's oral history interview are from this discussion.

49. Kwame Ture and Charles V. Hamilton, *Black Power: The Politics of Liberation* (New York: Random House, 1967); Peniel E. Joseph, ed., *The Black Power Movement: Rethinking the*

*Civil Rights–Black Power Era* (New York: Routledge, 2006); Peniel E. Joseph, *Waiting 'til the Midnight Hour: A Narrative History of Black Power in America* (New York: Macmillan, 2007).

50. Robert L. Crain and Jean Jenkins, "The Impact of School Characteristics on Student Dissatisfaction," in *Southern Schools: An Evaluation of the Effects of the Emergency Assistance Program and of School Desegregation* (Chicago: National Opinion Research Center, University of Chicago, 1973), 2:1–16.

51. *Daisy Chain*, 1969, 173.

52. Laurence A. Bradley and Gifford W. Bradley, "The Academic Achievement of Black Students in Desegregated Schools: A Critical Review," *Review of Educational Research* 47, no. 3 (1977): 399–449.

53. ArCasia D. James-Gallaway, "What Got Them Through: Community Cultural Wealth, Black Students, and Texas School Desegregation," *Race Ethnicity and Education* 25, no. 2 (2022): 173–91.

54. These trends in Black student achievement persisted decades later. See Dorinda Carter, "Achievement as Resistance: The Development of a Critical Race Achievement Ideology Among Black Achievers," *Harvard Educational Review* 78, no. 3 (2008): 466–97; Mavis Sanders, "Overcoming Obstacles: Academic Achievement as a Response to Racism and Discrimination," *Journal of Negro Education* 66, no. 1 (1997): 83–93; John Diamond, Amanda E. Lewis, and Lamont Gordon, "Race and School Achievement in a Desegregated Suburb: Reconsidering the Oppositional Culture Explanation," *International Journal of Qualitative Studies in Education* 20, no. 6 (2007): 655–79; and Greg Wiggan, "From Opposition to Engagement: Lessons from High Achieving African American Students," *Urban Review* 40, no. 4 (2008): 317–49.

55. Richard Jenkins, in discussion with the author, October 2023. All references in this chapter to Richard Jenkins's oral history interview are from this discussion.

56. David K. Wiggins, "'The Year of Awakening': Black Athletes, Racial Unrest and the Civil Rights Movement of 1968," *International Journal of the History of Sport* 9, no. 2 (1992): 188–208; Maureen Margaret Smith, "The 'Revolt of the Black Athlete': Tommie Smith and John Carlos's 1968 Black Power Salute Reconsidered," in *Myths and Milestones in the History of Sport*, ed. Stephen Wagg (London: Macmillan, 2011), 159–84; Douglas Hartmann, *Race, Culture, and the Revolt of the Black Athlete: The 1968 Olympic Protests and Their Aftermath* (Chicago: University of Chicago Press, 2003).

57. E. Lawrence Abel, *Singing the New Nation: How Music Shaped the Confederacy* (Mechanicsburg, PA: Stackpole Books, 2000); John Bush Jones, *Reinventing Dixie: Tin Pan Alley's Songs and the Creation of the Mythic South* (Baton Rouge: Louisiana State University Press, 2015).

58. Derrick E. White, "From Desegregation to Integration: Race, Football, and 'Dixie' at the University of Florida," *Florida Historical Quarterly* 88, no. 4 (2010): 476.

59. Robert E. Anderson Jr., ed., *The South and Her Children: School Desegregation, 1970–1971* (Atlanta: Southern Regional Council, 1971), 11, http://files.eric.ed.gov/fulltext/ED049327.pdf.

60. Derrick E. White, "From Desegregation to Integration," 477.

61. Joseph M. Thompson and Nate Beaty, "The 'Good Old Rebel' at the Heart of the Radical Right," *Southern Cultures* 26, no. 4 (2020): 124.

62. Derrick E. White, "From Desegregation to Integration," 477.

63. Anderson, *South and Her Children*, 12.

64. Gardner had been employed at Waco High since at least 1952, when the school was a segregated, non-Black school. See *Daisy Chain*, 1952–79.

65. *Daisy Chain*, 1966–68.

66. The Adamses were members of Toliver Chapel, a local Black church where they and other church members developed a plan to voluntarily desegregate schools in Waco. These families planned a carpool because the district was not yet using buses to achieve racial desegregation (this was before the 1971 decision of *Swann v. Charlotte-Mecklenburg Board of Education* and its busing mandate), and they thought it best to get an early start on desegregating in light of the better resources awaiting children at previously segregated white schools.

67. Charlotte Adams, in discussion with the author, December 2018. All references in this chapter to Charlotte Adams's oral history interview are from this discussion.

68. *Daisy Chain*, 1973, 109 (Service League), 114 (library assistant), 116 (Future Homemakers of America).

69. This relationship between Charlotte and Nolte is discussed at length in chapter 3.

70. *Daisy Chain*, 1973, 182.

71. For Russell's National Honor Society involvement, see *Daisy Chain*, 1971, 54; for his participation in Corrigan, see *Daisy Chain*, 1972, 35; and for his Key Club activity, see *Daisy Chain*, 1973, 68. Corrigan was the name Waco ISD gave its dance and associated events in which girls invite boys as their dates, reversing the conventional arrangement in which boys ask girls.

72. Sarah Johnson and Gladys Johnson in discussion with the author, November 2018. All references in this chapter to Sarah Johnson's and Gladys Johnson's oral history interview are from this discussion. This interview is noteworthy for a few reasons, one of which relates to its intergenerational nature. Reluctant about my interviewing her alone, Sarah consented to the interview provided that I allow her mother, Gladys Johnson, to participate with her to help her clarify her thoughts and memories.

73. Carolyn M. West, "Mammy, Sapphire, and Jezebel: Historical Images of Black Women and Their Implications for Psychotherapy," *Psychotherapy* 32, no. 3 (1995): 459–61, 462–63; Deborah Gray White, *Ar'n't I a Woman? Female Slaves in the Plantation South* (New York: W. W. Norton, 1999), 27–61; ArCasia D. James-Gallaway, "Alive and Well: Enduring Stereotypes in School Desegregation," *American Educational History Journal* 46, no. 1–2 (2019): 41–44, 46–47.

74. See *The Lion*, yearbook, 1972–79, Jefferson-Moore High School, Waco, Texas; Rosalind Russell, in discussion with the author, March 2019.

75. These girls are featured in chapter 4.

76. An analysis of yearbooks from the 1970s reveals that Jefferson-Moore had a higher number of Black school personnel than other high schools in Waco ISD. See *Lion*, 1972–83.

77. Darrick Bledsoe, in discussion with the author, October 2018. All references in this chapter to Darrick Bledsoe's oral history interview are from this discussion. In the school yearbook, Darrick is shown as a member of the junior varsity basketball team in the 1981–82 school year. *Lion*, 1982, 79.

78. Johnny Tusa was Jefferson-Moore's head football coach in 1980, 1981, and 1982. See *Lion*, 1980, 68, 106; 1982, 19, 103; and 1981, 48, 66.

79. Richard Majors, "Cool Pose: Black Masculinity and Sports," in *Contemporary Themes: African Americans in Sport*, ed. Gary A. Sailes (New York: Routledge, 1998), 15.

80. Keith Mayes, *The Unteachables: Disability Rights and the Invention of Black Special Education* (Minneapolis: University of Minnesota Press, 2023). See also Beth Harry and Janette Klingner, *Why Are So Many Students of Color in Special Education? Understanding Race and Disability in Schools* (New York: Teachers College Press, 2022).

81. Elverna Williams Jr.'s tenure at Jefferson-Moore High is documented in minutes, March 15, 1979, 87, WISD Trustees; and *Lion*, 1980, 67.

82. *Lion*, 1982, 121.

## CONCLUSION

1. Vanessa Siddle Walker, *Their Highest Potential: An African American School Community in the Segregated South* (Chapel Hill: University of North Carolina Press, 1996).

2. David. S. Cecelski, *Along Freedom Road: Hyde County, North Carolina, and the Fate of Black Schools in the South* (Chapel Hill: University of North Carolina Press, 1994).

3. Richard Kluger, *Simple Justice: The History of Brown v. Board of Education and Black America's Struggle for Equality* (New York: Vintage Books, 1976); Mark V. Tushnet, *The NAACP's Legal Strategy Against Segregated Education, 1925–1950* (Chapel Hill: University of North Carolina Press, 1987); James T. Patterson, *Brown v. Board of Education: A Civil Rights Milestone and Its Troubled Legacy* (New York: Oxford University Press, 2001); J. Harvie Wilkinson III, *From Brown to Bakke: The Supreme Court and School Integration: 1954–1978* (New York: Oxford University Press, 1979); Davison M. Douglas, *Reading, Writing, and Race: The Desegregation of the Charlotte Schools* (Chapel Hill: University of North Carolina Press, 1995).

4. Rachel Devlin, *A Girl Stands at the Door: The Generation of Young Women Who Desegregated America's Schools* (New York: Basic Books, 2018); Karen Anderson, *Little Rock: Race and Resistance at Central High School* (Princeton, NJ: Princeton University Press, 2010); Elizabeth Gillespie McRae, *Mothers of Massive Resistance: White Women and the Politics of White Supremacy* (Oxford: Oxford University Press, 2018). ArCasia D. James-Gallaway, "A Case for Interrogating the Relationships of Patriarchy, Masculinity, and Whiteness to Structural Power in the History of Education," *History of Education Quarterly* 66, no. 1 (2026): 112–19.

5. Anna Victoria Wilson and William E. Segall, *Oh, Do I Remember! Experiences of Teachers During the Desegregation of Austin's Schools, 1964–1971* (Albany: State University of New York Press, 2001); William Henry Kellar, *Make Haste Slowly: Moderates, Conservatives, and School Desegregation in Houston* (College Station: Texas A&M University Press, 1999); Guadalupe San Miguel, *Brown, Not White: School Integration and the Chicano Movement in Houston* (College Station: Texas A&M University Press, 2005); Glenn M. Linden, *Desegregating Schools in Dallas: Four Decades in the Federal Courts* (Dallas, TX: Three Forks, 1995); Robyn Duff Ladino, *Desegregating Texas Schools: Eisenhower, Shivers, and the Crisis at Mansfield High* (Austin: University of Texas Press, 1996); Dwonna Naomi Goldstone, *Integrating the 40 Acres: The Fifty-Year Struggle for Racial Equality at the University of Texas* (Athens: University of Georgia Press, 2006); Amilcar Shabazz, *Advancing Democracy: African Americans and the Struggle for Access and Equity in Higher Education in Texas* (Chapel Hill: University of North Carolina Press, 2004); Merline Pitre, *Born to Serve: A History of Texas Southern University* (Norman: University of Oklahoma Press, 2018).

6. ArCasia D. James-Gallaway and Adah Ward Randolph, "Critical Race Theory and Education History: Constructing a Race-Centered History of School Desegregation," in *Handbook of Critical Race Theory in Education*, ed. Marvin Lynn and Adrienne D. Dixson (New York: Routledge, 2021); ArCasia D. James-Gallaway and Francena F. L. Turner, "Towards a Racial Justice Project: Oral History Methodology, Critical Race Theory, and African American Education," *Paedagogica Historica* 60, no. 3 (2024): 414–38.

7. This immediately disrupted what I thought I knew as a Wacoan myself about Waco's Black educational history—chiefly, that it was far more linear than it actually was.

8. Evelyn Brooks Higginbotham, "African-American Women's History and the Metalanguage of Race," *Signs* 17, no. 2 (1992): 251–74; Francena F. L. Turner and ArCasia D. James-Gallaway, "Black Baby Boomers, Gender, and Southern Education: Navigating Tensions in Oral History Methodology," *Oral History Review* 49, no. 1 (2022): 77–96.

9. Saidiya Hartman, *Lose Your Mother: A Journey Along the Atlantic Slave Route* (New York: Farrar, Straus and Giroux, 2007); Saidiya Hartman, "The Time of Slavery," *South Atlantic Quarterly* 101, no. 4 (2002): 757–77; Orlando Patterson, *Slavery and Social Death: A Comparative Study* (Cambridge, MA: Harvard University Press, 1982).

10. Kevin Quashie, *Black Aliveness, or a Poetics of Being* (Durham, NC: Duke University Press, 2021); Katherine McKittrick, "Dear Science and Other Stories," in *Dear Science and Other Stories* (Durham, NC: Duke University Press, 2020).

11. Jeannie Oakes, *Keeping Track: How Schools Structure Inequality* (New Haven, CT: Yale University Press, 1985); Douglas D. Ready, Valerie E. Lee, and Kevin G. Welner, "Educational Equity and School Structure: School Size, Overcrowding, and Schools-Within-Schools," *Teachers College Record* 106, no. 10 (2004): 1989–2014; Carol Corbett Burris, *On the Same Track: How Schools Can Join the Twenty-First-Century Struggle Against Resegregation* (Boston: Beacon, 2014).

12. Russell Skiba and Ashley White, "Ever Since Little Rock: The History of Disciplinary Disparities in America's Schools," in *Disproportionality and Social Justice in Education*, ed. Nicholas Gage, Luke J. Rapa, Denise K. Whitford, and Antonis Katsiyanis (Cham, Switzerland: Springer International, 2022); Chaddrick D. James-Gallaway, ArCasia D. James-Gallaway, and Autumn A. Griffin, "'It's in [Their] Roots': A Critical Race Discourse Analysis of Media Accounts Depicting Black Hair Discrimination in K–12 School," *Urban Review* 56, no. 1 (2024): 35–58.

13. Gary Orfield, *Reviving the Goal of an Integrated Society: A 21st Century Challenge* (Los Angeles, CA: The Civil Rights Project, 2009), https://civilrightsproject.ucla.edu/reports/reviving-the-goal-of-an-integrated-society-a-21st-century-challenge. See also Genevieve Siegel-Hawley, *When the Fences Come Down: Twenty-First Century Lessons from Metropolitan School Desegregation* (Chapel Hill: University of North Carolina Press, 2016); Jamel K. Donnor and Adrienne D. Dixson, eds., *The Resegregation of Schools: Education and Race in the Twenty-First Century* (New York: Routledge, 2013); Gary Orfield and Susan E. Eaton, *Dismantling Desegregation: The Quiet Reversal of Brown v. Board of Education* (New York: New Press, 1996); and Charles T. Clotfelter, *After Brown: The Rise and Retreat of School Desegregation* (Princeton, NJ: Princeton University Press, 2006).

14. Bettina L. Love, *Punished for Dreaming: How School Reform Harms Black Children and How We Heal* (New York: St. Martin's, 2023); Wayne Au and Joseph J. Ferrare, eds., *Mapping Corporate Education Reform: Power and Policy Networks in the Neoliberal State* (New York: Routledge, 2015).

15. ArCasia D. James-Gallaway, "Waco's First Black School Board Trustees: Navigating Institutional White Supremacy in 1970s Texas," *History of Education Quarterly* 63, no. 1 (2023): 59–83.

16. W. E. B. Du Bois, "Does the Negro Need Separate Schools?," *Journal of Negro Education* 4, no. 3 (1935): 328–35.

# INDEX

www.ingramcontent.com/pod-product-compliance
Lightning Source LLC
LaVergne TN
LVHW101548020926
846999LV00029B/271